COMMUNICATION
AND DESIGN
WITH THE INTERNET

COMMUNICATION AND DESIGN WITH THE INTERNET

JONATHAN COHEN

W. W. NORTON & COMPANY

NEW YORK • LONDON

Copyright © 2000 by Jonathan W. Cohen

All rights reserved
Printed in the United States of America
First Edition

For information about permission to reproduce selections from this book, write to Permissions, W. W. Norton & Company, Inc., 500 Fifth Avenue, New York, NY 10110

The text of this book is composed in Sabon
with the display set in Sabon Bold
Manufacturing by Courier
Book design and composition by Abigail Sturges Design

Library of Congress Cataloging-in-Publication Data

Cohen, Jonathan, 1948–
Communication and design with the Internet : a guide for architects, planners and building professionals / Jonathan Cohen
p. cm.
Includes bibliographical references and index.
ISBN 0-393-73043-3
1. Architecture—Computer network resources. 2. Web sites—Directories. 3. Information storage and retrieval systems—Architecture. 4. Internet (Computer network) 5. World Wide Web. I. Title.

NA2728 .C62 2000
720'.285'4678—dc21   99-086574

W. W. Norton & Company, Inc., 500 Fifth Avenue, New York, N.Y. 10110
  www.norton.com
W. W. Norton & Company, Ltd., 10 Coptic Street, London WC1A 1PU

0 9 8 7 6 5 4 3 2 1

Acknowledgments

I would like to acknowledge a few of the scores of people who contributed to this book.

For allowing themselves to be interviewed at length, thanks to Cheryl Parker, Roy Chan, David Baker, Michel J. Bocchicchio, Bob Kraiss, Brian Orland, Wayne Goldberg, Paul M. Teicholz, Michael Tardif, Michael J. Shiffer, James R. Brogan, William Tucker, Robert Johnson, Robert C. Schulz, Randy Tsuda, Ellen Miller, Keith A. Kurtz, Tim Clark, Richard Kingston, Gary J. Jastrzab, Charlie Kuffner, Elizabeth Hanson, Jill Rothenberg, Linda Joy Weinstein, Ken Sanders, Ray Quay, Mark Herman, Dan Young, Philip Crompton, Andy Ball, Colin Gilboy, Ronald Hicks, Margaret R. Goglia, Hamid Pouyed, John Swett, and Ken Grobman.

For reviewing the manuscript, special thanks to Jerry Laiserin, Carol Whitescarver, Peter R. Nobile III, and David Lindemulder.

For valuable help in assembling the illustrations, thanks to Stephen Lauf, John Danahy, Pablo Monzon, Paul Kahn, Matthew Chalmers, Mark Lawton, David Colleen, Tamara Munzner, Vassilis Bourdakis, Bart A. Hall, Maia Engeli, Manfred Koob, Naveen Jamal, Michal Jacovi, Dan Taylor, Ellen Dozier, Martin Fischer, Alan Day, Matiu Carr, Santiago Ribas, Lex van der Sluijs, Jonas Kronlund, and Jay Mazzarella.

For software support, thanks to Louise Ann Miller, Adobe Systems; Doug DeRusha, Squamish Media Group; Kim Walker Borst, Allaire Corporation; Matthew Bowe, Filemaker Inc.; Emily Naranjo, Apple Computer; Dan Monaghan, Diehl Graphsoft; Walter Neals, VR Toolbox; Joseph L. Ortiz, Interactive Pictures; Ryan Kish, AEC Software; Phil Chouinard, Bentley Systems; Ted Florence, Avenza Software; Bill Tucker, Evolv; Michael Trupiano, Netopia; Paige Farsad, Primavera Systems; Allen Bannon, Symantec Corporation; Holly Nichols, White Pine Software; Bill Rothenberg, Cephren; Jay

Gonzales, StarNine Technologies; Dale Weisman, Pervasive Software; Dan Rampe, Bidcom; Gwen Marker, Cubus; Bill Doerrfeld, Blue World Communications; Arjan Timmermans, Cyco International; Catharine Reynolds, Framework Technologies.

For help in directing me to resources I would otherwise have missed, thanks to Jonathan Coopersmith, Catherine Tranmer, Nate Gilbertson, Richard Kingston, Stephen Ervin, Frits Tolman, Robert Amor, Mike Kagioglou, Wayne M. Senville, Lee Wolfe, William George Paul, and Carla Bailey.

I thank copy editor Linda Venator, book designer Abigail Sturges, and the fine team at W. W. Norton & Company: editorial assistant Christine Habermaas, jacket designer Debra Morton Hoyt, and above all senior editor Nancy Green, for having the foresight to recognize the value of this project.

Finally, thanks to my loving family, Raphael, Nat, and Ariel, for their patience and support.

Contents

Preface

The means by which architects, planners, and builders communicate—with clients, with each other, with government agencies, and with the public—are changing. For the first time in history, design professionals have a powerful, interactive, multimedia communication channel: the Internet. Direct, two-way communication of visual and spatial ideas with clients, building users, public officials, and ordinary citizens is now possible. Moreover, hypertext gives designers the ability to make powerful connections between isolated pieces of information, supporting collaborative design and group decision making.

Designers have unique communication requirements. Most of our work is described using graphical two- and three-dimensional media. These forms of communication—plan, section, and elevation—are optimized for building three-dimensional buildings and spaces using two-dimensional documentation, but they are largely ineffective for communicating with ordinary people. Three-dimensional models are better, but their physical limitations make them useful mainly in small group situations, not as mass media. In a connected society, one in which stakeholders are demanding more participation than ever in planning and design, the Internet is giving everyone in the building enterprise a chance to communicate more effectively to an expanded audience.

Two broad trends in communication, audiovisual media and networked computing, are converging at the beginning of this new century. During the twentieth century, movies and television became the main venues for cultural expression in Western society, surpassing literature and live performance. People began to receive more of their information and entertainment from screens and less from paper. No one doubted the power of these media to persuade and inform, but access to audiovisual media production was limited and expensive; one needed a movie studio or a broadcast license. An architect may have

The emergence of a new electronic communication system characterized by its global reach, its integration of all communication media, and its potential interactivity is changing and will change forever our culture.

—Manuel Castells, *The Rise of the Network Society*

realized the immense potential of multimedia to simulate physical space, for example, but had little opportunity to use it. Besides, architects needed to communicate with only a few people at a time, the client mainly; certainly not neighbors, building users, faculty committees, or politicians.

The convergence of audiovisual media with the Internet makes powerful communication tools far more accessible, just at a time when architects, planners, and builders find they need to communicate with a more diverse audience than ever before. The media convergence is most developed on the World Wide Web, which integrates text, images, video, and sound into an interactive global network that is cheap, easy to use, and almost universally available. It is an excellent time for design professionals to acquaint themselves with new means of communicating.

For city planners, such tools as geographic information systems (GIS), plus new techniques for urban visualization, when coupled with the Internet, become powerful instruments for analysis and simulation. On-line access to rich, previously inaccessible information about cities and their inhabitants helps improve planners' understanding of the complex factors at work in human communities.

For builders and building owners, the Internet provides the opportunity to gain control over vital information about facilities that has been hidden behind walls of incompatible data formats. Information can now more easily be captured, stored, and reused throughout a building's life cycle.

And for architects, the Internet may be the means by which the profession reasserts a central place in the direction of projects by assuming an important new role—that of project information manager.

The explosive pace of Internet technology (and the more leisurely pace at which books are published) means that some of the material in this book may be out of date by the time it is published. Don't worry: the buzzwords and acronyms may change, but the principles remain. Information technology should be empowering, not intimidating. This book is not about having the latest release of this, or the most megahertz of that; rather it is about recognizing new possibilities and harnessing the opportunities that this revolution in communication offers to everyone in the building enterprise.

This book will focus on concepts—ways that design and building professionals are using Internet technology to address some long-standing communication issues in our industry—as well as the tools and techniques you need to implement these ideas within your own firm. When glossary terms are first introduced, they are set in **bold type**. Up-to-date information will be available on the *Communication and Design with the Internet* Web site at www.communication-design.net.

It is anticipated that the readers of this book will have widely different degrees of previous experience with the Internet and computing and will come from all corners of the AEC industry. Some of you will already be familiar with many of the concepts discussed here, others will be learning them for the first time. Some of you will be managers charged with setting an Internet direction for your firm; others will be

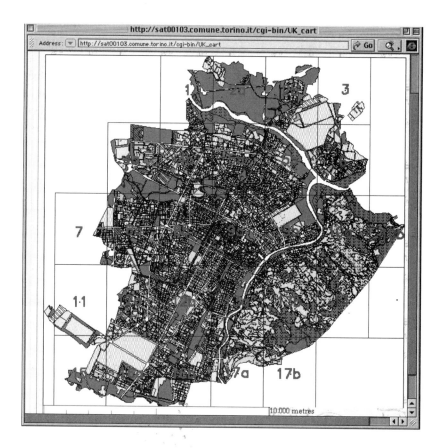

(Right and opposite) The on-line Geographical Information System for Turin, Italy.

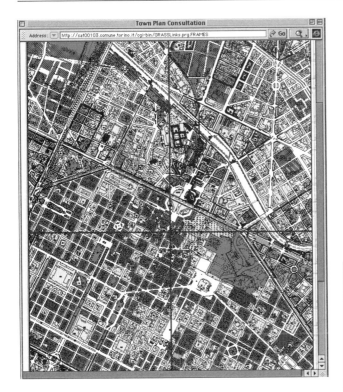

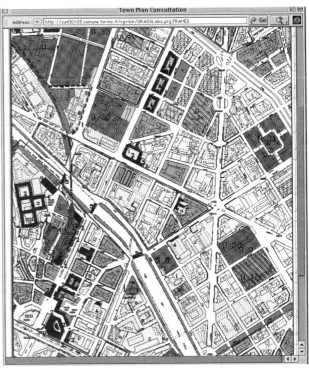

students wanting to learn new skills. In the process, you may be surprised to discover that creating Web sites, the core skill you need to participate in the connected world, is surprisingly easy and fun.

Feel free to read the book in any order you like. The nuts and bolts of getting connected, using Internet services, and building and managing Web sites is covered in chapters 2 through 6. In chapters 7 through 12, you will see how architects, planners, and builders are using these tools to deliver services and communicate with clients, collaborators, and the public in innovative ways that may challenge your notion of how getting on-line can help your firm succeed.

1 Architecture

Integration and synthesis are the core skills of a designer. Taking disparate bits of information, making trade-offs, synthesizing them into a cohesive realization: their training uniquely prepares architects for this kind of problem solving. Architectural design can be thought of as the ability to make connections—among a client's needs and budget, a site, a palette of materials, code requirements—and to shape those connections into a tangible piece of the built environment. But no design can be realized without the ability to first communicate it to others, because building is a collaborative art.

A good design means there has been successful communication between the owner and designer. And a project that is delivered on time and budget represents successful communication between the design team and the contractor. From the client's point of view, such successful communication forms the kernel of a successful project, even more so, one might argue, than an award-winning design, an efficient document creation phase, or a profitable year for the contractor.

Much has been written about the apparent disconnection between how architects are trained and the work they actually do. The Carnegie Foundation report *Building Communities: A New Future for Architecture Education and Practice* (Mitgang 1994) describes an educational setting in which students are trained in a studio system that rewards individual creative expression, then find themselves working in a profession that best succeeds when individual goals are subsumed to those of the team and the client. In recent years the profession has renounced as archaic the "lone creator" myth of architecture portrayed in Ayn Rand's *The Fountainhead*. But architects still think of themselves as visionaries, the one generalist in the entire design and construction process who is able to conceptualize the whole. Indeed, many architects are attracted to

and Communication

the field precisely because of the opportunities it offers for integrative problem solving.

An architect's skill in coordinating the work of specialists required to design any modern building adds value to those projects. Her ability to communicate the clients' requirements successfully to those who will design and build it is critical. The architect's ability to satisfy a client's needs is therefore directly tied to the ability to communicate effectively.

Buildings designed by architects today are rarely products of standard construction practices. As building technology advances, systems become more specialized and complex. No architect can be completely up to date about every aspect of design. Instead, the highly technical tasks of designing complex building systems falls to outside consultants.

Such fragmentation of the design process is relatively new. Until the first decade of the twentieth century, not even structural engineers were consulted in the design of typical buildings. Today a dozen or more specialists are routinely consulted, from acoustical engineers to permit expediters. As Robert Gutman noted in *Architectural Practice: A Critical View* (1988), even during periods when the demand for architectural services is increasing, the proportion of the total project that the architect *actually designs* is steadily decreasing. As the percentage of the project that the architect is qualified to design diminishes, however, the job of managing and coordinating the ever-growing number of specialists grows larger.

Every architect has handled a drawing set from an older building. How few drawings were needed back then—and the contract was a few pages at most! The older the building, it seems, the less documentation was needed to produce it. Over time, the amount of information required for building projects has steadily increased. The number of players involved in the process has also increased, and consequently the task of coordination has increased exponentially. Indeed, the American Institute of Architects, in its September 1996 "Redefinition of the Profession," sets out a vision of the architect of the future, who will increasingly be called upon to manage complex, interwoven professional relationships and to assume a central role as the facilitator and integrator of the knowledge and disciplines needed.

Virtual teaming is a buzzword very much in vogue throughout industry, but it is nothing new in the design field. Teams of specialists that are assembled to create one project and then disbanded have been the norm for some time. Architects have long known that such project teams require an intense coordination of efforts. What is new is that such virtual teams can now be free from the constraints of physical co-location or even organizational affiliation. The Internet becomes both the source of new-found managerial complexity and the means of controlling it. It is certain that the function of coordination is more important than ever, but will that role continue to be the architect's, or will a new kind of professional—the project information manager—be needed?

The Power of Networks

You are undoubtedly considering the potential applications of Internet technology to your own practice. The full significance of the Internet is not easy to grasp because it does not have a single, identifiable purpose. It is an open conduit, ready for any kind of digital content to be poured in. Compare it to an earlier communication tool, the telephone. Is it a marketing tool? A project management tool? A research tool? Obviously the telephone is used for all those things and much more. What if you could have a multimedia telephone that allowed you to talk and draw and model and photograph all at once? What if that telephone connected you seamlessly to your clients, your employees, and your consultants? What if you could link together an elevation sketch to a photo of the site to a material sample to a model of your proposed building? What if such a fantastic system for communicating were so cheap as to be available even to the smallest firm or sole practitioner?

The Internet combines interpersonal communication with collaborative work support and mass media. It is frequently compared to broadcasting and publishing, but unlike these models, the Web also allows for two-way communication. It makes the active creation and sharing of information as easy as merely receiving it. Communication can be as private or as public as you wish. One can use the Internet in an entirely passive way, for example, to research products or code requirements, or in an active way, to distribute project information to a geographically dispersed design team.

Such versatility is possible because the Internet is not one, but several, media combined. Communication theorists talk of *media richness*, in which *lean channels*, such as e-mail, are best used for communicating simple and unequivocal messages, while *rich media*, such as the Web, are needed for information that is ambiguous, emotional, or requires complex "hints" to supplement the basic message. E-mail may suffice for giving clear directives, but broader communication, particularly the ability to persuade, requires a more compelling presentation. If the Internet is to be used for managing professional relationships, a mastery of rich media will be required to substitute for the subtle but essential nonverbal cues that accompany face-to-face interaction.

Today most design professionals' work products consist of computer files, and while the Internet is the perfect delivery channel for digital content, electronic media are still routinely exchanged via paper-based formats. Most of the anticipated productivity gain from automating design tasks is lost when computer-generated work must be reduced to paper. Just as CAD has shown that a line need be drawn only once, so the Internet allows information to remain in a continuous digital stream throughout the life span of a project.

CAD taught designers the value of layering information. Derived from overlay drafting in the analog world, CAD layers allow designers to present information spatially. They can be inserted and removed, made visible or invisible, and be stacked in any order desired. The Web offers another means for visualizing information spatially: **hyperlinks**. Layering and linking expand your understanding of information by moving you beyond what the painter Frank Stella calls "flatland." Layering allows you to recognize the depth of the information, and linking allows you to jump directly to related information, even if it is in a different form and in a different location. Hyperlinks become the connective tissue between related bits of information. The ability to link information is crucial to anyone whose work depends on making connections, such as between a drawing and a specification, between a zoning map and a land-use table, or between a schedule and a contract.

While hypertext helps people overcome spatial constraints, by connecting related information wherever it may reside, the Internet also helps connect people by changing the temporal aspect of information exchange. The Internet supports teamwork by replacing **synchronous** communication (such as meetings in the construction trailer) with **asynchronous** communication. Team members can work together without being in the same room or the same time zone. You can participate in that job-site meeting at 3 A.M. if you must. Each participant in a multiplayer design project can make a contribution on his own time, via the network.

Old and New Means of Communication

Many business and professional people are still more comfortable with the phone and fax machine than they are with the Internet. Some are skeptical or downright suspicious: will cyberpunks steal vital business information? Will employees spend their days downloading pornography or wasting time in chat rooms? Will competitors steal ideas and clients?

People were similarly suspicious of the telephone at first: sending your voice off into the ethereal space, going where? Communication experts of the time thought the telephone would be used mainly to allow telegraph operators to talk to each other. The telephone was initially considered a "womanly" means of communicating and therefore unsuitable for business (Brooks 1975). While the telephone did help relieve the social isolation of housewives, no one today would seriously consider it a gender-biased means of communication.

Think about how fleeting a telephone conversation can be—it leaves no physical trace. Yet you entrust the telephone with some of your most important messages. E-mail, on the other hand, provides a permanent, accurate record of an exchange, done with the speed of the telephone and without the bother of note taking. But as with the telephone years ago, some still think of e-mail as a toy.

A similar level of skepticism prevailed when the telegraph was introduced in the nineteenth century. Astounding claims were made about the transformative power of this new invention. Hype and hucksterism were rampant. The telegraph was hailed as a panacea for all the world's problems, and its spread was thought to be the harbinger of a golden age of peace and prosperity. At first, many businessmen were deeply suspicious, but they soon became the most enthusiastic adopters, because they began to understand the time value of information. Companies were beginning to understand that only fresh information had value, and those who did not have it were at a competitive disadvantage.

The telegraph did not bring world peace (in fact, it proved to have great military value), but it did transform the world in very real ways. Before the telegraph, news could travel only as fast as horse or steamship. Once global, real-time communication became available, the form of cities and organizations changed dramatically. The modern corporation, built on centralized control, became possible. Manufacturing functions could be physically separated from sales and management, helping to create the downtown office district, symbolic of the modern city. The Internet, by transforming communication again, will undoubtedly have similarly profound but unforeseeable effects on how we live and work.

The telegraph, moreover, was an expensive way to communicate. In contrast, one of the main drivers of the Internet explosion has been its low cost. Economists use the concept of *network externalities* to explain how the value of a network is a function of the number of people using it. Network in this sense refers broadly to the constellation of people who share a common technology. The value of a piece of software, for example, increases when users know that a large number of other people are also using it. Especially with regard to communications, a network's value for one user depends entirely on how many others are also using it. The value of a network increases exponentially as the number of subscribers increases, in a snowball effect. A tenfold increase in the size of a network leads to a hundredfold increase in its value.

Fax machines offer a classic illustration of network externalities at work. A precursor of the modern fax machine was invented by 1902, but unlike the telephone and telegraph, the fax remained little more than a curiosity for decades. The value of having a fax depended on two very important conditions: enough people had to have them to make them a viable way to communicate, and every fax machine had to be able to talk to all the other fax machines. That second condition was not achieved until 1980, when an international standard for fax transmission was established. After that, growth began slowly, then accelerated until eventually reaching a point of complete market saturation, described by the classic **S** curve (fig. 1-1). The number of faxed pages doubled between 1980 and 1985 and increased by eleven times between 1985 and 1991 (Coopersmith 1993). All of a sudden, one couldn't seriously do business without a fax machine.

The Internet snowball has been rolling throughout the second half of the 1990s. (It must be getting bigger; one manufacturer is designing an Internet-enabled refrigerator that senses when you are low on milk and orders it from Webvan.com.) Although Internet use has increased dramatically in only a few years, its true value will emerge

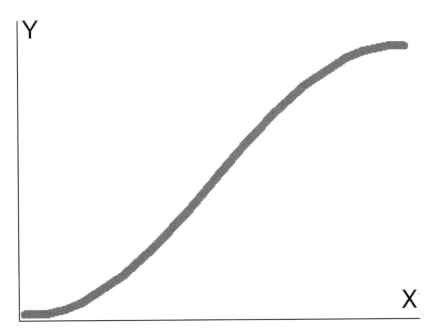

1-1. The S curve describes the growth of and eventual market saturation by the fax machine. Will the Internet follow the same pattern?

A 1997 AIA firm survey reported that 57 percent of firms (and 95 percent of large firms) were using the Internet in 1996; the percentage is surely much higher now. In 1996, 57 percent of large firms had a Web site, and three-quarters of the remainder were planning one.

when industry-specific solutions become part of standard practice. Linking together all the participants in a building project with an **extranet**, for example, dramatically increases the value of the network to all of them. Network externalities kick in even if no new content is available and the quality of the information is the same—the network adds value just by offering a new channel of communication. A point will soon be reached, if it hasn't already, where *not* being Internet savvy will be a major handicap to any business.

Computers in the Design Studio

Before the Internet, computers already had a well-established place in the studio, but many in the design professions felt vaguely uneasy with them. For architects, switching to computer-aided design represented a radical change from time-honored practice. Skills that were acquired through long training and experience had to be abandoned, and new skills learned. Many architects felt the loss of a craft tradition built on drawing by hand and constructing models of balsa and chipboard. Moreover, some architects viewed technology as detrimental to the artistic, intuitive nature of architectural creation. A distinct generation gap arose between those who had been trained in hand drawing and a younger group whose education had included computer methods. Even architects who were eager to adopt computer tools for management and support tasks were hesitant when it came to design. That domain, many felt, would be corrupted by the new tools. Computers would lead to cookie-cutter, assembly-line architecture. Attitudes started to change when architects saw that such visionaries as Frank Gehry not only supported their design work with computers but were positively energized by the freedom they gave to create. Computing, it now seemed, could be empowering (fig. 1-2).

Even so, the switch to CAD was painful because it was an abrupt, revolutionary change. For revolutionary changes to be successful, the new technology must offer clearly superior performance to compensate for the effort involved in implementing the technology, what economists call *switching costs*. For many, CAD did not offer an obvious performance enhancement, and its advantages were difficult to measure. Although electronic drawings could be changed more easily, starting them seemed to take far longer. File management, storage, layering—all offered convenience and efficiency over conventional methods, but they had to be balanced against the enormous cost of retraining personnel. And many early adopters of CAD were burned: they bought expensive proprietary systems that locked them in, limited their upgrade options, and introduced frustrating compatibility issues with collaborators on different systems. Not until the price/performance equation for CAD dropped substantially did widespread adoption occur. Some architects learned the hard way that the switching costs associated with adopting

©CASA 1995

1-2. Plan of the VRML model of the city of Bath in the United Kingdom (shown in color on the back of the dustjacket). (Courtesy of The Centre for Advanced Studies in Architecture, University of Bath, UK)

new technology can be astronomical, and many still argue that the touted advantages of CAD have not been achieved.

That's because CAD does not address the design tasks that would most benefit from information technology: coordination and project management. In its present form, CAD automates what had previously been a manual operation, but it does not address a fundamental issue: every element within a building must still be drawn or described not once, but many different times during design, construction, and in the operation of the building. A CAD program can draw a window, for example, with an exquisite degree of geometric precision, but it cannot write a specification for the window or add the window to the manufacturer's order book or schedule the window's delivery and installation or supply its U-value or the expected life of its painted finish. Every element of a designed physical environment must be translated, recompiled, and redescribed in many ways during the course of a project. Each time a building component is rendered from one mode to another, the opportunity for error, whether from misinterpretation or mistranslation, is introduced. Such errors have a way of revealing themselves late in the process, when they are very expensive to fix. The Internet, when coupled with such emerging technologies as object-oriented CAD and XML, has the potential to chain together all these separate representations of building elements into a seamless continuum. This second wave of computing in the studio promises to achieve what CAD alone never could: to unify a highly fragmented process.

Historically project information has been kept behind the walls of discrete disciplines—planning, architecture, engineering, construction management. When one discipline is finished with it, it is thrown over the transom to the next fellow. Usually these mode changes are marked by printing on paper a static snapshot of a design, and a meeting is held in which participants try to explain to each other what they have done in language the other participants will understand. Communication frequently takes place "off-line" and is never documented or captured into a comprehensive knowledge base that could be used throughout the lifetime of a building.

Every aspect of the highly distributed building enterprise—design, planning, development, financing, construction, materials—now uses information technology in some form, but the efficiency gains that were expected to flow have been imperfectly achieved. There is little *integration* of project information across disciplines. The boundaries around information are still defined by age-old craft and professional divisions, each with its own language and tools. The architect "owns" the plans, the contractor "owns" the schedule, and the owner is not well served. An integrator is sorely needed, but who will step into this role?

This fragmentation of the design and construction process has caused the AEC industry to lag in productivity behind other sectors of the economy. One of the biggest obstacles to productivity growth has been poor communication along the chain of activity, from programming to design to construction and occupancy of buildings. Until recently, information technology had not begun to address this issue; indeed, it aggravated it by erecting new barriers of technical incompatibility between systems that should work together. The result for the AEC industry has been lower quality, higher costs, and longer time to market than might otherwise be possible. The Internet, by supporting communication throughout the development process, holds the potential to bring about the kind of integration that could make this entire industry more productive.

For many organizations, the globalization of the marketplace has demanded a complete rethinking of business practices, leading to restructuring on a large scale. Perhaps not coincidentally, the Internet fits very well with modern management theories. Companies are flattening their organizational structures and moving toward decentralized decision making and closer rapport with customers.

Responsibility is being devolved to business units and away from headquarters. Internet-based communication is playing a key role in supporting these changes, by putting enterprise-wide knowledge and experience into the hands of many more people within the organization. In business and government, the pressure to reduce costs and increase flexibility and responsiveness is now being turned to facilities. Those in the building professions who serve these organizations need to speak this new language. And they need to show their clients that they've applied the same principles of reengineering—supported by Internet-based communication—to their own businesses.

2 An Internet

In recent years there has been a dramatic shift from computing as a standalone activity to networked computing. During the 1980s computing focused on automating specific tasks, such as word processing, financial analysis, drawing, scheduling, and modeling. Specialized software tools were used on standalone computer systems. In the early 1990s, that focus changed; for the first time, computers became powerful communication devices and enablers of collaboration and teamwork. To understand how this change came about, let's review a bit of Internet history.

In the 1960s the foundations of the Internet were laid at an elite Pentagon laboratory: the Defense Advanced Research Projects Agency (DARPA). In those early days of computing, each machine was a unique system. Programs were written in machine languages custom-designed for each computer. A common **operating system** used by millions of people, such as Windows, Macintosh, or Unix, was unknown. Computers were expensive, trouble prone, and unreliable, and there were too few of them to meet the demand. To increase the availability of limited resources, a system of time sharing was developed, in which access to computers was carefully rationed among the researchers who needed it. A system was needed that would extend time sharing geographically, by connecting the major computer-science research centers within a **network**. Researchers at MIT, for example, would then be able to exchange files and share computer time with their colleagues at UCLA.

A *distributed* networking system was devised. Unlike a hierarchical or radial network, in a distributed network each **node** and link has equal status with all the others. Such a system has multiple redundancies, like the structure of a wood-frame house. Network redundancy offered a more reliable design than one based on fixed links: if a single link were lost, it would not bring down the entire

Introduction

system. Because the Internet was devised during the height of the Cold War, it has been widely and incorrectly assumed that the distributed network model was chosen because a headless system might better survive a nuclear attack. In truth, it was a response to the unreliable nature of early computing. The Internet was designed to be a decentralized, **peer-to-peer system,** like a city's street grid (fig. 2-1). If Second Street is blocked, you can always take First Street or Third Street. This underlying design made the Internet highly fault tolerant, robust, and flexible.

The second key idea behind the Internet was **packet switching.** Messages would be disassembled into small pieces, or packets, and then sent via network links over telephone lines to their destination, where the pieces would be reassembled into the complete message. Packets would not take a fixed, predetermined route to their destination; instead, they would follow the path of least resistance to skirt any trouble on the line (figs. 2-2 and 2-3). The different packets constituting a message might follow different routes to the same destination. Routing tables, updated every fraction of a second, would determine the best path for each departing packet to follow. Identifiers in each packet would keep track of its origin and destination.

Packet switching enabled far more efficient use of telephone lines than is the case in voice communication, which relies on **circuit switching.** When you make a telephone call, you tie up the entire line even during your most pregnant pauses. In contrast, packet switching allows many different messages to crisscross simultaneously on a single line. Telephone experts of the time were skeptical that packet switching was even possible, but they were proved wrong.

Packet switching became the basis of Transmission Control Protocol/Internet Protocol (**TCP/IP**), the foundation of today's

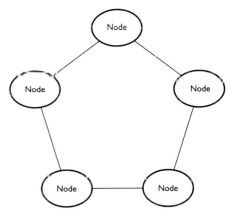

2-1. A peer-to-peer system.

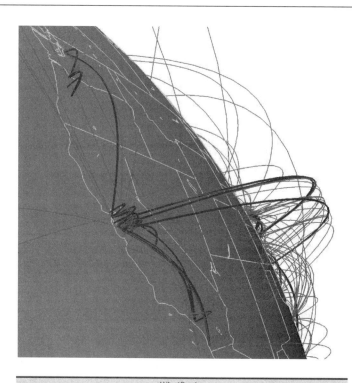

2-2. "Planet Multicast" illustrates the "hops" between servers on the Internet. (Courtesy Tamara Munzner, Stanford University; Eric Hoffman, Ipsilon Networks; K. Claffy, NLANR; and Bill Fenner, Xerox Palo Alto Research Center)

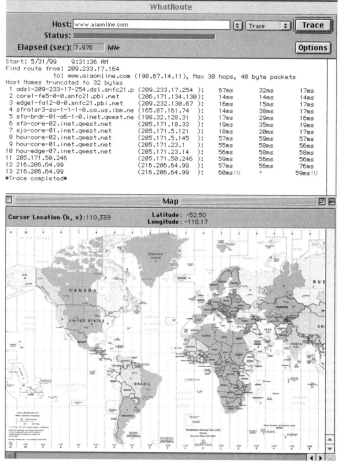

2-3. WhatRoute traces the "hops" that an Internet packet makes as it goes around the world. In this case, a request to www.aiaonline.com made thirteen hops to the author's computer. (Courtesy Brian R. Christianson)

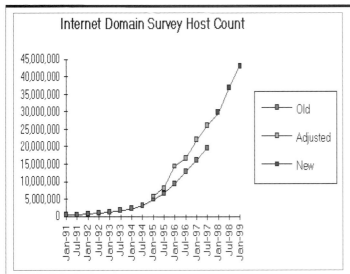

2-4. The growth of Internet hosts during the 1990s.

How Many People Are on the Internet?

For information on the number of people currently using the Internet, go to Matrix Information and Directory Services (www.mids.org) or Network Wizards (www.nw.com). From the mid-1980s to the mid-1990s, the number of people using the Internet doubled every twelve months. The World Wide Web Consortium has predicted that the number of users worldwide will exceed 300 million in the first few years of the new century. All such predictions are educated guesses, because there is no way to be certain how many people use the Internet. But the number of host servers is a known fact: from January 1993 to July 1999, that number increased fifty times, according to the Internet Software Consortium (figs. 2-4 and 2-5).

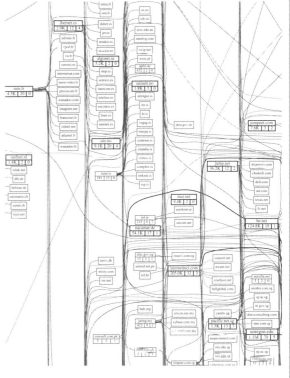

2-5. The topology of Usenet hosts. (Courtesy Naveen Jamal; ©Naveen Jamal, Bitmap Organization)

Internet. Because none of the early computers had common operating systems that would enable them to speak with each other directly, a kind of digital Esperanto was needed to enable basic communication. Like all of the underlying technology of the Internet, TCP/IP was designed as a public-domain, open standard, permitting all types of computers to share information easily.

ARPANET, the forerunner of the Internet, grew slowly at first. It began with four nodes, and by 1973 only twenty-five computers formed the entire network (fig. 2-6). By the early 1980s, it consisted of, at most, a few hundred host computers with no more than a few thousand regular users.

ARPANET was designed for resource sharing, but it quickly became clear that its most compelling application was human communication. Electronic mail, or **e-mail,** became the most widespread function of the network, as scientists grasped the potential of this convenient and powerful new tool for collaboration. They discovered the advantages of asynchronous communication and of one-to-many communication,

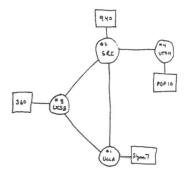

2-6. ARPANET, the forerunner of the Internet, began with only four nodes.

the ability to send a message to a group of people as easily as to an individual recipient. E-mail became the first of the **Internet services**.

The public Internet, as well as private **intranets** and **extranets**, is powered by the underlying communication technology of TCP/IP. Built on top of this foundation are the Internet services, the actual working applications of the Internet used on a daily basis. These services include:

- E-mail: text messages sent to individuals and groups; files can be attached to e-mails as enclosures
- File Transfer Protocol (FTP): a system that **uploads** and **downloads** files to and from a **server**; FTP is used, for example, to place files (or upload them) on a Web site
- Network newsgroups (Usenet): electronic bulletin boards; discussion systems built around interests and affinities, which can be public or private
- World Wide Web: the interactive, multimedia, and hyperlinked component of the Internet

Each of these services is discussed in detail in chapter 3.

In 1989 the Internet was still known only within academic and government circles. By this time, private on-line services, such as CompuServe and America Online, had begun to catch on with computer enthusiasts, offering information services and e-mail. But these were closed systems; one could only send e-mail to other subscribers of the same service, and the content comprised only a small fraction of the resources available on the Internet itself. **Internet service providers** (ISPs) then began offering direct access to the Internet to private individuals and companies. By the early 1990s, AOL's and CompuServe's customers began clamoring for the "real" Internet. To keep their subscribers, these services started building gateways from their closed systems to the Internet.

Still, the Internet was a black-and-white world of plain text and **command-line interfaces**. For the Internet to take off in a big way, people needed an easier, more intuitive way to use it—the World Wide Web.

In 1989 at CERN, the European Laboratory for Particle Physics in Geneva, Tim Berners-Lee envisioned a means of using hypertext links to allow researchers to collaborate with each other and share both text-based and graphic information. Several thousand CERN researchers were attempting to work together toward a common goal, but as people came and went, information was being irretrievably lost. When new people arrived, they were given a few hints about who was working on what or where various resources were located, but for the most part they were left to figure things out for themselves. Through gossip and informal conversations, information flowed through the organization, slowly and imperfectly. Sometimes effort was duplicated, and when people left the organization, vital knowledge left with them. The hierarchical management structure of this huge scientific effort did not mesh very well with the way people actually worked. A means of collecting the knowledge assets of this massive project and making it accessible throughout the organization was needed. Berners-Lee found that the scientists' real pattern of communicating was a "multiply connected Web," a network whose complex linkages evolved over time (Berners-Lee 1989). He proposed a new information management system called *distributed hypertext*. He noticed that when people attempted to describe the interrelationship of pieces of the project, they often drew diagrams with arrows and circles. They were trying to describe the linkages between things, something that could not be easily shown in a table or a flow chart. The *connections* mattered as much as the information itself.

Berners-Lee invented a system that would allow information in various forms to be connected in nonlinear, even random ways. The Hypertext Transfer Protocol (**HTTP**) was built on top of TCP/IP so that the existing Internet infrastructure could be used to transmit and display multimedia content along with associative links. A new kind of software application, called a **browser,** was needed to provide access to the distributed pieces of information and the links between them. At the same time, a new method of assigning addresses to resources on the Internet was developed, called Uniform Resource Locators (**URLs**). Berners-Lee named his invention the World Wide Web.

The first Web browser was Mosaic, developed at the University of Illinois National Center for Supercomputing Applications. The core of the Mosaic team of computer scientists later founded Netscape. Today the browser market is divided between Mosaic's descendant, Netscape Communicator, and Microsoft's Internet Explorer. The browser made the Internet easy and fun, and by the mid-1990s, the Web became its primary gateway.

The Web has four distinguishing characteristics that set it apart from the rest of the Internet:

- *Multimedia*: The Web revolutionized the Internet by allowing formatted text, graphics, photos, sound, and video to be displayed simultaneously with a single piece of software.
- *Hyperlinking*: The Web supports an intuitive, nonlinear way of navigating information. Links are made between pieces of information in different data formats, without regard for their physical location.
- *Platform independence:* Compatible browsers are available for all kinds of computers, removing the barriers imposed by the mixture of computing **platforms** typically found in organizations and work teams. A Web site created on a Macintosh, for example, can be hosted on a Unix server and viewed on a Windows PC, with no loss of content or need for file translation.

The Origins of Hypertext

Despite the hype that has surrounded the Web, the importance of its single most powerful feature, hypertext, is often understated. The idea of linking together disparate pieces of information held in different media was first proposed in a July 1945 article by Vannevar Bush, director of the Office of Science and Research Development under President Franklin D. Roosevelt. He wanted to build something called a *memex* (for memory extender):

> A memex is a device in which an individual stores all his books, records, and communications, and which is mechanized so that it may be consulted with exceeding speed and flexibility. It is an enlarged intimate supplement to his memory....The process of tying two items together is the important thing....When the user is building a trail, he names it, inserts the name in his code book, and taps it out on his keyboard. Before him are the two items to be joined, projected onto adjacent viewing positions....Thereafter, at any time, when one of these items is in view, the other can be instantly recalled merely by tapping a button below the corresponding code space. Moreover, when numerous items have been thus joined together to form a trail, they can be reviewed in turn, rapidly or slowly, by deflecting a lever like that used for turning the pages of a book. It is exactly as though the physical items had been gathered together to form a new book.

Clearly, the memex was ahead of its time.

In the mid-1960s, the information visionary Ted Nelson coined the term *hypertext*. He foresaw an entirely networked culture in which "there would be new documents, a new literary genre, of branching, non-sequential writings on the computer screen. Second, these branching documents would constitute a great new literature, but they would subsume the old, since all words, all literature would go on-line and extend to a new branching generality" (Nelson 1970).

The first commercial product to employ hypertext was Apple Computer's HyperCard, which used the visual metaphor of 3-by-5 cards holding both text and media, which could be randomly accessed in any order.

The Importance of Standards

The open standards of the Internet recall the struggle to standardize track gauges in the early days of railroads. In mid-nineteenth-century America, many incompatible gauges existed, requiring long-distance passengers and cargo to be loaded and unloaded many times during a long trip for "breaks in gauge." The most prevalent gauge was the English standard, 4 feet 8½ inches from rail to rail, said to derive from the axle width of Roman war chariots, but each railroad was free to adopt whatever gauge it desired. Many pressed for a wider gauge, arguing that the extra width was better technology, providing more stability and a higher carrying capacity. The obvious inefficiency of nonstandard gauges was widely recognized, but debate about how to resolve it lasted for over thirty years. In 1873 the entire country reverted to the English standard, still in use today. That agreement made a national railroad system possible, and with it, the settlement of the West.

2-7. A Web page is an HTML document plus all the linked files and formatting instructions.

2-8. The same page in raw HTML.

■ *Interactivity:* The Web supports two-way communication, like a multi-media, hyperlinked telephone system. It blurs the boundary between information provider and information consumer. All of a sudden, everyone is both a publisher and a subscriber.

A Web page (a document written in Hypertext Markup Language, or **HTML**) uses hyperlinks to connect visitors to other files and media resources that may be stored *locally*, within the same Web site, or *remotely*, on another server (figs. 2-7 and 2-8).

Internet computing is based on a **client-server** paradigm (fig. 2-9). The content of a Web site is kept on a server and made available on demand to client computers on the network. (Confusingly, *server* and *client* refer both to software and hardware.) Thus, the Internet consists of different, connected hosts, or servers, each of which in turn is connected to a series of clients (fig. 2-10). Web browsers are sometimes called *thin clients*, meaning they are viewing and navigating tools that do not create or modify information themselves. They are universal, because they span multiple hardware platforms, operating systems, applications, and users.

The Web browser has been called the Swiss army knife of computing. It is a wonderfully versatile, easy to-use tool that allows the viewing of a wide variety of media types within its own windows by employing **plug-ins** or by handing them off to **helper applications**.

Specialized software applications are still needed to *create* different kinds of content—CAD for drawings, word processors for specifications, and so on—but now the content created by others can be viewed through the windows of a browser. And hyperlinks allow seamless connections between pieces of information. Not only does the browser navigate and display various media, it maintains a history of visited Web sites, like a trail of electronic bread crumbs.

Two other freely distributed, public-domain computing standards paved the way for the Internet. Unix, invented by Bell Labs with government funding, is the prevalent operating system used by Internet servers, or hosts. And the **modem**, which permits direct communication between computers over ordinary telephone lines, was invented by two University of Chicago students, Ward Christensen and Randy Suess, in 1978. In the spirit of utopian cooperation that prevailed in those early days, they freely gave away their invention.

Key to the success of the Internet is its basis in open, public standards, free from proprietary technology under the control of one company. The advantage of open standards should be obvious to designers who were early adopters of CAD and found themselves locked in to technology that was incompatible with other systems. On the Internet, open standards have resulted in more choices and greater compatibility than would have been the case had proprietary technology won the day. When different proprietary standards compete, some companies may gain or lose a short-term advantage. But when open, public standards are set, the entire economy benefits.

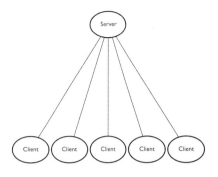

2-9. A client-server system.

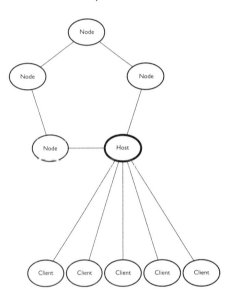

2-10. The Internet is both a peer-to-peer and client-server system.

3 Getting

The first step toward using the Internet to expand your business practice is to get connected. To begin, you will need some hardware, software, and an Internet connection. For hardware, almost any new computer will suffice. Even your old standby is probably up to the task if it is a Pentium-based PC running Windows 95 or later or a Power Macintosh computer running Mac OS 7.6 or later. Web authoring, especially if you are using graphics and multimedia, will require more horsepower than the minimum, and hosting a Web server still more. Virtually all the software you need for basic Internet connectivity—e-mail client, Web browser, **newsreader**, and basic networking software—is free or included as part of your operating system.

Next, you will need an **Internet service provider** (ISP). These companies provide Internet connections at the retail level to businesses and individuals. A wide selection of both national and regional ISPs is available. Don't assume that a national company with a recognizable brand name will be better for your firm than a smaller outfit that serves only your local area—often the opposite is true. A local ISP, particularly one specializing in business customers, may provide better service with little or no extra expense. Rely heavily on recommendations from colleagues; take advertised claims with a grain of salt. Local computer magazines available free at newsstands regularly run user satisfaction surveys of ISPs. The List (http://thelist.internet.com) is an on-line resource that maintains a comprehensive database of ISPs (fig. 3-1). Simply type in your area code and receive a list of providers, services, and fees, with links to their Web sites. The appendix contains a detailed list of questions to help you to find an ISP that is right for your firm.

Each ISP offers a range of service options, from the cheapest (and slowest) to the most expensive (and fastest). The two broad

Connected

categories of connectivity are **dial-up** and **dedicated**. Dial-up connections are intermittent; you have to initiate an Internet session by using a modem to make a telephone call to your ISP. When you are done, you disconnect. In contrast, a dedicated connection remains open at all times. Each category offers choices of price and **bandwidth**, the speed and capacity of information flow. Service may be

Company	Dial-Up Services	Dedicated Services
A-Link Network Services, Inc.	28.8, 33.6, 56K(56Kflex), V90, ISDN	56K, ISDN, DSL, FracT1, T1, FracT3, T3, Frame Relay
A000111ACCESS	28.8, 33.6, 56K(X2), 56K(56Kflex), V90, ISDN	56K, ISDN, DSL, FracT1, T1, FracT3, T3, Frame Relay
a01-Michigan Connect	28.8, 33.6, 56K(X2), 56K(56Kflex), V90, ISDN	56K, ISDN, FracT1, T1, FracT3, T3, Frame Relay
A1-Ampro Net	28.8, 33.6, 56K(X2), 56K(56Kflex), V90, ISDN	
A1699 Access	28.8, 33.6, 56K(X2), 56K(56Kflex), V90, ISDN	56K, ISDN, FracT1, T1, FracT3, T3, Frame Relay
A1 Internet Service Provider	28.8, 33.6, 56K(56Kflex), V90, ISDN	
A Abaca	28.8, 33.6, 56K(56Kflex), ISDN	56K, ISDN, FracT1
A Access USA	28.8, 33.6, 56K(X2), 56K(56Kflex), V90, ISDN	56K, ISDN
A.B.I. Marketing Group	56K(56Kflex), V90	
A FlashNet Dist.	28.8, 33.6, 56K(56Kflex), V90, ISDN	56K, ISDN, FracT1
A FlashNet Ind. Distributor	28.8, 33.6, 56K(56Kflex), V90, ISDN	

3-1. The List provides information and links about ISPs, sorted by area code.

symmetric or **asymmetric**, that is, the speed in the downstream and upstream directions may be the same or different. Bandwidth is typically expressed as a pair of numbers, signifying the capacity of the connection in each direction in bits per second, or bps. For example, the designation 1.5 Mbps/384 Kbps means 1.5 *million* bits per second downstream, 384 *thousand* bits per second upstream. The second number is especially important if you decide, now or later, to run your own server to host Web, e-mail, or other Internet services (see Chapter 6 for more information about having your own server). Since most ISPs offer a selection of bandwidth options, it's best to choose one for its good customer service and the range of options it offers, rather than for a specific type of service. That way, if you need to upgrade your service later, you will not have to switch ISPs.

Dial-up Connections

With a dial-up connection, you use ordinary telephone lines to call your ISP, which then connects you with the Internet. Your computer uses a modem, which may be built in or external, to convert digital signals to analog sounds; the screeching you hear is your modem negotiating the terms of the conversation with another modem at the other end of the line. This digital-to-analog-and-back translation takes a heavy toll on the capacity of the phone line to transmit information. The highest-speed modem converses with the Internet at 56 Kbps, or 56,000 bits per second, in the downstream direction and perhaps 33.6 Kbps upstream. Most users cannot reliably achieve these theoretical transmission rates because of the uneven quality of telephone lines.

ISDN is the second type of dial-up connection. It achieves higher speeds by conversing strictly in digital 1s and 0s, bypassing the digital-to-analog conversion process. ISDN requires a dedicated telephone line that cannot simultaneously be used for voice or fax communication. At the time of this writing, it appears that ISDN will soon be supplanted by **DSL** (Digital Subscriber Line), a dedicated service that offers significant advantages of cost and speed. At the moment, however, ISDN is more widely available than DSL and remains a viable option for small businesses in the near term.

Dial-up accounts may be limited to a fixed number of hours of usage per month, after which additional charges apply. Some ISPs offer unlimited usage. When comparing the monthly cost of dial-up connectivity options, consider local telephone usage charges as well. While most residential service is flat rate within a local calling area, business telephone users pay per-minute charges, which add up when your firm is spending serious time on the Internet and can easily exceed the cost of your basic ISP service.

Dedicated Access

The second class of Internet service is *dedicated*, meaning always available, as opposed to dial-up connections, which must be initiated by a phone call. With a dedicated connection, the Internet is not only faster but far more convenient. More frequent and even casual use is much easier, making the Internet a resource that is always at hand. These higher-speed kinds of connections are sometimes referred to as *broadband*.

A dedicated Internet connection is not the same as an open telephone line. Because voice communication uses circuit switching, when you are on the phone, you are consuming all the available bandwidth as long as you are connected; your silences consume just as much as your most intense conversation. You may use the full capacity of your connection only rarely and then in short bursts. In contrast, a dedicated Internet connection is in standby mode at all times but does not consume bandwidth when inactive. Dedicated service is not portable; it is hard-wired to one location. It does, however, normally include an additional dial-up account for access when traveling.

An important difference between dial-up and dedicated access is the way in which **IP addresses** are assigned. Every host computer on the Internet must have a unique address in the form of four groups of numbers, such as *140.174.162.14*. A **virtual domain name**, such as

3-2 and 3-3. TCP/IP preference settings in Windows

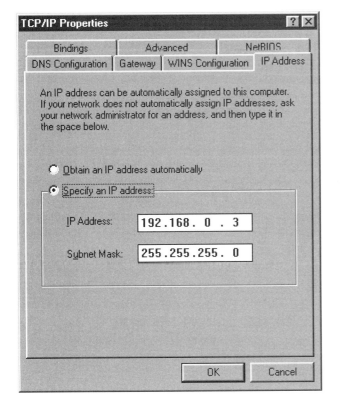

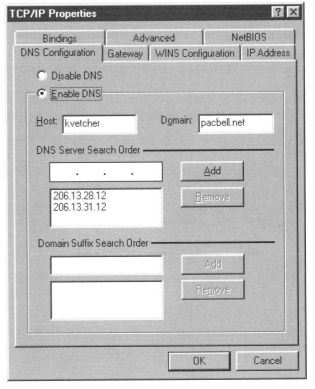

architecture.com, is an **alias** for this numeric IP address. Most dial-up Internet services use a system of *dynamic addressing*, in which an IP address is assigned for that session only. Dedicated connections use *static addressing*, in which each networked computer has a permanently assigned address (figs. 3-2 and 3-3, page 33). Having a fixed IP address is a requirement for hosting a Web site or other Internet services on your own server.

DSL and **frame relay** are two types of dedicated connections that are point-to-point, in effect creating a virtual pipeline between your location and the telephone central office in your neighborhood. DSL works over normal telephone lines simultaneously with voice, fax, or modem communication by employing much higher frequencies and special switches. DSL installation consists of splitting off the data component from the voice component in the phone line, then bringing the split line to a small device known as a DSL "modem," or network terminator (it's not really a modem because no sound is generated). From there, the signal is fed via **Ethernet** into an individual computer or a local area network (**LAN**). The low cost and high bandwidth of DSL, and its use of standard telephone lines, make it a very attractive option for even the smallest firm or sole practitioner.

The most commonly available type of DSL service in the United States is ADSL (the *A* stands for *asymmetric*). ADSL moves information faster downstream than it does upstream. Thus, it will download information very quickly, but its upstream capacity may be much slower, sometimes too slow for hosting a Web server. DSL requires that you arrange with the telephone company (which may also provide Internet access through a subsidiary) to bring the basic service to your location and then establish an account with an ISP. Every regional telephone company, it seems, offers different variations of DSL. Check the speeds offered in both directions when you order. The telephone company may guarantee a minimum speed that you may be able to exceed in practice.

Some DSL providers, such as Pacific Bell, are also ISPs, and they may offer a discount when you order both services. Choose your ISP wisely, because once DSL is installed, you may not be able to move your service to another ISP. You may be locked in, either by dedicated hardware or a service contract, to one provider of DSL. For example, in the San Francisco Bay area, two DSL providers, PacBell and Covad, split the market, and each is allied with its own group of ISPs. The current situation is similar to the confusing array of cellular telephone systems now in operation. At the time of this writing, telephone companies are trying to agree on a new form of universal DSL, which, if adopted, may remove the concern about lock-in by standardizing DSL service across the country.

Frame relay, a second type of dedicated Internet service, is *symmetric*, and therefore supports the higher speeds upstream needed to host Internet services. It differs from higher and more expensive forms of connectivity in that it is not a leased line for the exclusive use of one company but instead makes use of the public telephone network. Frame relay customers typically have a choice of bandwidth capacities, from 56 Kbps up to 1.5 Mbps. Frame relay is an appropriate choice for setting up a wide area network (**WAN**) or for linking more than one LAN to an ISP. When several branch offices of a company (or several temporary job-site offices) need to share a single high-speed Internet connection, the company can install a single T1 connection to the main office that is shared by the various branch offices using frame relay. Such an arrangement avoids duplicating the considerable expense of installing special equipment at each location.

Cable TV systems provide another kind of dedicated, high-speed access. If you've noticed that the coaxial cable used by your TV is much thicker than the thin pair of copper wires used by the telephone, you have an inkling of how much more information can pour through these bigger pipes. In fact, just one cable channel is capable of carrying data hundreds of times faster than a 56K modem. Unfortunately, cable was designed for one-way communication only, so cable Internet access is available only where cable companies have invested in converting their systems to two-way, and even then the system is likely to be drastically asymmetric, with much slower speeds upstream. The interface between the "cable modem" and your computer is similar to DSL; the signal is fed into a new or existing LAN using standard Ethernet. A TV cable brought into an apartment complex or office building can distribute high-bandwidth connectivity throughout the facility using a LAN.

Unlike DSL, cable systems share lines among their subscribers, and performance can vary unpredictably, depending on how many users are connected at one time. Some corporate tech managers also have concerns about the relative lack of security inherent in this kind of party line arrangement, although encryption systems with decoders built in to the cable modem can solve this problem. Even so, many business locations lack cable access completely.

Cable's arch rival, satellite TV, has rolled out Internet services of its own. Satellite, which requires a dish antenna, is very fast in the downstream direction but nonexistent in the upstream. To upload files (or even just to send an e-mail) requires a separate modem connection.

T1 (1.5 Mbps) and **T3** (45 Mbps) services, the fastest of all, use leased telephone lines, that is, lines laid for the exclusive use of one subscribing company. As with frame relay, different data rates are available in the form of fractional T1 lines. T1 remains the preferred alternative for those companies wanting to host their own servers. It is a proven, reliable technology with a large installed base and enjoys wide support from ISPs and hardware manufacturers. But its price is out of the range of many small businesses: expect to pay $1,000 per month plus hefty installation and equipment charges.

Wireless connectivity is starting to emerge as a viable option, espe-

Should AOL Be Your ISP?

America Online, along with CompuServe and Prodigy, are on-line services that developed parallel to, not as part of, the Internet. AOL was planned as a closed system, with its own proprietary content, software, and interface. Originally, subscribers could send e-mail only to other subscribers on the same service. As the Internet grew in visibility and the World Wide Web gave it a user-friendly interface, these services began losing customers. So AOL and the others responded by adding a gateway to the Internet as part of their service. But subscribers still had to pass through AOL's portal first, instead of getting on the Internet directly.

AOL makes the sometimes chaotic Internet a little more manageable for consumers, but it is not necessarily the best way for businesses to use the Internet, particularly if they plan to do more than just consume information. Some of the limitations that an AOL account will impose include:

- Multitasking is impossible. You cannot perform multiple functions simultaneously, such as downloading files via FTP, reading e-mail, and Web browsing all at the same time.
- Advanced services are not supported. You cannot, for example, use CGI scripts to run the forms on your interactive Web site.
- Contacting live support personnel is next to impossible.
- AOL supports only a limited range of software—you must use AOL's own browser, e-mail application, and newsreader—and these are sometimes a generation behind those offered for free by ISPs.
- Both AOL and CompuServe use their own **encoding** and **compression** protocols for e-mail attachments. You may have a great deal of difficulty exchanging files with other people unless they happen to be on the same service.
- AOL does not provide virtual domain names. Not only can you not be www.bestarchitect.com, but if you want to change your ISP later, you cannot take your e-mail address with you—and AOL will not forward your mail to the new address.

cially for professionals who find themselves frequently on the road. Wireless modems are available in small packages for notebook computers, with connection speeds and service plans that are roughly comparable in cost to conventional dial-up access. Mobile users can also exchange files with each other without engaging the public Internet. As with cellular telephones, though, security is an issue. The latest Palm hand-held devices support wireless Internet access through a dedicated national network, enabling users to receive e-mail and specially formatted Web pages. These devices are smaller and cheaper than a laptop and might prove useful to workers in the field who need connectivity to a project extranet from construction job sites. Such portable, connected devices may someday replace the rolls of drawings that construction personnel are expected to handle now.

New kinds of wireless satellite and radio transmission options are arriving almost every day, some of them as fast and priced only slightly higher than such land-based services as T1. With these, branch offices can connect themselves wirelessly with Ethernet transmitters having a range of several miles.

How Is Your ISP Connected?

The most important thing to know about your ISP, aside from its reputation for customer service, is its total bandwidth divided by the number of its subscribers. In other words, how well is *it* connected to the Internet?

Your ISP has a **point of presence** that may consist of one or more high-speed links to the major arterial data lines of the Internet (called the "backbone"). The fastest connection an ISP can have is via a T3 line. Most ISPs have something well short of that, usually one or more T1 lines. The ISP is able to sell this capacity several times over because traffic is "bursty"—most customers use their full bandwidth only intermittently, leaving plenty of spare capacity. Studies have shown that an ISP can safely sell up to fourteen times its capacity with no measurable loss of performance. But some ISPs oversell their available bandwidth to too many subscribers, causing sporadic performance hits.

A good ISP will also have redundant sources of upstream connectivity, giving customers a backup when trouble hits. In August 1999, MCI Worldcom's part of the Internet backbone was down for ten days, throwing an estimated 250,000 subscribers off the 'Net. ISPs without redundant suppliers were shut down completely during that period.

Ask a potential ISP for a bandwidth usage report, which gives an indication of peak times and overall usage compared to capacity. Smaller ISPs may have several layers of middlemen between them and the Internet backbone. An evaluation of the entire stream of data from your site to the backbone may uncover some potential bottlenecks. You may get better performance if you, your partners, and clients are all using the same ISP or perhaps different ISPs that rent basic capacity from the same wholesale provider.

Internet Services

Once you have arranged for basic connectivity, you are ready to begin using Internet services such as e-mail and the Web. These are the applications that you use to perform specific communication tasks. Although this book focuses mainly on the Web, the other Internet services each have a place in an overall communication strategy for your firm. All of these services are normally included in the basic package offered by an ISP. You may need to install a different application program on your computer to run each of them, however. **Shareware** or commercial versions of these applications are normally provided free of charge by your ISP, either on a disk you are given when you enroll or by download from your ISP's server.

E-mail

E-mail has always been the Internet's single most popular component. Since e-mail is fast and cheap, people tend to use it much more frequently than postal mail. It can substitute very well for the kind of routine phone calls that seem to take up so much of everyone's working time. Because it leaves a permanent written record, it is far easier to reconstruct past e-mail exchanges accurately than it is to recall week-old telephone conversations. A log of e-mail exchanges often provides an excellent overview of the history of a project.

Setting up an e-mail program is normally a matter of following the prompts to enter a few items of information, such as the name of your ISP's incoming and outgoing mail servers (typically in the form of mail.domain.com), the telephone number to be called, where downloaded files are to be placed on your hard drive, and your reply-to e-mail address (figs. 3-4, 3-5, 3-6, and 3-7, pages 38–39). All of this information will be supplied to you when you open an account.

Mail programs include an address book, which not only retains the e-mail addresses of your correspondents but allows you to sort them into groups. For example, all the members of a project design team might be part of a group, so you can easily broadcast messages to all of them at once. Sent and received messages can also be saved and sorted into folders. You may want to create a folder for each project or sort messages by any categories you choose. Most e-mail programs also provide a search function, so that stored messages can be easily retrieved (try doing that with phone message slips!).

When responding to e-mail, it's a good idea to quote part or all of the original message, to remind the recipient of the thread of discussion that may eventually extend over several messages back and forth. E-mail programs can be configured to add > characters to all, or a

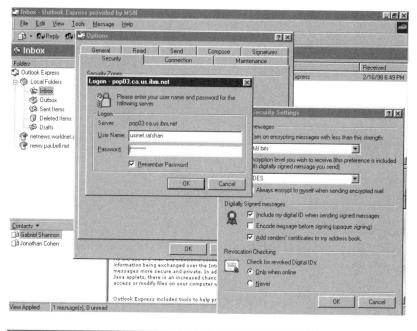

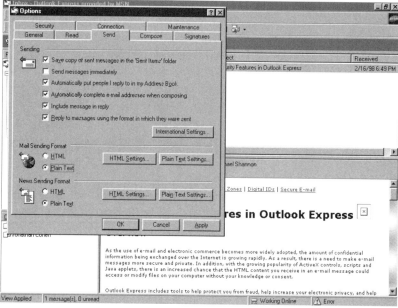

3-4 through 3-7. Setting e-mail preferences in Outlook Express.

selection of, a quoted message to set it off within the new message (fig. 3-8, page 40). Some display quoted text in different colors to help sort out threads several generations deep.

An e-mail message consists of three parts: a *header*, which identifies the sender and recipient and shows the servers and nodes through which the message passed; the *body* of the message itself; and, optionally, a *signature*. The full header is normally not shown, because it contains information that most people don't need, and it tends to clutters the message. Most e-mail programs give the option

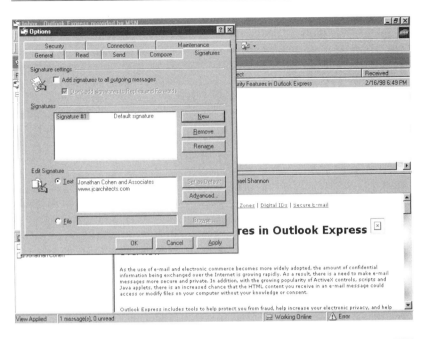

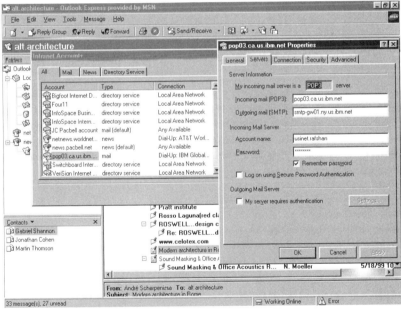

of either not displaying headers at all or showing an abbreviated header with just the identity of the sender and the date and time. The signature (called a *sig* in Internet shorthand), which typically contains contact information for the sender, is normally appended to the message by the sender's e-mail program automatically. Most e-mail programs provide options for adding different signatures to business and personal messages.

Messages can be forwarded to additional recipients. Most e-mail programs permit additional recipients to receive copies, using the old

3-8. Outlook Express displays quoted text from previous posts in a thread.

typewriter terminology for carbon copy, *cc*, or blind carbon copy, *bcc*. Sending a blind carbon copy conceals from the recipient who else is receiving the message, keeping your mailing list private.

One of the most useful applications of e-mail is for subscribed mailing lists. These can be public or private, moderated or unmoderated. Many such lists are in use on the Internet, covering a wide range of interests and affinities. One joins a list by sending a message to the server hosting the list, using a command to its list server software (Listserv and Majordomo are the most popular). If the list is public and unmoderated, the subscription is entered automatically. Subscribers to unmoderated lists can add contributions whenever they wish; when they do, their message is automatically sent to all subscribers. Moderated lists have a human gatekeeper, someone who has been appointed to review messages before they are sent along to the subscribers.

E-mail lists do not require the subscriber to actively seek out the discussion; messages are sent automatically to each subscriber. If you are running a server on the Internet or an intranet, it is easy to create your own mailing lists organized around projects. List server programs permit subscribers to receive mailings in digest form, a single mailing with all of the messages sent that day.

Unlike the Web, e-mail is for text only, but additional files can be sent as e-mail attachments or enclosures. Many firms rely on e-mail attachments to distribute CAD files or meeting minutes to project participants, for example. You need to tell your e-mail program about which helper applications to use to open any attachments you receive (figs. 3-9 and 3-10). For example, you can configure your e-mail program to hand off graphics files to Photoshop, word-processing files to Microsoft Word, and spreadsheets to Excel.

Attachments sometimes become a problem when different com-

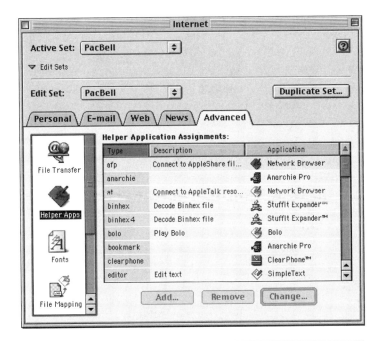

3-9. Choosing helper applications for attached files.

3-10 Assigning applications to handle files with particular suffixes.

puter platforms, or even different e-mail programs, are in use. This is because the Internet was originally set up to transfer only simple, unformatted text known as **ASCII**. ASCII uses seven bits of data to specify each character in the alphabet as a pattern of 1s and 0s. But many files, such as graphics, databases, and CAD drawings, contain much more than plain text. Data in these files are stored in a binary format that uses not seven but eight bits to define each piece of information. So how do you transmit eight-bit data through a seven-bit system? That's where **encoding** comes in. When nontext files are attached to e-mails, they are encoded, which temporarily turns the attached file into a text document made up of ASCII characters, text that can travel intact across any file server, through any mail gateway, and into any e-mail program, regardless of whether it is running on a Mac, a PC, or a Unix computer. When an encoded file arrives at its destination, the recipient's e-mail program detects the encoding system used and converts the file back into its original eight-bit form. This process is supposed to happen transparently, without users being aware of it, and it usually does. But sometimes problems arise when the particular encoding system used by the sender is not recognized by the recipient's e-mail program.

Three types of encoding are commonly used to send attached files via e-mail: MIME (also called Base64), UUencode, and BinHex. All three can potentially leave you with attachments that look like unintelligible garbage if your software program does not know how to decode them. The problem arises most often when either the sender or recipient is on CompuServe or AOL, which each use their own proprietary encoding schemes. If you cannot get your e-mail program to correctly decode attachments, you may still be able to open them with a utility program such as Mpack, WinZip, or Stuffit Expander.

Another twist is added when e-mail programs use **compression**. Compression temporarily reduces the size of an attached file so that it is transmitted faster. Many e-mail programs compress attached files automatically and decompress received files. When you first configure your e-mail software, you are given options about which encoding and compression schemes to use by default. Unless you are certain about your recipients' e-mail capabilities or you are sending an e-mail attachment to multiple recipients, its best to turn off compression and set the encoding protocol to Base64 or MIME.

MIME also comes into play when configuring a Web server. The server must be told about special file types so that it can instruct the browser to "hand it off" to the appropriate helper application or plug-in.

File Transfer Protocol

If dealing with the encoding and compression of e-mail attachments is too much trouble, you can use File Transfer Protocol, or FTP, to move files to your project team. FTP is used for transferring files via a server as well as for uploading and downloading files to your Web site.

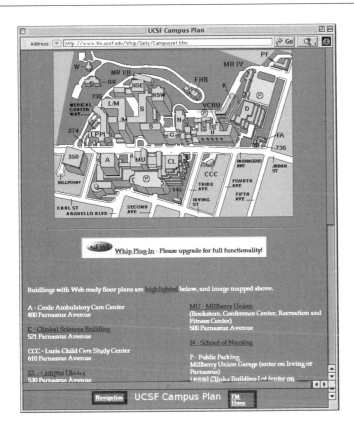

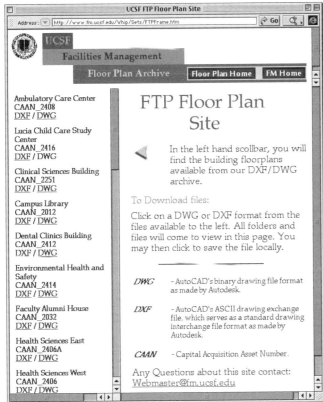

3-11 and 3-12. The University of California at San Francisco provides downloadable as-built drawings of its facilities on an FTP site. A clickable map of the campus leads to FTP directories for each building. (Courtesy of UCSF Facilities Management)

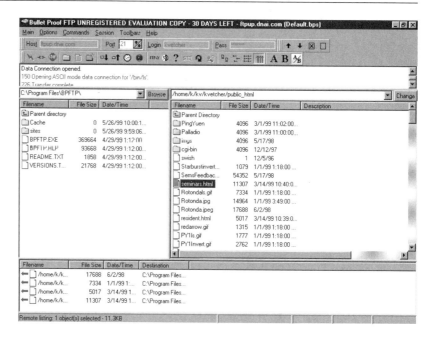

3-13. Bullet Proof FTP for Windows allows you to see local and remote directories side by side. (Courtesy Bullet Proof FTP)

Most Web browsers can handle the download part of an FTP transaction, but uploading requires software designed for this purpose. Popular FTP programs include Fetch and Anarchie for the Macintosh and Internet Neighborhood and Bullet Proof FTP for Windows.

The simplest kind of project meeting place is an FTP site, where architects, contractors, subs, and consultants can exchange files, creating in effect a virtual plan room. FTP can be *anonymous*, in which any client on the network can have access to files, or it can be configured to accept only **authenticated** visitors. When investigating potential ISPs, make sure they will allot you space on their FTP server, and find out how much space you will have. If you decide to run your own Web server, it is easy to add FTP capability to it, and you will be able to log visits and password-protect the site (figs. 3-11 and 3-12, page 43).

FTP is the usual method for uploading material to Web sites, and it is now integrated into most Web page design software. Many Webmasters like to duplicate, or "mirror," their Web site on a computer off the network, and they use FTP to synchronize the two sets of files (fig. 3-13). That way, changes to the Web site can be modeled and studied off the network, then when a change is accepted, it can be published on the Web server. The mirror site also serves as an additional backup copy.

Like the Web, FTP is a client-server system. Any FTP client application can get the job done, but the good ones support such advanced features as:

- *Auto resume*, which prevents having to reconnect to a server and begin again if an FTP file transfer is interrupted. The down- or upload is resumed at the point of interruption.

- *Recursive directory transfers,* which allow you to transfer en masse entire Web site directory structures, that is, folders with all subfolders and files.
- *Drag and drop,* which allows you to treat the remote FTP server as if it were a computer on the local area network. Simply drop your files into the appropriate folder on the FTP server.
- *Address book (bookmarks),* which enable you to reconnect to a previously visited FTP site with one click.
- *ASCII/binary options,* which allows the FTP client to differentiate between text files and files that must be opened by a helper application.

A number of commercial Web sites providing free or low-cost remote file storage, such as FreeDrive, X:drive, and @Backup, have positioned themselves as an alternative to FTP. As the sheer volume of data on hard drives has grown, a new business called data vaulting has appeared, offering secure, encrypted Web backup for large businesses. Instead of backing up data to tapes or other media, companies simply program their computers to upload the contents of their hard drives nightly to these data vaults. Most offer a limited version of their services for free, allowing up to 50 MB of storage on their servers and only obliging you to look at some advertising in return. Many individuals and small businesses use these Web sites to exchange files with clients and partners.

Network Newsgroups (Usenet)

Newsgroups are bulletin board discussion lists built around shared interests, or affinities. At the time of this writing, more than forty thousand publicly available newsgroups were on-line, ranging from alt.barney.die.die.die to zoom.cheesedog (fig. 3-14). Newsgroups can

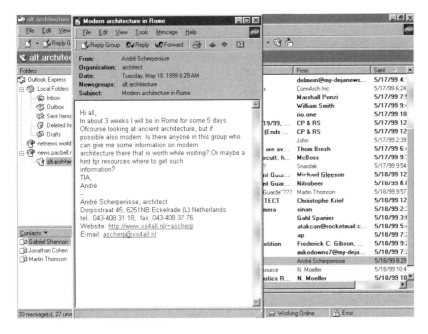

3-14. A post in the alt.architecture newsgroup.

3-15. A directory of newsgroup posts in Outlook Express. Responses in a thread are nested under the original posting.

also be used for serious business purposes, and you can host your own private newsgroups by running news server software on your intranet or extranet. Another option is to use a news-hosting service that will provide space on their server, usually with the requirement that you

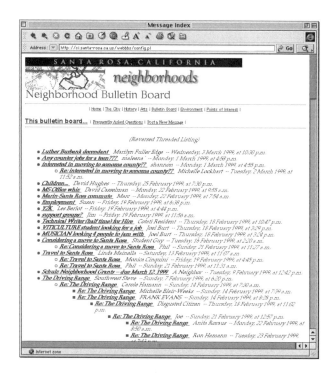

3-16. A threaded discussion in a Web browser window.

accept advertising banners. Companies that provide subscription-based project extranets commercially, such as Cephren and Evolv, allow you to set up newsgroups specific to your project. Discussions are **threaded**, that is, as particular topics of discussion are raised, replies to the original post are grouped together, allowing readers to follow the discussion of that topic as it unfolds (fig. 3-15). Architects and planners are using threaded discussion groups to collect programming information from stakeholder groups for projects. In such cases, access is restricted to those with a password.

A key difference between newsgroups and e-mail lists is that the former requires you to actively seek out the discussion by logging on. A moderator may be needed to keep discussions on topic or to suggest new topics when discussion falters. A capacity for threaded discussions can also be added to a Web site with a **CGI** script. This enables people to participate through their browser, obviating the need for a separate news reader program (fig. 3-16).

Other Internet Applications

Many other peripheral applications run on the Internet, with more added each day. Some require special software or a high-bandwidth connection. A sampling of these other Internet services include:

- *Internet relay chat*: Connected users participate in live group chat sessions, that is, they send typed messages to each other. Teenagers love it. A related technology, called *instant messaging,* allows users to send messages directly to each other without the use of a mail server, provided they are on-line at the same time.
- *Videoconferencing:* Not for low-bandwidth connections, but an increasingly viable option for high-speed intranets and extranets. Videoconferencing applications such as CUSeeMe require each partic-

Performance, Bandwidth, and the Internet

Much has been written about the "world wide wait"—network bottlenecks that sometimes seem to slow the information flow on the Web to a crawl. So many variables affect network performance that the cause of an Internet slowdown is almost impossible to pinpoint. Because of its decentralized design, Internet packet traffic might follow a circuitous route from sender to receiver, passing through many routers and traversing a great deal of territory. Sometimes the problem is local, sometimes it is regional or national, as was true when I was presenting a seminar in Chicago on the same day that Ken Starr's report, with its salacious details of presidential sex romps, was being released. The entire Internet slowed to a crawl as millions of Bill and Monica fans downloaded the report.

Bandwidth is the measure of capacity for a network. Think of it as the diameter of the pipe through which your information flows. With a slow modem connected to the Internet, you are drinking a thick milkshake through a narrow straw. In the computer industry, bandwidth has become a metaphor for all scarce resources: bandwidth is to the Internet what water is to the West. Internet visionaries dream about a future time when bandwidth is cheap and abundant. With the advent of widespread DSL and cable modem service, that future may be here soon.

3-17. CUSeeMe from White Pine Software is a popular videoconferencing application.

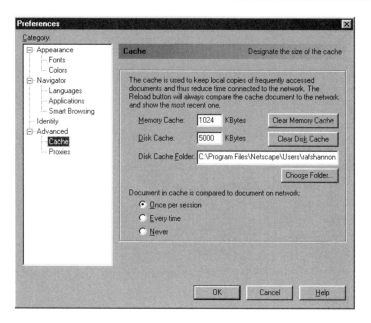

3-18, 3-19, and 3-20. Setting browser preferences in Netscape Navigator.

ipant to have a small video camera attached to the computer (fig. 3-17, page 47). Video quality is still poor.

- *Audioconferencing:* Participants can speak to each other, using a microphone attached or built in to their computers. Such applications as Microsoft NetMeeting also support shared whiteboarding whereby participants in an audioconference can mark up a drawing, for example, as they discuss a proposed design. The marked-up drawing is then saved as an image file and distributed to the participants as a record of the meeting.
- *Streaming audio and video:* These technologies try to overcome the bandwidth limitations of dial-up connections by allowing users to begin viewing or hearing a file before it is completely downloaded. They require a plug-in for the browser and special software installed on the server. Real Networks, Apple's QuickTime, and Windows Media Player are the leaders in streaming media.

The World Wide Web

Most of the remainder of this book will concern itself with the Web, because the Web browser has become the jack-of-all-trades client application for most of the Internet activities discussed in this book. With the aid of plug-ins (or Microsoft's ActiveX) and helper applications, Web browsers allow you to view and interact with virtually any kind of content that is created on computers (figs. 3-18, 3-19, and 3-20).

Since both Microsoft Internet Explorer and Netscape Communicator are distributed free of charge, there's really no reason not to use the current version. All new PCs come with at least one browser preinstalled, and ISPs provide disks with browser software to

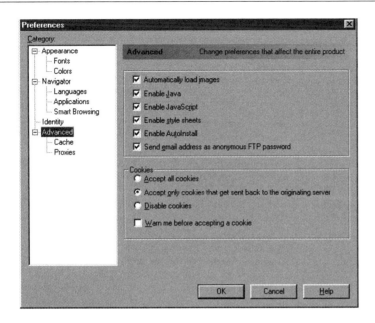

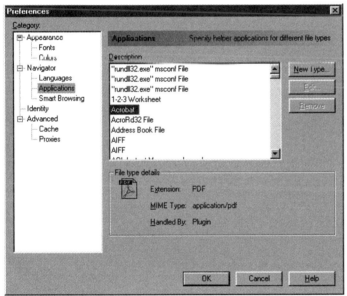

new subscribers. A click on the Netscape or Microsoft logo in the upper right corner of a browser window will bring the user to an update page for downloading the latest version. The intense competition between these rivals for dominance of the browser market has led to a dizzying pace of innovation. Many of the new features are more hype than substance, but real improvements have been made in stability and ease of configuration.

Why do these industry titans battle so fiercely to give away their products? The browser's universality has made it an all-purpose tool not only for millions of people on the Internet, but for millions more on corporate intranets, who use their browsers every day to check

Searching the Web

The difference between a library and a pile of books on the floor is an indexing system. As the amount of content on the Web grows, the problem of finding information becomes ever more acute. By mid-1999 the Web consisted of about 800 million pages, containing six **terabytes** of text information, hosted on millions of servers. What will replace the Dewey decimal system and the card catalog? Most Internet users rely on search engines.

A controlled survey of eleven of the most popular search sites published by the science journal *Nature* in July 1999 found a significant disparity in results between the most effective, Northern Light (www.northernlight.com), and the least, Euroseek. But even Northern Light indexed less than 20 percent of the estimated amount of data on the Web. The study also found that overlap between the search engines was relatively low, suggesting that an effective search should always include at least two sites. As the Web matures, another criterion for effective searching will become more important: how good are the search engines at culling pages that have moved or no longer exist? There is nothing more worthless than a page of outdated links.

An Internet search engine has three components:

1. A program, variously called a spider, a crawler, or a bot, that visits every page, reads it, compiles its text, and follows every link. The major search sites each claim to have searched nearly every publicly accessible page on the World Wide Web, but as the *Nature* study showed, they do not come close to achieving this feat.
2. An index or catalog of all the pages that have been visited.
3. A program for receiving search requests, comparing them to the index, and returning responses in the form of a page of links.

Popular keyword search engines include AltaVista, Hotbot, Infoseek, and Excite. A second type of search resource is a structured directory, such as Yahoo, the Web's equivalent of the Yellow Pages.

The key to finding results is to know how to perform a search. Each of the search engines uses its own method of compiling content, so effective searching requires knowing the peculiarities of each site. Each maintains pages with advanced searching tips, and it pays to read them.

In general, searches are begun when the user enters a search argument, which may be just a single word. Some search engines, such as Hotbot, allow searching by exact phrase, so that a search for the phrase "Bauhaus architecture" will produce specific results, not just a list of pages that include the words *Bauhaus* and *architecture*.

Most search sites also permit Boolean queries. The nineteenth-century English mathematician George Boole developed a system of logical thought employing operators between words or values. Boolean operators include AND, OR, and NOT. A search for "apples AND oranges" will return pages containing both words,

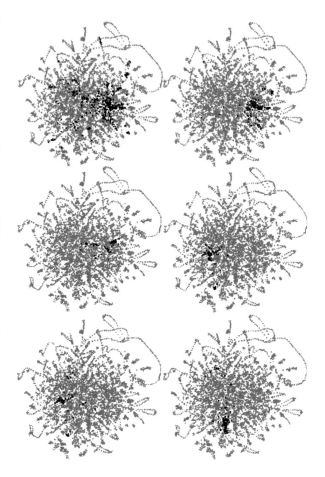

3-21. A layout of 4,558 URLs, with matches for each of six searches highlighted. From *The Order of Things: Activity-Centred Information Access*, by Matthew Chalmers, Kerry Rodden, and Dominique Brodbeck. (Courtesy Matthew Chalmers, Glasgow University)

while "apples OR oranges" returns pages with either term, and "apples NOT oranges" returns pages that contain apples but exclude oranges. On some search sites, separating two words by a space (or sometimes a comma) is understood to be the same as the Boolean operator AND. A few search sites permit questions in "natural language," that is, plain English phrases such as "Who is the most fashionable architect in New York?"

A second generation of search resources uses more sophisticated methods to find relevant pages. For example, Google (www.google.com) rates the relevance of a Web page to a particular query by examining how many other pages link to that page (fig. 3-21).

their retirement fund or access monthly sales data. The browser is the gateway to the connected world, and whoever controls the gateway has an immense commercial advantage. In the 1980s Microsoft saw that dominating the market for PC operating systems would give it an advantage in selling its (much more lucrative) application software, and it viewed Netscape's early lead in browsers as a threat to its control of the desktop. Thus, the browser war began, which led to the antitrust suit against Microsoft.

In truth, the two major browsers have similar feature sets, and both are remarkably powerful pieces of software. Since most people use their browsers primarily to find information on the Internet or intranets, future improvements in browser technology will likely focus on enhanced search capabilities. For those in the fields of planning, design, and development, the browser is the tool we use for finding zoning information, downloading GIS maps, searching products, and locating suppliers.

So far, we've discussed selecting an ISP and using different software programs to access the basic Internet services of e-mail, FTP, newsgroups, and the Web. You should now feel confident that you can use the Internet to communicate with colleagues, join discussion groups, and do research on the Web. But that's only half the story. Finding information is one thing; but how do you bring your own information to the Web? The next chapter introduces the fundamentals of creating Web sites.

Creating

Now you are connected to the Internet and ready to put it to work. In the networked economy, the ability to create Web sites will be an essential business skill. Web sites will all but replace most other kinds of business communication. Proposals and statements of qualifications, even construction documents, will take the form of Web sites, taking advantage of the power of hyperlinking and multimedia. Fortunately, the tools now available make creating Web sites both easy and fun, and anyone with basic computer skills can do it.

Building a Web site requires a design process with distinct steps, not unlike the phased design process architects use to design a building. The process can be summarized as follows:

- Know your audience
- Plan a structure
- Design an interface
- Assemble resources
- Build pages and sites
- Upload to a server
- Evaluate and revise

Setting Goals

The first questions in any design problem are whom is this for and what is its function? Your first step should be to develop an idea of the Web site's purpose, objectives, and target audience. List the kinds of informational transactions that will occur on the site. Is it a hyperlinked statement of qualifications for a potential project? Is it a place for file exchange among project team members? Is it an advertisement for your firm's services? Or a site designed to explain a design proposal and solicit comment from stakeholders? A statement of purpose will

Effective Web Sites

help clarify your objectives before you begin and can be used later to evaluate how well the site is achieving them. If the site is designed to meet specific quantitative goals of time savings, expense reduction, or schedule compression, state these goals explicitly.

Your assessment of an intended audience will include knowledge of the kind of information sought by your visitors. Some sites will be designed for a quick scan, others for a more leisurely encounter. It may help to think about what problems your visitors are trying to solve. Your task as a site designer is to know your intended audience so that you can develop a site that helps visitors find the information they need. Questions to ask yourself include: Is the site designed to be used by a limited number of people on a regular basis, or is it one that will be accessed by new visitors all the time? Will people be visiting the site several times a day over a long period, or will they visit one time only? Will visitors likely be on high-bandwidth connections, or dialing in on modems? Will visitors be consuming information onscreen, or will they be printing pages for later reference?

Software engineers classify computer users as dedicated or casual. The former are people who will be frequent and heavy users of specific programs and can be expected to spend considerable time becoming familiar with them. Casual users are infrequent or occasional users who need access to the most basic features without having to read a manual. In the same way, a well-designed site should accommodate users with different levels of expertise. Its layout should be quickly discernible to "power users" looking to get in and out as quickly as possible but not be intimidating to users with more limited Internet experience.

Consider the speed at which visitors are connecting. If the site is intended for a high-speed corporate intranet, you have more freedom to use graphics-intensive pages than if the expected audience is a construction superintendent using a modem to connect from the job-site trailer. Consider the limitations of international connections as well. Aside from the obvious language barriers, many countries simply lack the high-speed telecommunications infrastructure we take for granted in the United States. Foreign visitors may experience slower Internet performance overall. If you have international partners or are routinely engaged in international projects, you may need to slim down and design your site for lower bandwidths.

After you have completed a first draft of a site, test it. Try imagining yourself as a visitor to the site, looking for different kinds of information. See how long it takes for each kind of expected user to "score." Compressing the path from home page to the needed information is your objective. Try **beta-testing** your site on people whose profile matches the planned audience.

Diagramming Your Site

Your next task before creating content is to design a structure for your Web site. Here design professionals have a distinct advantage: they are trained to understand complex design issues and see the structural and spatial relationships between elements.

A Web site begins at an entry point, or **home page**. The home page has been likened to the front door of a house. When you enter a well-designed house, its plan unfolds before you. You have no problem finding the kitchen or the bathroom. But in a poorly designed house, you may have to open and close doors and retrace steps before you find what you are looking for.

In the same way, when you enter a Web site at the home page, you should grasp its structure immediately. Just as Le Corbusier called a house "a machine for living," so a Web site is a machine for delivering information. You are designing an effective delivery system that takes visitors where they need to go in the fewest mouse clicks.

Site Maps

A Web site is a collection of electronic files, including pages, images, and other types of media, organized by a system that links the material together. The links from and between the various elements *within* the Web site are called *local links*. Links to resources *outside* of the Web site are *remote links*. A diagram of the site is essential to grasp the relationship between pages and to design for maximum efficiency of use (figs. 4-1, 4-2, and 4-3).

Therefore, an important early step is to draw a site map, which graphically plots the linked relationship of pages within a Web site. Building a Web site without a site map is akin to constructing a building without a plan. Diagramming these relationships forces the Web designer to think about navigation and to begin visualizing the information delivery system, even before any pages have been designed.

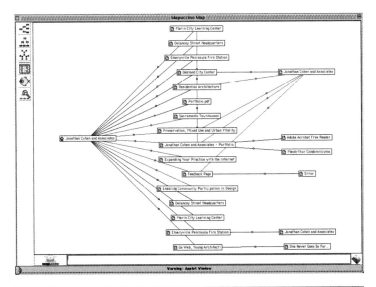

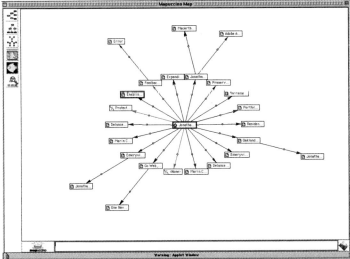

4-1 and 4-2. Mapuccino from IBM is a Java program that charts Web sites in a variety of ways. (Mapuccino was developed by IBM Haifa Research Lab. © IBM Corporation)

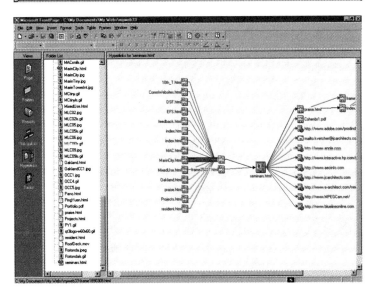

4-3. Microsoft FrontPage allows Web authors to inspect the links to and from a page.

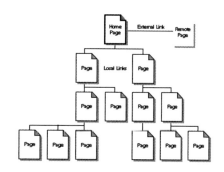

4-4. A hierarchical Web site structure.

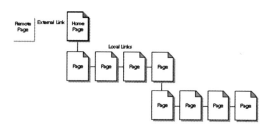

4-5. A sequential structure.

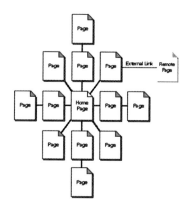

4-6. A matrix structure.

Because of the nonlinear structure of most Web sites, it is especially important to organize information in a logical way.

Figure 4-4 shows a *hierarchical* "trunk and branch" organization, the most common structural organization for Web sites. It offers plenty of potential to channel visitors into different directions from a home page. Most people can intuitively grasp this kind of organization, similar as it is to the classic "org chart," and keep it in mind as they move through the site. It also takes good advantage of hyperlinking.

A *sequential* organization, as shown in figure 4-5, is not unlike a slide show or PowerPoint presentation. It is appropriate when the order of progression through a site is important, as, for example, with an on-line training course, or when presenting information in chronological order. If you are telling a story with a Web site, then the organization should be sequential, with movement through the site aided by BACK and FORWARD buttons. Any presentation intended to lead a visitor through a logical progression lends itself to a sequential organization. At times, a combination of sequential and nonlinear movement through the site will be needed. For example, you may be presenting a narrative, such as the history of your firm, but still want to allow the visitor to be able to move to related topics or remote sites.

Other sites are both nonsequential and nonhierarchical: a construction specification, a catalog of fabric samples, and an on-line planning code are all examples. When the information consists of items of approximately equal size and importance, a *matrix* type of organization is appropriate, as shown in figure 4-6. This kind of organization, which allows random access to any part of the site, really demonstrates the power of hyperlinks. An entry page to such a site might display a grid of thumbnail graphics linked to each piece of information. No logical progression is being imposed, and visitors can proceed through the site any way they like (figs. 4-9 and 4-10, page 58).

Very complex sites may require more sophisticated ways of visualizing their structures than simple diagrams allow. Figures 4-7 and 4-8 show three-dimensional isometric views of a Web site link hierarchy, which help to illustrate the spatial component of the information.

A good plan for a Web site considers the type of content and the expectations that site visitors will have about how that content should be organized. Project-specific Web sites, for example, can be modeled on existing paper-based project management systems. You could begin diagramming a site map by taking the file directory you already use to categorize project information. If you can "flatten" the site hierarchy without losing its logical structure, people will find the information they want in fewer steps. Figures 4-11 and 4-12 (page 59) show how a "flat" structure differs from a "deep" one.

A complex Web site will necessarily have a deeper structure than a simple one does. But always keep in mind how frustrating it can be to sift through page after page to find something hidden many levels deep. The shortest, most direct route from the entry page to the desired infor-

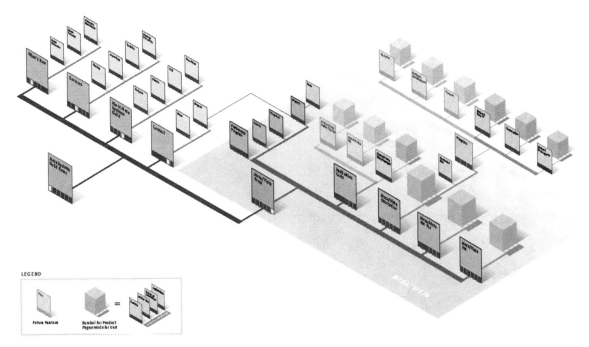

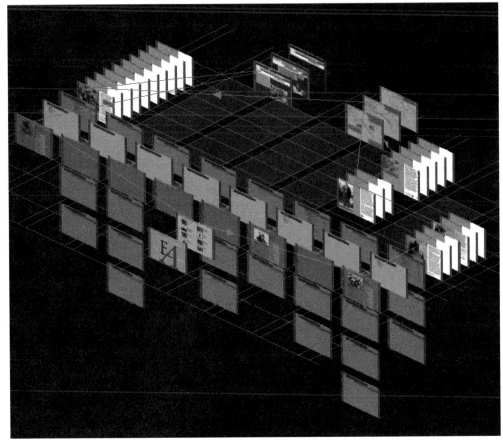

4-7 and 4-8. Three-dimensional isometric diagrams of more complex Web site structures. (Courtesy Dynamic Diagrams)

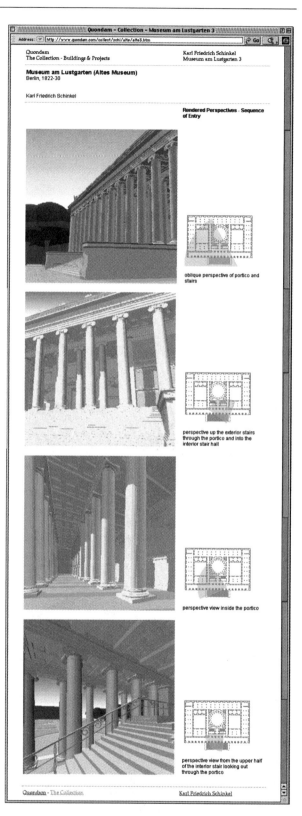

4-9. A Catalog of Courtyard Types, part of the Urban Design Precedents project at the Center for Landscape Research, University of Toronto.

4-10. Schinkel's Altes Museum from Quondam, a virtual museum of architecture.

mation should always be the goal. Try drawing storyboards of each page on 3- by 5-inch index cards, so that you can experiment with different navigational schemes to track a visitor's progress through a site.

The site map does not have to be fixed and unchanging. It is more like a living ecosystem, where old pages die and new ones take their place. Because Web sites tend to grow incrementally, you have to remain vigilant that the underlying structure you established does not get lost. The ease of making changes means that a Web site need never be considered finished. After a Web site's launch, test the effectiveness of its structure and adjust if necessary. Rearranging the elements in a Web site is easy, but always keep your plan in mind.

Information is easiest to use when it is presented in small pieces. A Web page can be of any length, but consider the advantage of breaking up material into easily absorbed and logical segments. Instead of placing an entire specification on one page, for example, place each CSI section on a separate page. Think about the smallest chunks of information your viewers need at a time, and divide your Web site accordingly. Be consistent, so that readers know what to expect when they ask for the next chunk. It's a balancing act: if too little information is provided, the viewer will become frustrated. No one wants to wait for another page to load just to read another paragraph. On the other hand, readers find it annoying to have to scroll through long blocks of text and graphics to find a link to needed information. Keep in mind that, on-line, the threshold of frustration is low, and the attention span is short.

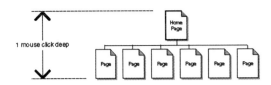

4-11. A flat structure.

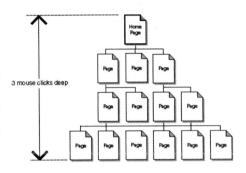

4-12. A deep structure.

Interface Design

After the development of a site map, the next step is to design an interface, the so-called "look and feel" of the Web site. Again, take your cues from a careful analysis of the site's purpose and intended audience. A site designed to catch the eye of a potential client with snappy graphics has a different look and feel than one designed to distribute documents to a project team. The latter will likely be lean on graphic accoutrements that might slow down a site intended for quick information exchange.

The interface is the mechanism through which visitors understand and interact with the site. A good interface gives visitors assurance that they will be able to find the information they need when they need it. The design problem lies in integrating all elements into an easily comprehensible and consistent information space. You want to give visitors a sense of control; they are making the choices about where to go and what to see. You also want clients and business partners to be comfortable there. The interface you design can be a graphical representation of your signature mode of operating. Just as clients become familiar with the names and faces of your firm, they will also know you by the interface you create.

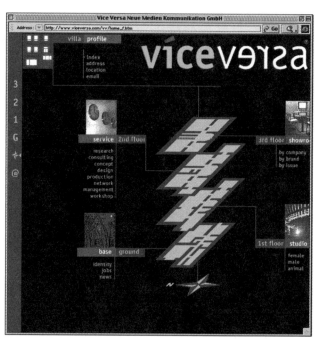

4-13 through 4-16. The Web site of this German design firm uses the spatial metaphor of a multi-level building to aid site navigation. (© ViceVersa Neue Medien Kommunikation GmbH)

In interface design, predictability matters as much as clarity. Once your users have learned how to use your system to access a particular kind of information, don't make them relearn a new way for similar information. For example, if they pull down a menu for this, don't make them click a button for that.

Interface design is more than two-dimensional graphic design. Information space reveals itself to the user just as architectural space unfolds as one walks through a building or landscape. In the same way that visual and spatial cues help to guide people through physical space, good interface design can convey to Web site visitors where they are within the information space of the site. The interface may even have a spatial characteristic; after all, it might be a substitute for the meeting room, the drafting room, or the job-site trailer.

Everyone is familiar with how to navigate a book; the conventions of using tables of contents, indexes, page numbers, and the like evolved over a long period of time. But visitors interact with Web sites in ways that are not possible on paper. The Web is too new to have its own widely accepted standards, which is why good site design is so important (figs. 4-13, 4-14, 4-15, and 4-16).

Elements of Interface Design

Page elements should be visualized on paper before building them in the computer. Just as you drew a site map to plan the site, use cartoons and storyboards to begin blocking out the site's appearance and navigational scheme. Many interface elements use visual metaphors, such as the classic Macintosh trash can. The Windows desktop is a metaphor for a

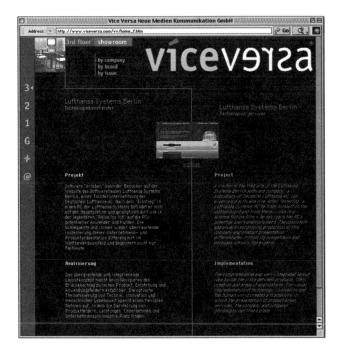

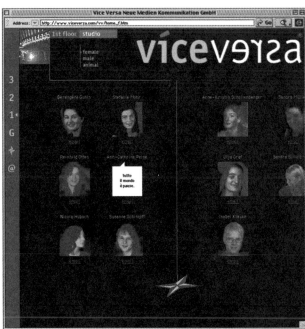

familiar work space, enabling people to think of computing as an extension of their traditional work environment. When you design interface elements, tailor them to your expected audience. For building professionals, why not use visual metaphors for the hanging plan file, the flat file, the drafting board, and the product library? When presenting information about architectural space, why not stairways, doors, and hallways? A great example of adapting visual metaphors can be seen on the Chiat/Day Web site, which uses the metaphor of a factory to talk about advertising in a very effective way (fig. 4-17).

4-17. This advertising agency uses visual metaphors to explain its services.

4-18. The QuickTime Player interface includes a time bar.

Elements of interface design used on Web sites include:

- *File directories*: using nested folders, for example, allows visitors to see several layers of the directory structure, graphically displaying how the information is stored.
- *Menus*, including menu bars, text and iconic, at the top, side, and/or bottom of a window; pull-down menus; tear-off menus; cascading menus; and contextual (pop-up) menus
- *Dialogue boxes*
- *Paging and scrolling devices*
- *Split-screen and windowing capabilities*, such as HTML frames (discussed later in this chapter)
- *On-line form elements*, including text blocks, buttons, check boxes, pop-up selectors, and submit/reset buttons
- *Navigational graphics*, such as buttons, imagemaps, and icons
- *Progress bars*, which add a time element to the information mix, by providing information about the status of downloads, volume adjustment, jump to end, jump to start, and the like (fig. 4-18). Much information is displayed in a small area of screen space.
- *Customizable features*, which allow users to interact with the interface by changing the way information is presented to them.

Assemble Resources

After organizing your site with a site map and blocking out your design ideas on storyboards, your final preparatory step is to assemble the raw material that will make up your site. In all likelihood most of this material will already be on hand. For many companies the first Web site is an electronic version of an existing printed document, such as a brochure or portfolio. In this case you'll be using existing resources in the form of text documents and graphics that were originally created for printing.

If you are preparing new written or graphic material for the Web site, do this first, using tools meant for the job. Write your copy with a word processor. Scan your photographs. (Preparing images and multimedia files for the Web is discussed in chapter 5.) Copies of text files, illustrations, photographs, and other electronic media that may be used on the site should then be assembled and placed in a single **root folder** on your hard drive. As you build pages from this material, you will be creating links between items in this root folder and then transferring the whole folder en masse to the server. Keeping everything in one place minimizes the likelihood of misplacing files or breaking links.

</HTML>: The Web's Native Language

Before beginning to construct a page, let's learn a bit about how the Web really works. A Web page is simply a text document written in **HTML**, or Hypertext Markup Language. HTML tags are embedded instructions that tell the browser how to display text, where to find and how to display graphics and media, and how to link to other pages. For example, the following two HTML tags tell the browser that the title of the page is "Andrea Palladio" and that the background color of the page is blue:

```
<TITLE>Andrea Palladio</TITLE>
<BODY BGCOLOR="#6666ff">
```

The browser knows that everything within brackets is an instruction, not part of the content of the page. The < >(opening) and </ > (closing) brackets mark the beginning and end of each instruction. Tags such as <TITLE> and <BODY BGCOLOR> are agreed upon by convention, and all browsers recognize them.

A minimum, but complete, HTML document would be:

```
<HTML>
<HEAD>
<TITLE>Andrea Palladio</TITLE>
</HEAD>
<BODY>
<P>Andrea Palladio was a noted architect of the 16th Century.</P>
<P>He designed many buildings that still influence architecture today.</P>
</BODY>
</HTML>
```

You can see the underlying HTML code of any page you visit by selecting SOURCE (in Internet Explorer) or PAGE SOURCE (in Netscape) from the VIEW menu of your Web browser.

During the first few years of the Web, creating pages required hand-coding the HTML with a text editor. Web authors had to know arcane

HTML commands, such as the ones above, to make pages. With Adobe's introduction of PageMill in 1994, creating Web pages became almost as easy as word processing. Visual, intuitive page-creation tools now allowed users to build pages graphically, without knowledge of HTML. These new tools did for Web authoring what Pagemaker and QuarkXpress did for desktop publishing ten years earlier. Now, building Web sites could become a mainstream business skill.

Many professional Web designers still edit their HTML by hand, but you don't have to. It does help to have a minimum understanding of how HTML works, however, in the same way that knowing a few things about what goes on under the hood makes you a more informed automobile driver.

All the modern Web-authoring applications allow you to design documents visually, and as you work, the underlying HTML code is written for you in the background. When you drag and drop a graphic into a page or use a color palette to change its appearance, the appropriate HTML code is added to the page automatically. You can, however, view and work with the raw HTML if you want to. Some page-authoring tools allow you to simultaneously view the HTML source code on one side of the screen and, on the other, preview how the page will appear in a Web browser. As you make a change graphically, you can see the HTML working. Other software lets you toggle back and forth between HTML view and preview mode. Even with these handy tools, it's a good idea to always preview your pages in the Web browsers themselves before you put them on-line.

Creating Pages

For those who pine for the craft traditions of the old days, when architects in smock and beret produced beautiful sketches and watercolors, the Web can restore some of the fun and opportunity for creative expression that may have drawn you to the field in the first place.

Begin by selecting one of the excellent Web-authoring applications now on the market, such as Adobe PageMill and GoLive, Microsoft FrontPage, Claris Home Page, Macromedia Dreamweaver, NetObjects Fusion, or Allaire HomeSite. Assemble a toolbox of helper applications, such as Adobe Photoshop, for image manipulation.

Some of the best resources for learning the rudiments of Web design are, not surprisingly, on the Web itself, such as the excellent Yale C/AIM *WWW Style Manual*, the NCSA *Beginner's Guide to HTML*, Rick Levine's *Sun Web Style Guide*, and David Siegel's *Creating Killer Web Sites* (figs. 4-19 and 4-20).

In many ways, some quite subtle, creating content for the Web is different from designing a printed page. Yet the principles of good graphic design still apply: achieving a balance between graphics and text; paying attention to shape, color, and contrast; using thoughtful

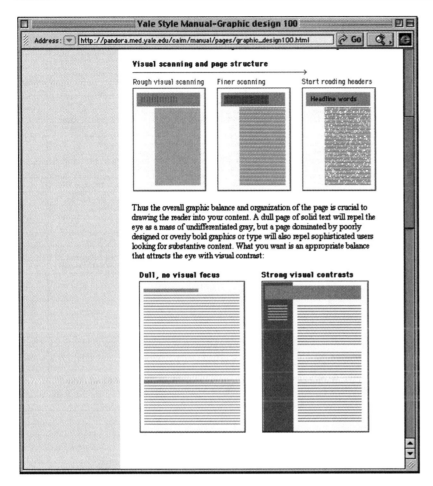

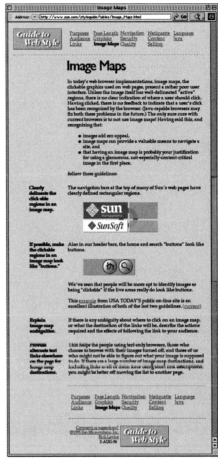

layout and typography; and having consideration for the reader, whose eyes are strained by the low resolution of computer screens.

To illustrate some of these concepts, let's build a page about the sixteenth-century Italian architect Andrea Palladio, using Adobe PageMill 3.0, a simple and inexpensive (under $100) Web-authoring application available for both Windows and Macintosh. If you have that software installed, I suggest you follow the discussion below with your computer in front of you, so that you can practice the techniques as we proceed. This example will provide an overview of the process, intended to show that building Web pages is not so difficult and to encourage you to try it. As with learning to swim, there is no substitute for just getting wet. PageMill and the other software applications mentioned above come with excellent tutorials and documentation, and classes in Web authoring are available at university extension programs and at art and technical colleges around the country.

Let's say you have already created a word-processing document that contains the text for the page. Although PageMill allows you to type directly into a page, it is best to prepare text documents in advance

4-19. The Yale Style Manual by Patrick Lynch is one of the best resources for Web authors on the Internet. (©1999, Patrick Lynch; all rights reserved)

4-20. The Guide to Web Style from Sun Microsystems (Courtesy Sun Microsystems, Inc.)

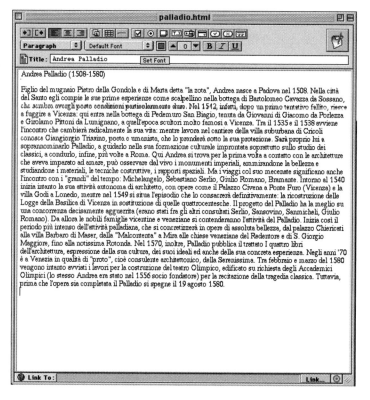

4-21. Text has been brought into a new PageMill document. It is displayed as Times New Roman, 12 point—the default font of Web browsers.

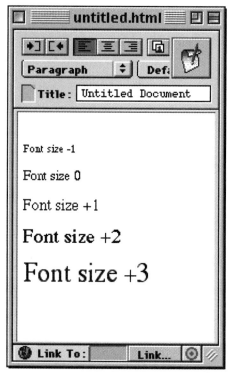

4-22. Web authors control the relative, not the absolute, size of type.

with a word processor. Proofread your document carefully, with a printed copy—it is difficult to spot errors onscreen.

In your word processor, select the text, then drag and drop it into a new PageMill document. As you do so, the appearance of the text changes: it reverts to the default formatting that Web browsers use to display text (fig. 4-21).

Fonts and Typography

HTML does not give you absolute control over how every aspect of a page will appear in a Web browser. Text size and style, for example, is determined both by choices you make as a designer and the settings and preferences of your readers, as well as the characteristics of their systems. When you use a word-processing application, you can specify an exact font and size and establish styles. With HTML, however, you control only the *relative* weight of text, for example, between a headline and body text, without necessarily specifying particular fonts and sizes (fig. 4-22).

Let's take the headline text of your page, and make it two sizes larger than the default setting. In PageMill's menu bar, up and down arrows set the size of text. A relative font size has been specified, so that the HTML is written:

```
<font size="2"/font>
```

HTML handles text very differently from graphics. To facilitate

4-23. The headline has been made two font sizes larger and the typeface has been changed to Palatino.

quick loading of pages into the browser, HTML was designed to hand off the chore of rendering text to the end user's computer. A choice was made to favor speed over design control. End users set their browsers to a default setting, choosing one fixed-width font and one proportional font, and that is how text will appear on their screens. In the illustrations below, notice how the relationship of text to images changes with variations in font settings and window size.

Web page designers can override the default fonts with *font tags*, but these work only if viewers have the specified font installed on their systems. Let's change all the text on the page to Palatino. In PageMill select some text, then choose the font using the drop-down font menu in the toolbar (fig. 4-23). The HTML tag is:

```
<font face="Palatino"/font>
```

In order for the text to appear in viewers' browsers in Palatino, they must have that font installed in their system or the text will revert to the default font. Web browsers on both Windows and Macintosh systems default to Times New Roman unless the user has specified otherwise in his browser PREFERENCE panels (figs. 4-24 and 4-25). When you call for particular fonts by name, assume that viewers have only those most commonly available. Be sure to use the exact, full name as defined in the system software: Times will not invoke Times New Roman, or vice versa. Watch for spaces and capitalization of the font name.

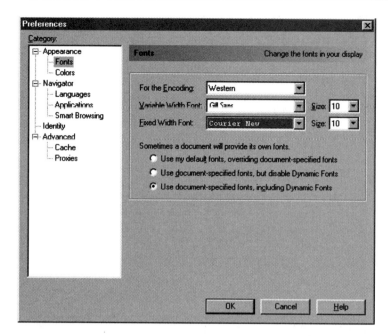

4-24. Users can select one proportional and one fixed-width font to be the default ways in which text is displayed in their browser.

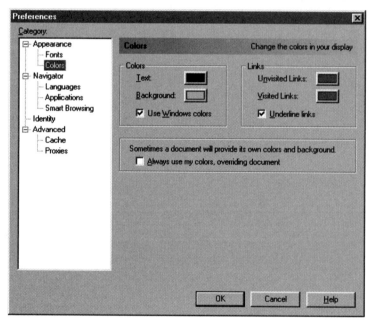

4-25. Another preference panel lets users change the default color of text, linked text, and page background.

One solution is to use *font sets,* which allow you to call for second and third choices if the preferred font is not available on the viewer's system. An example of an HTML tag for a font set is:

```
<font face="GillSans,Palatino,Helvetica,Verdana"/font>
```

The browser will look for the requested fonts in the order given and use the first one it finds.

Be aware that typefaces that are legible on paper are not necessarily as readable on screens, and vice versa. Some new typefaces (such as Verdana and Georgia) have been developed specifically for use on Web pages.

To complicate matters further, a specified font does not always look the same on different computers and monitors. In the United States, 72 points equals 1 inch, so that the designation "12 point Times Roman" describes accurately the physical size of text on a printed page, but it tells little about the size of the text on computer screens. There, the units of measurement are *pixels*, not points, inches, or centimeters.

The number of pixels per inch on a particular screen varies depending on the hardware and operating system. For example, Microsoft Windows assumes that 96 pixels equal 1 inch of screen space, while Macintoshes assume that 72 pixels equals 1 inch. With multisync displays, a given monitor can display screens with a varying number of pixels (screen resolution) within a fixed physical area. Macs treat screen resolution and point sizes of type the same way: 72-point type will use 72 pixels. But Windows differentiates points from pixels: 72-point type may in fact use 96 pixels, but that relationship can be changed in the DISPLAY control panel. Thus, Web pages designed on Windows computers often use type sizes that are too small to be read comfortably on Macs.

One way to ensure that the font you specify is the one that the viewer sees is to create headlines or small amounts of copy in Photoshop using any font you like and saving their images as **GIFs**. Your headlines will now look precisely the way you planned them on all browsers, regardless of which fonts may be available on the viewer's system. If your firm uses a particular typeface for all its printed materials, this technique allows you to bring that visual identity to the Web. Don't do this for large blocks of text, because the pages that result will take much longer to load. This method is especially effective for large headlines or when text is used as part of an imagemap. Special effects, such as drop shadows, can also be added. GIFs, imagemaps, and drop shadows are discussed in chapter 5.

Linking

Linking different items together is one of the most powerful things HTML allows Web designers to do. In PageMill, to create a text link to another page within your Web site, select the text that you wish to link, then drag the icon of the page to which you are linking over the selected text. When you release the mouse button, the text is highlighted and underlined, indicating that it holds a link (figs. 4-26 and 4-27). You can check this link by switching to the PREVIEW mode and clicking on it. You have successfully created a local link between one page and another within your Web site. The link tag looks like this:

```
<A HREF="andrea.html">Andrea Palladio (1508–1580)</A>
```

Here we see that the text "Andrea Palladio (1508–1580)" is being

---

What Is a Font?

A font is a set of text characters in a specific style and size, for example, Palatino, 12 point. Points and picas are units of measure; 1 pica equals 12 points and is approximately ¹/₆ inch. The type design for a set of fonts is called a typeface. In practice the terms typeface and font are often used interchangeably.

The two broad categories of typefaces are *serif* and *sans serif*, indicative of whether or not the typeface uses serifs, or cross-lines, at the end of a stroke. Palatino, for example, is a serif typeface, and Helvetica is a sans serif typeface. Computer systems also distinguish between *monospaced* type, in which each letter uses an equal width, as with a typewriter, and *proportional* type, such as the type in this book, in which the width of individual letters varies. Courier is a monospaced, fixed-width typeface; Garamond is an example of a proportional typeface.

Several technologies for computerized type have been developed. *Bitmap* type is composed of pixels, and it is intended only for display on screens; it looks jagged when printed, particularly at large font sizes. Postscript (developed by Adobe) and TrueType (developed by Microsoft and Apple) are two kinds of *outline* type technology; they describe mathematically the shapes and curves of the type. They are scalable, meaning they can be made larger or smaller and still appear sharp, both on screens and when printed. The difference between bitmap fonts and outline fonts is analogous to the distinction between raster graphics and vector graphics, which will be discussed in chapter 5.

linked to another page, named andrea.html, within the same Web site. We could also make a remote link, that is, link the text to an external Web site:

```
<A HREF="http://www.palladio.com/">Andrea Palladio (1508–1580)</A>
```

In this case the text "Andrea Palladio (1508–1580)" is being linked to a remote Web site, with the URL www.palladio.com.

4-26. Text has been selected.

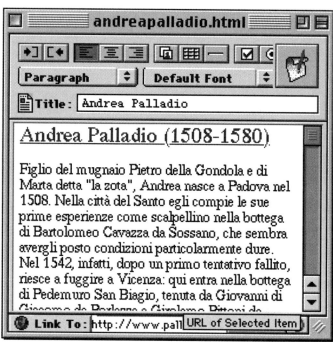

4-27. The selected text is now highlighted and underlined, the default way in which browsers display linked text.

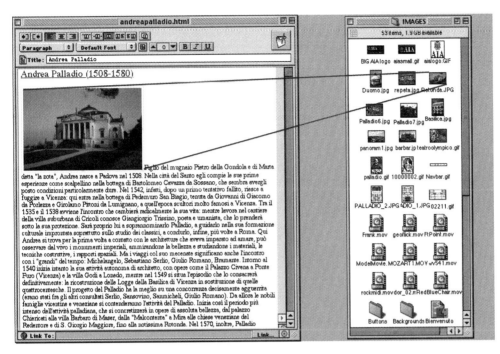

4-28. To insert an image in a Web page, drag and drop the file's icon into the page.

4-29, 4-30, and 4-31. Text can align left or right and wrap around images.

All of the images and other media elements that appear to the viewer to be part of a Web page are in fact separate files that are linked to the page. An image on a page can in turn be linked to another page or another graphic. To do that in PageMill, you must first insert the desired image onto your page (creating and editing graphics is covered in chapter 5; for now, let's assume you already have some image files that are Web-ready). Within your root folder is the subfolder of images that you have prepared for your site. Select the file containing the image you want, and drag its icon into your Web page (fig. 4-28). Once on the page, you can resize the graphic, adjust its alignment, and change the way text wraps around it (figs. 4-29, 4-30, and 4-31). As you do these things, the HTML is written for you. For example, an image is placed on an HTML page with the following tag:

<IMG SRC="//images/JCAlogo.gif" WIDTH="80" HEIGHT="80"
ALIGN="BOTTOM">

Several instructions are given here: the name of the file to be placed is "JCAlogo.gif"; the folder containing it, from which the browser must fetch it, is called "images" and the two backslashes indicate the location of that folder relative to the location of the page itself. The instruction "width="80" height="80"" is a size tag that defines the space in pixels to be given to the image on the page. The final instruction sets the alignment of the image with respect to text on the page.

To link this image to another Web site, select it, and then enter the URL of the remote site in the LINK TO bar at the bottom of the window. Hit the return key, and the link is made (fig. 4-32).

So far, you have been working in PageMill's EDIT mode. By clicking the icon at the upper right of the window, you can move to PREVIEW mode and see how the page will look and behave in the Web browser. When you click on the image for which you have just created a link, a new Web browser window will open, and you will be taken to the linked Web site.

Absolute and Relative Links

The links you make from one item to another create a road map, called a *directory path*, that the browser must follow to locate the file being linked to. In the following example, we create a link from the text

4-32. The image has been linked to a remote Web site whose URL is shown in the LINK TO bar.

"Duomo" to an image file called "duomo.jpg," which can be found in the subfolder "images" within the enclosing folder "palladio" :

```
<A HREF="//palladio/images/duomo.jpg"><Duomo</A
```

Having been told what to look for and where to look, the browser finds "duomo.jpg" and jumps to it when the viewer clicks on the linked text. The two kinds of directory paths that might be used are called *absolute* and *relative*. In the above example, we have indicated a relative path because the location of the linked item is given relative to the Web page containing the link. As you build a Web site, you are in effect staging it on one computer and then transferring it to a second computer, a server. When relative links are made, they point to a location relative to the page itself, and that relative location must be replicated on the server.

An absolute link is used when the browser must go to a new Web site to find a linked item. An absolute link is expressed in HTML as:

```
<A HREF="http://www.jcarchitects.com/palladio/images/duomo.jpg">
<Duomo</A
```

Now the full URL of the link is given so that the browser can find the external Web site and follow the directory path to locate the desired file.

If this sounds complicated, don't worry. The software takes care of these links for you. However, it's important to understand that linking a graphic to a page, for example, is not the same thing as embedding it within the page. It remains a separate file and must be placed on the server along with the Web page itself.

Hyperlinks are unquestionably powerful, enabling the connection of information in ways that were impossible in print media. You can point a reader to other sites that support a point, for example, without cluttering your site with extraneous material. But links can also be a distraction that may cause visitors to lose focus. When creating pages, avoid overlinking within text. It's difficult enough to read text on screens without having to contend with too many links sprinkled throughout it, especially for visitors with itchy fingers who feel compelled to jump to every link. Consider placing links in a separate area of the page, such as the left or right margin.

Make sure your writing is clear *without* the links. Jumping to a link should be optional: don't force your reader to follow a link just to finish your thought. Always link to a keyword or phrase within your text that gives readers a clue as to where the link will lead. Do this:

> **"It's good to use <u>hyperlinks</u> to let readers jump to the definition of a word."**

Instead of this:

> **"To find out what hyperlinks are, click <u>here</u>!"**

Just as bibliographies and appendices in books point readers to other sources, appended lists of links to other Web sites can be easily

Keeping Links Current

Remember that remote links can be changed without notice, so to keep your site current, you must frequently check remote links to be sure they are still working and still relevant. Nothing will undermine the credibility of your Web site more than broken links. Many Web designers add a link to the Webmaster's e-mail at the bottom of each page, so that visitors can report broken links and other problems.

What Is a Cache?

The browser stores recently visited pages and images in a cache on the hard drive. When revisiting a page, it will display the cached version to save time, rather than downloading it from the server again. If the contents of the page have changed since it was last visited by this user, she may not see the latest version. The Web author can add a tag that overrides this feature and compels the browser to reload the page each time.

When a nav bar or any graphic is used repeatedly, the browser will load it from the cache after the first page and subsequent pages will load much faster.

4-33. The Macintosh Web color picker. (Screen shot reprinted with permission from Apple Computer, Inc.)

assembled to augment or support the material in the main body of your site. In this way, you can more fully annotate your material than is possible on paper, if only because the high cost of printing and distribution is avoided. An example is a statement of qualifications that links to the various team participants, without incurring the bulk and expense of photocopying reams of supporting information. Think of whole forests of saved trees!

Color and Backgrounds

One way to enliven your pages is to add areas of color, sometimes in combination with tables (discussed later in this chapter). Unlike graphic files added either as in-line images or background images, color adds nothing to download time and may be all you need to turn a dull, text-heavy page into something people will want to look at twice. Adding some color to sidebars or sections of a page, such as the header, foot-

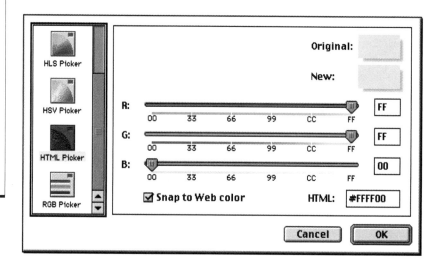

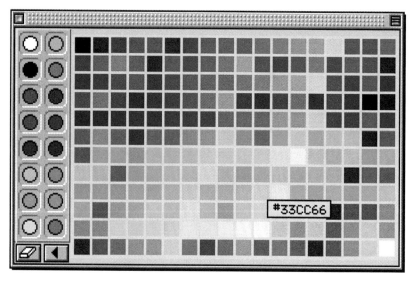

4-34. PageMill's color palette. As the cursor passes over a color sample, its HTML code is displayed.

er, or links bar, can enhance contrast and clarify the organization. Go easy, though, since black text on a white background is already difficult enough to read on screens.

In the old days, when HTML coding was done by hand, colors had to be represented by arcane hexadecimal codes such as **#0099ff**, which the Web browser understood to be blue (fig. 4-33). Adding color using Web-authoring software is much easier. In PageMill, for example, you can color the background of your page by selecting the desired color from PageMill's floating color palette and dropping a sample of it into the BACKGROUND well of the PAGE tab in the INSPECTOR window. The corresponding hexadecimal code is automatically inserted into the HTML for you (fig. 4-34).

Adding a *background graphic* is also easy, but doing so will have an impact on download time. Background graphics are small **GIF** or **JPEG** files that *tile*, or repeat down and across as many times as necessary to fill the full browser window. Too much of this can easily ruin a page, so go easy. The best background graphics are small texture or atmospheric images such as sky or water. If you drag one of the these files into the BACKGROUND well in the INSPECTOR window, your page will include it (figs. 4-35 and 4-36). Such image files are available for download from a number of Internet sites, including Adobe and Microsoft, or you can create your own from photographs or illustrations. Samples may be provided on the disks that come with your Web-authoring software.

The background image usually loads after the Web browser has already displayed the page, so if the page design includes a background image, be aware that viewers will not even see it at first. If you do use backgrounds, use them consistently on every page. That way, the graphic file will be kept in the browser's **cache** and will load much more quickly after the first time. As with other graphic devices that require time to download, this technique is more appropriate for a presentation Web site than for an informational one.

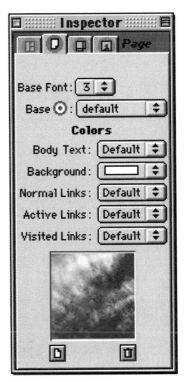

4-35. An image file has been dropped into the BACKGROUND well of PageMill's INSPECTOR window.

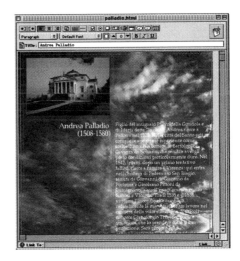

4-36. The background image fills the page.

Tables and Layout Grids

If you want to add tabular material such as a spreadsheet to a Web page, PageMill, FrontPage, and other such programs allow you to just drag-and-drop it into the page. It will be converted on the fly to an HTML table, a grid of cells in a row-and-column format. In fact, recent versions of Excel allow you to save a spreadsheet in HTML. But in Web page design, tables are also frequently used as a formatting device. Without tables, the relationship of text to images will be completely uncontrolled, leading to haphazard and unpredictable results (figs. 4-37 and 4-38). Tables are a useful device for controlling placement of elements on the page, whether text or graphics, and they are the only way to create columns and sidebars. Without them, HTML simply displays one continuous column of text and graphics, at whatever the width of the open window is, starting at the top left of the page and proceeding to the bottom right.

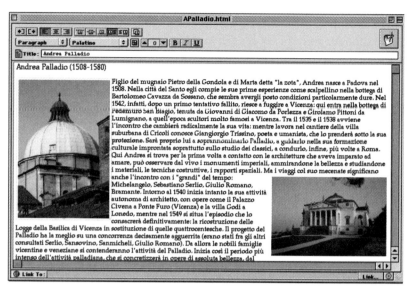

4-37 and 4-38. Without tables, the relationship of text to graphics is affected by the browser window size and shape.

Tables are used to create multiple text columns as well as vertical margins, which make text easier to read (fig. 4-39). Without control over the width of text columns, your text will run across the full width of the browser window. On a large monitor, such lengthy lines of copy can be difficult to read. Wider line lengths force readers to move their heads to read a whole line, making finding the beginning of the next line more difficult. Tables also allow page designers to use blocks of color and multiple columns of text and graphics to format a page, and the formatting does not vary with the size of the browser window (figs. 4-40, 4-41, 4-42, and 4-43).

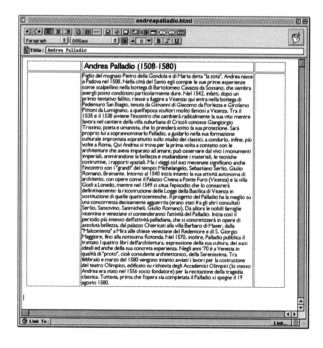

4-39. Here a table is used to fix the width of a block of text and to preserve left and right margins.

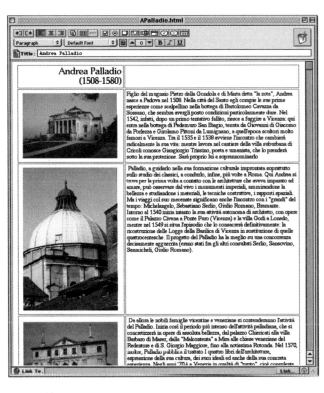

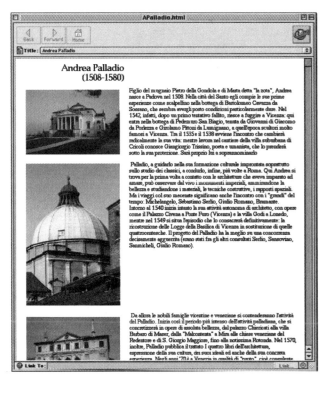

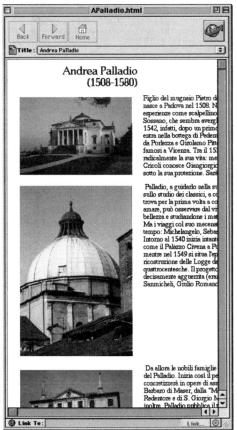

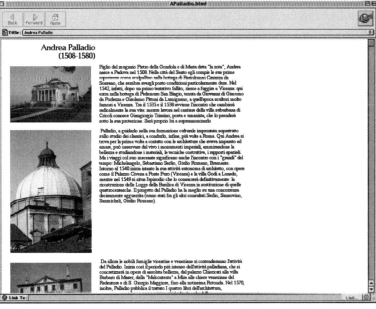

4-40 (top left). A table has been used to create a two-column page. In the EDIT mode, cell borders are visible.

4-41 (top right). The same page in PREVIEW mode. Cell borders are no longer visible. This is how the page will appear in a Web browser.

4-42 and 4-43 (above). With tables, formatting is not changed as the browser window is resized.

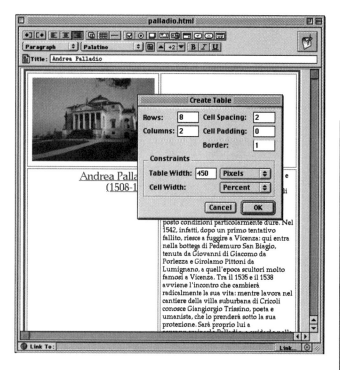

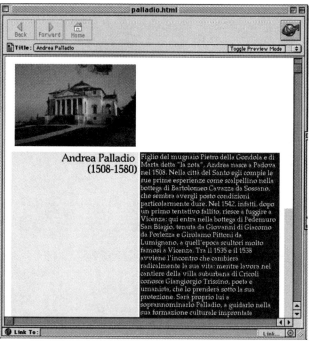

4-44. HTML tables permit Web authors to control formatting.

4-45. Individual cells or groups of cells can be colored.

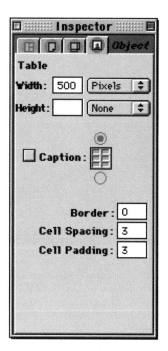

4-46. Setting cell borders to zero makes them invisible in browsers.

Let's reformat our Palladio page with a table. In PageMill, select the TABLE tool in the menu bar and drag out the desired number of cells down and across (fig. 4-44). You can add or delete, combine or divide, or resize table cells later. Text and graphics can be inserted into cells by dragging and dropping a selection into a cell. You can color table cells (or entire rows or columns) and individually format them for text alignment (fig. 4-45). To color a cell or a range of cells, select them and then drop a sample from the color palette into the BACKGROUND well in the INSPECTOR window. With a cell or range of cells selected, adjust the alignment of text and graphics within the cells using the controls available in the INSPECTOR window. In figure 4-41 (page 77), the thumbnail images in the leftmost column were set to align center. The text in the next column to the right was set to align left. You can add a white gutter by inserting a blank column of cells between them.

You can also change the appearance of tables in a Web page by controlling the size of the cell walls and by varying the spacing between cell walls and the contents of cells. With an entire table selected (not just a range of cells), the INSPECTOR window offers three new controls: border, cell spacing, and cell padding. By setting borders to a value of

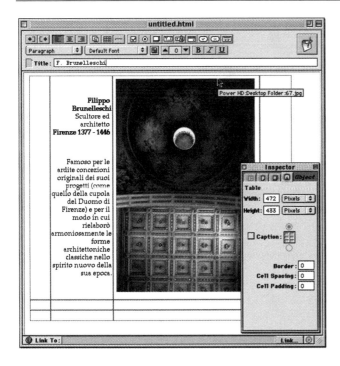

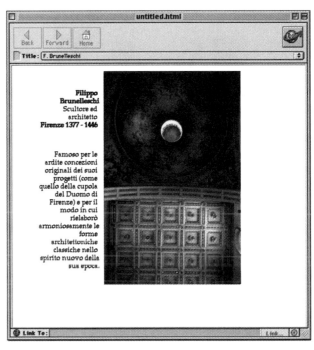

0, the grid of cells becomes invisible when viewed in the PREVIEW mode or in a Web browser (fig. 4-45). *Cell spacing* creates a white space (of *X* pixels) around the outside of a cell, while *cell padding* adds a margin around the contents (whether text or graphics) inside the cell. The overall width and height of a table can be set as either a percentage of the screen or a fixed dimension in pixels. By using percentages, a white margin can be preserved on both sides of a text column, even when the window size is reduced (fig. 4-39, page 76).

You may not always be aware that you are viewing a page containing tables. To find out, check the HTML source of any page you visit. Look for the ‹TABLE› tag to see if hidden tables are being used to block out areas of the page.

An advanced table trick is to mortise images with table cells turned off. Text can be made to wrap around images in interesting ways, and a number of neat effects can be achieved by mixing animated GIFs with stills in a collage. Tables can also be used to attach captions to illustrations and maintain their relationship to each other (figs. 4-47 and 4-48).

Although effective, using tables for layout can be a time-consuming

4-47 and 4-48. An HTML table is used to attach a caption to an image.

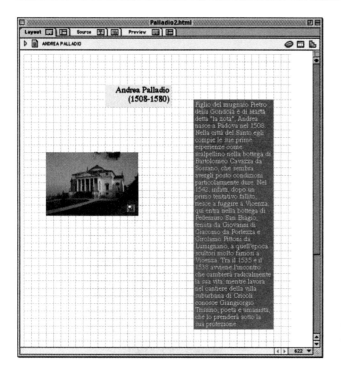
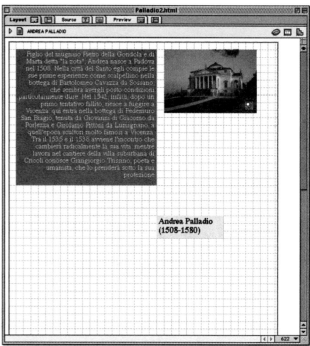

4-49, 4-50, and 4-51. In GoLive, two text blocks and an image are arranged in different ways on a layout grid.

chore. Wouldn't it be better to be able to position elements on a page however you like? After all, you can do that with desktop-publishing programs such as PageMaker and QuarkXpress. More complex and expensive Web-authoring software, such as GoLive and Dreamweaver, allow page designers to work with layout grids or pasteboards. Elements can be snapped to the grid, just as they can with CAD programs. Figures 4-49, 4-50, and 4-51 show an image and two text blocks being manipulated on a layout grid in GoLive. These elements can be moved and resized as necessary, allowing more facility with layout options than is possible when using tables. As you manipulate the elements, the many lines of elaborate HTML code required to provide these effects are written in the background (fig. 4-52).

Frames

It is disorienting to scroll down a page or click on a new page and thereby lose the menu of links or other navigational aids that were guiding you through a Web site. Consequently, some Web designers prefer to limit pages to the size of one screen. But such a limitation taxes viewers, who must continually download new pages for each bit of content. It is particularly inconvenient for long documents, such as specifications or code sections. *Framing* is a browser feature that allows visitors to view multiple Web pages within a single browser window. When different parts of a browser window are separately framed, one frame can change independently of the others. A menu of

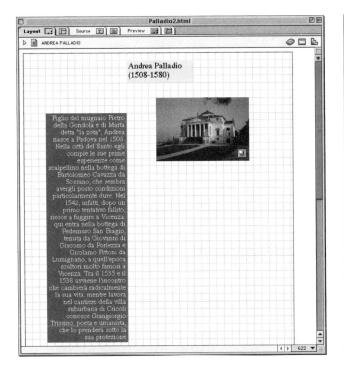

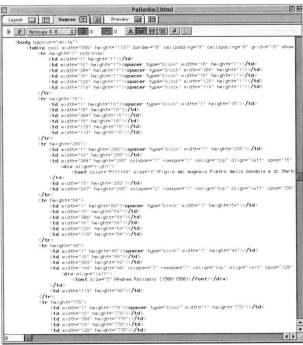

4-52. The HTML code for figure 4-51. GoLive writes elaborate code in the background, giving the page designer freedom to move elements on a grid.

links, or a series of thumbnails, for example, can remain on a portion of the screen while visitors move through a site.

Frames provide two significant advantages that cannot otherwise be achieved. First, they allow visitors to stay on your site while at the same time linking to remote sites in another frame. For example, you may be constructing a statement of qualifications in the form of a Web site. You want to provide links to the Web sites of your proposed subconsultants, but you don't want to send your potential client off to your structural engineer and forget about you. With frames, you can set the engineer's Web site to appear in one frame, on only a portion of the visitor's screen, while elements of your site are still displayed. In effect you have allowed your visitor to check out the engineer without feeling that she has left your site. With frames, you don't have to repeat headers, footers, links, menus, and navigation bars on each page. These elements can be displayed in static frames, while content changes in another frame. Sites that are updated frequently, such project-specific Web sites, benefit greatly from this feature, because you need to change navigational elements only once, rather than on every page.

In one common framing format, a header frame is created at the top of the screen, a footer frame at the bottom, a links frame on the left, and a target frame in the center. The target frame is where the changing content of the site is revealed, while the other frames remain as stationary menus or other fixed items.

Making frames is easy in PageMill. To illustrate, let's create a framed

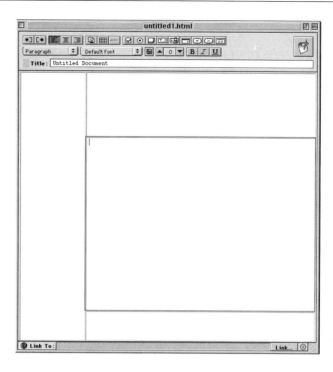

4-53. Four frames have been created by option-dragging from the window edges.

project directory. In a new window, begin by option-dragging frame borders from the edge of the window, creating an arrangement of four panels (fig. 4-53). As you do this, PageMill creates a new HTML document for each frame, giving each file a temporary name, which you can change later. Now the page you are working on becomes a *frame set*. The frame set is the HTML file that describes the arrangement of the frames; each frame is a separate document. The frame-set page is the one to which you want people to link, as it will invoke the other files that make up the arrangement of frames. When you finish creating the frame set, PageMill will ask you if you want to save each individual frame, as well as the frame set itself. All of these pages must be placed on the server together for the frames to work. If the frame set page is your home page, you will want to name it *index.html*.

Let's say you have already prepared a file directory in the form of an HTML document, which you will use to create links to various content areas of your Web site, and you placed this document in the root folder. Now drag and drop that file's icon into the leftmost frame. Then place your nav bar with logo in the topmost frame (fig. 4-54; creating nav bars is discussed in chapter 5). Now you want to turn the file directory into a menu of linked items that, when clicked, will appear in the "target" frame in the center. Suppose, for example, you want to link a directory item for construction sketches to a roofing detail. First, select the text *CSKs*. Now go back to the root folder, select the roofing detail, and drag its icon over the selected text. When you click on this linked text now, a new contextual menu appears giving a thumbnail view of

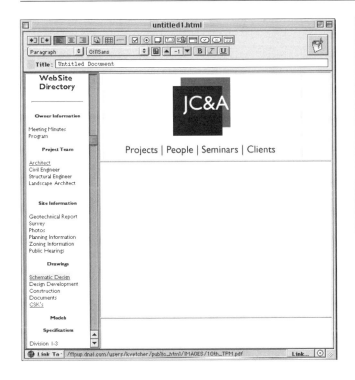

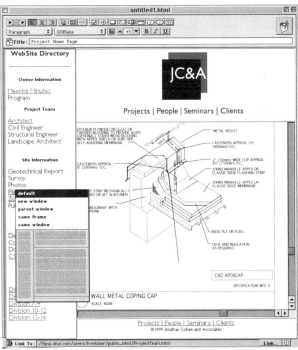

your frame set. Now, select the target frame for this link from among the choices shown on the thumbnail. Figure 4-55 shows the framed page with the link appearing in the selected target frame. You can also cause the link to appear in a new window instead of a frame.

Every frame can be individually formatted, because each is in fact a separate page. You can turn frame borders on and off and make frames with or without scroll bars. In PageMill, with a frame selected, the INSPECTOR window's FRAME tab gives you control over the frame width and frame border thickness, as well as options for turning scroll bars on or off within frames (fig. 4-56). In the example, scroll bars are not needed in the top and bottom frames, and you can save precious screen space by turning them off. When frames are given the same background color and borders are turned off, Web site visitors cannot even tell they are looking at a framed page.

Frames are useful for comparing alternatives side by side. The existing condition can be shown in one frame, for example, with a series of alternate proposals shown in another. Manufacturers can use frames to allow customers to compare two or more product options.

If your visitors will likely be printing pages from your site, and you can't be sure which browser they will be using, consider *not* using frames, as they do not print well from some browsers. Or provide a "printer-friendly" alternative version of each page without frames that will fit on an 8$\frac{1}{2}$- by 11-inch sheet of paper. For pages intended primarily for printing, consider using Adobe's Portable Document Format (discussed in chapter 5).

4-54. A nav bar has been inserted into the topmost frame, and a text menu, in the leftmost frame.

4-55. A floating menu allows the page designer to set any frame as the "target" frame for a link.

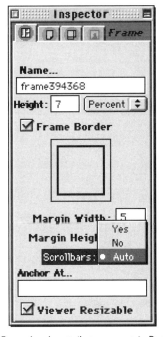

4-56. Frame border attributes are set in PageMill's frame INSPECTOR.

Page Layout

Layout, typography, and illustration are all tools for leading a viewer through a page. Readers will first look at a page, taking in large blocks of space, before choosing sections for closer examination. Even if your site is primarily text, a consistent page layout will make it easier to use.

A page of unrelieved plain text may be boring, but some pages err in the opposite direction, with overstimulating graphics that detract from the content. Contrast, especially between text and background, usually must be emphasized on a Web page more than on paper.

Because reading text for long periods on a computer screen is uncomfortable, you must convey your message quickly. Try to make your main points without expecting the viewer to scroll down to the next screen, in the same way that newspapers place the major stories of the day "above the fold." Viewers do not know how much of the full page they are seeing and may never scroll down to find out. Because text is read from top to bottom and left to right, the most valuable "real estate" on a page is the upper left corner. Web designers will usually try to fit the most important information within a 640- by 480-pixel space, the equivalent of one screenful on a 14-inch monitor (fig. 4-57). In addition, within this limited amount of space, the browser's menu bar and window borders will consume up to 40 pixels of width and 120 pixels of height, leaving an actual usable space of about 600 by 360 pixels.

Layout grids, consistently applied, are a good way to begin organizing your pages into an easily followed pattern. Your grid may consist simply of a standardized header, footer, and navigational buttons

4-57. Visitors with small monitors will not see important information on this Web page because it falls outside their maximum screen area. The highlighted area is **480 by 640** pixels, the typical resolution for a 12- to 14-inch monitor.

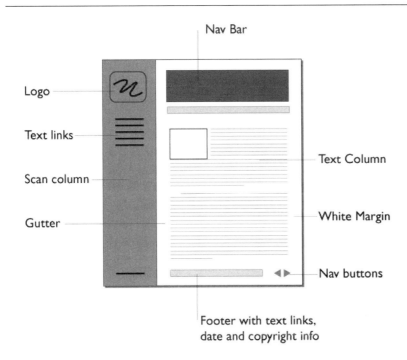

Nav Bar

Logo

Text links

Scan column

Gutter

Text Column

White Margin

Nav buttons

Footer with text links,
date and copyright info

4-58. A Web page layout grid

or toolbar placed in a consistent location on every page (fig. 4-58). Once you have applied a layout to one page, be consistent in applying it, with perhaps minor variation, to all the pages on the site. Template pages make this easy. Since Web sites tend to grow over time, a consistent page layout will help maintain continuity. Consider the following points when planning your layout:

- Sometimes the ease with which links can be made results in a graphical nightmare of linked words in every sentence. If the page requires many links, try placing them on a region of the page outside of the main body text.
- Variations in browser software, operating systems, and the font preferences set by individual readers make text columns difficult to control. Consider limiting blocks of text to a width that can comfortably be scanned by the eye, typically not more than sixty characters per line, which is much less than a full screen width.
- Tables and frames allow you to format pages into blocks of text, graphics, links, headers, and footers. Tables also allow you to apply different background and text colors to different regions of a page, helping to visually organize it.

The layout and typographic limitations of HTML drive graphic designers crazy because they make sophisticated, subtle page design difficult. With **cascading style sheets**, designers can overcome many of these shortcomings, giving them a degree of control approximating that of desktop publishing. With this technique, a Web page references another document within the Web site, one that specifies such style properties as text attributes, alignment, margins, and other layout variables. Every page in a site can reference the same style sheet, in much the same way that layout styles can be saved and reused in a word processor. Web pages need have only content, with all formatting handed off to the style sheet. In this way, complex sites that grow over time can maintain a consistent look and feel by referencing style sheets. When different people within an organization are charged with creating sites for their projects or departments, style sheets enable them to apply consistent formatting easily. When the organization wants to revise its style globally, it need change only the style sheet, and all the pages will be updated (figs. 4-59 and 4-60). In this way, the style of the Web pages is separated from their substance.

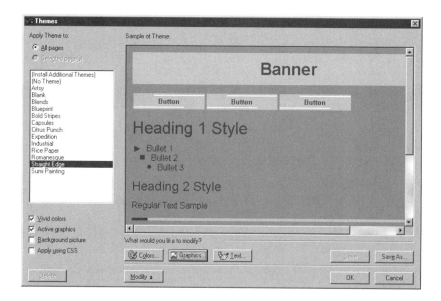

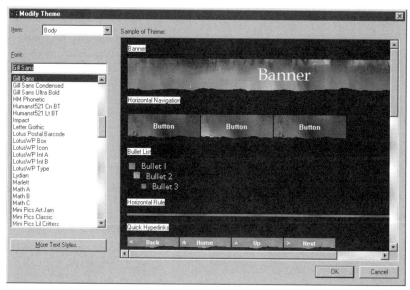

4-59 and 4-60. Web-authoring applications such as Microsoft FrontPage (shown) and NetObjects Fusion allow Web authors to apply styles globally to an entire site.

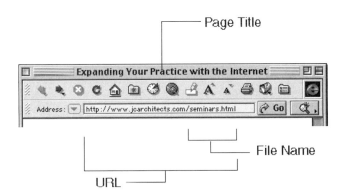

4-61. The page title appears at the top of the browser window; the URL and file name appear in the address bar.

Pages that will likely be printed require additional consideration in design. Assume that pages that are primarily text *will* be printed. Don't use graphics that are too wide to fit horizontally on a 8½- by 11-inch or A4 sheet of paper. Columns of text that are wider than about 530 pixels will not print on a single sheet of standard paper. Because of the potential difficulty of reconciling printed and onscreen versions of documents, consider using Adobe Acrobat to create downloadable PDF versions of text-rich pages.

Every page should have a title. The title appears in the top bar of the browser window displaying the page; it is *not* the same as the name of the file, or the URL (fig. 4-61). The title will be the first thing a visitor sees when clicking on a site and may be the only thing seen for several seconds as the page loads. When visitors save or print the page or save a bookmark for it, the title will remind them of the page contents and source. Thus, a single page may have a title such as "Palladio's Architecture," a URL such as http://www.palladio.com, and a file name (which the viewer never sees but the browser must find), such as "palladio.html." In PageMill the page title is entered in the menu bar in the EDIT mode.

Pages should also be dated, so the visitor can assess how fresh the information is. For example, crucial information may be added to an actively used project-specific Web site, where pages may be updated daily or hourly but look the same as they did before the changes. With extremely time-sensitive information, remember that browsers call up cached versions of pages rather than the new version. You may have to remind visitors to reload the page or add the HTML refresh tag to overrule the browser's preferences.

The Home Page

As the entry point to your site, the home page should provide an easily comprehensible map of the information you are making available. The home page sets the tone for the Web site. It is where you introduce your visitors to the information available and how to access it and show them the basic elements of the site's interface design. As such, it should include all of the structural and navigational elements that will be seen on subsequent pages. For example, including an imagemap for navigational purposes on the home page is a good idea—but make sure it appears in the same location on all the following pages. By placing it in a particular location on the home page, you have told the visitor always to look there for navigational cues.

The most important task of the home page is to present the visitor with choices of where to go next, so some kind of menu is essential. Menus can be organized in a variety of formats, from simple text links to elaborate clickable buttons and imagemaps. The first few vertical inches of the home page are the most important screen space on the Web site, and consequently Web designers put a great deal of effort into the graphics that offer the important first links to the interior of the site. These links may be repeated as text in a footer at the bottom of each page. When a site is complex, listing all its elements on the home page may not be practical, even with text links. Such a site can be divided into a series of subsites, with a subsidiary home page for each section. These subsidiary home pages may become the primary entry point for those users needing only that section. The more complex a site becomes, the more important it is to include a prominent link back to an index page or table of contents from every subsidiary page.

Your design of the home page will be informed by a number of criteria. If visual impact is important, then clearly you will want to use graphics. But you must make a trade-off between the graphic impact of

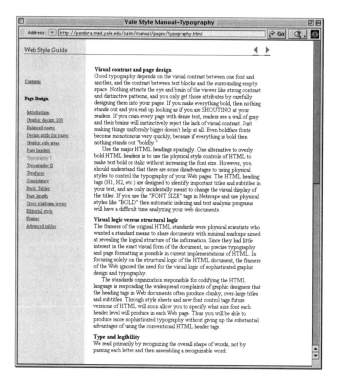

4-62. A page that is lean on graphics can still be well designed and easy to read. (©1999, Patrick Lynch; all rights reserved)

4-63. Example of a splash screen from Web Lab. A visitor can select a no-frames version if desired. (Courtesy of Web Lab)

the page and the time it takes to download. Consider the purposes of the site and its intended audience. A business-to-business information-al site assumes that a visitor is looking for specific information and wants it quickly, whereas a business-to-consumer site may sacrifice speed for entertainment value. Most companies try to impress with their public home page, using graphics and media to create an image of the firm and its capabilities. But for internal consumption, especially when some visitors may be using low-bandwidth dial-up connections, a leaner style that relies more heavily on text is preferable (fig. 4-62).

Avoid the temptation to impress visitors with all your most glam-orous material on the very first page. If visitors want graphics, let them move to a graphics-intensive portion of the site from the home page. Make sure that the visitor sees *something* before all images are loaded. A good rule of thumb is to create a home page that loads in 10 seconds or less over a 28.8 modem. All of the visual Web-authoring applica-tions allow you to estimate the download time for any page and its graphics. In PageMill, for example, DOWNLOAD STATISTICS under the VIEW menu gives you an approximation of download time for the page at different connection speeds. Be aware that tables do not appear on the page until all content within table cells is loaded. A home page con-sisting of one large table may present a visitor with a blank screen for an unacceptably long time.

Anything that prolongs the time visitors must spend to reach their destination should be avoided. Particularly annoying are splash screens, those mysterious pages that require you to click ENTER (or just wait) to see the *real* first page. But some sites use a splash page pro-ductively, for example, to allow visitors to choose between a high- or low-bandwidth version of the site before entering (fig. 4-63). Some sites take the splash screen much further, using site entry tunnels that flash a sequence of several pages at the visitor before showing any actual content. They may set an interesting tone, but doing so should be possible with careful design of the home page itself. Leave such devices to graphics-intensive entertainment sites, where the main design task is to lure people onto the site.

The URL of the home page is the Web address that points visitors to your site. You will probably put it on your stationery and business cards, and it will become an important part of your firm's identity. The virtual domain name you choose is an **alias** for the Web address of the root folder containing your Web site. When Web browsers are directed to folders on Web servers, they look for a file named *index.html* and open it by default. Thus, "www.greatbuildings.com," for instance, becomes an alias for your home page, whose much longer real Web address may be http://www.isp.net/users/~greatbuildings/index.html.

Accommodating User Differences

Accommodating user differences is an issue every Web designer must consider. With a book, you can be certain that every reader is seeing the same thing. Were that only the case on the Web! A visitor's perception of your Web site will vary because of factors beyond your control, but you can make allowances for them. Some of the variables that affect how visitors experience your site include:

- Screen resolution and size
- Color depth
- Processor speed
- Connection speed
- Computer platform and browser

Unlike a printed page, a Web page has no fixed width or height; information is presented on screens, so that viewers' experiences will vary with the screen size and display capabilities of their systems. And screens vary considerably. Someone viewing your page on a 12-inch screen at 256 colors will have a different experience than someone looking at a 21-inch screen with millions of colors. Remember too that viewers are not necessarily devoting their entire screen to your page—they may be viewing in a small window occupying just a corner of the desktop.

Although standard office and home monitors are tending to be bigger, with 17-inch screens of at least 832 by 624 pixels becoming the norm, a countervailing trend is the growing popularity of personal digital assistants, such as the Palm hand-held computer. These devices are adding more Internet capability, making them potentially useful extranet clients for field personnel, but their tiny screens severely limit the amount of information that can be displayed without scrolling.

Sometimes user differences can be overcome by providing alternative versions of a page or parts of a page. For those with slow connections or using text-only browsers, many home pages provide a prominent link to a text-only version of the page that has been designed especially for this purpose. The HTML *ALT* tag allows the designer to insert alternative messages, such as a line of descriptive text substituting for a graphic, which will display before or instead of an image:

    <IMG SRC="highres.jpg" ALT="Picture of Building">

The designer can also provide low-resolution black-and-white versions of images that will act as quick-loading place holders for the higher-quality version that will take longer to load:

    <IMG SRC="highres.jpg" LOW SRC="lowres.gif">

Now, *lowres.gif* will appear quickly, to be replaced by *highres.jpg* when it has finished loading.

These tags can be added to the HTML by hand, or if one is working with a high-end Web-authoring application such as Adobe GoLive, they can added when inserting the graphic into a page (fig. 4-64).

All of the visual Web-authoring applications allow page designers to view their pages in a preview mode that simulates a Web browser, but no software can accurately model all the different variables that may affect page appearance. Before placing your Web site on a server, it's always a good idea to preview it in both Internet Explorer and

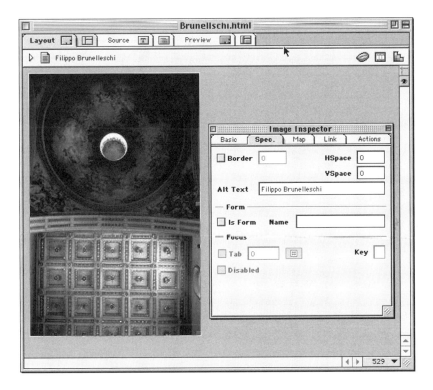

4-64. Adobe GoLive makes it easy to attach ALT TEXT to an image. Here, the text "Filippo Brunelleschi" can substitute for the image.

Netscape, on both Mac and Windows systems, and on a variety of screen sizes and color capabilities.

Site Navigation

Hypertext provides a nonlinear means of moving through information space, so clear navigation through a Web site is vitally important. BACK, FORWARD, and HOME buttons are useful when presenting sequential information. Suppose you have prepared a lecture with accompanying slides or a PowerPoint presentation. A Web version of the lecture can be easily created, using BACK and FORWARD buttons to preserve the desired order. Frequently used navigational graphics can be stored in PageMill's PASTEBOARD, which retains their embedded links for future use. Such buttons are easily made from small graphic files linked to the desired page. You can find small graphics for this purpose on many Internet sites, and a selection of them is typically bundled with Web-authoring software.

Although a home page is considered the beginning of a Web site, it does not follow that a site necessarily has a middle or an end. Visitors are free to jump around, taking the shortest route to the information they need, and sometimes it is easy for them to lose track of where there are. Remember that it is entirely possible for visitors to enter at a page other than the home page when, for example, a search engine links to a page in the middle of your site. To reorient this visitor, you must provide a clear path back to your home page from every subsidiary page in the site. Every page should have a HOME button or text link—without it, the orphaned page becomes a dead end.

A clickable trunk-and-branch diagram, serving as a schematic of your site, is another useful navigational aid. It is especially appropriate for large sites and those that serve multiple purposes. Pages that offer only a few navigational options at a time may frustrate expert users. They want to reach the information they need quickly, even when it's buried deep in the site. A hyperlinked site map enables these users to jump-start the site, bypassing the navigation scheme you have provided for novice users. Such diagrams can be made from the site map you created when planning the site, and some advanced software packages make them automatically. Don't put the site map on the home page, but do provide an obvious link to it from there.

A menu, either within a frame or as a pull-down, can also guide viewers through your site. Text menus load instantly and may be the best solution for sites offering multiple destinations to experienced users. As discussed in the frames exercise earlier in this chapter, a project home page that provides links to various types of project information benefits from including a quick-loading, comprehensive text menu on the home page.

Thumbnail images and icons, linked to different projects, regions of the site, departments, or document areas, can also act as site naviga-

tion buttons. When using icons, make sure their meaning is clear or supplement the graphic link with explanatory text.

Imagemaps serve a similar navigational function. These are graphics that have been "mapped" with embedded links to specific *X/Y* coordinates in the image, so that one image can provide numerous links. The most common use of imagemaps is for so-called navbars or banner graphics. A banner graphic is usually placed at the top of the home page, to provide point-and-click access to various parts of the site (fig. 4-65). The choices available on this navbar may vary as visitors move through the site, but because its location and appearance remain constant, visitors always know where to look. Creating imagemaps is covered in chapter 5.

Finally, a page with frequently asked questions (**FAQ**s), preferably with embedded hyperlinks, will orient visitors and allow them to jump to parts of the Web site directly. A good FAQ page can be extremely useful to first-time users of a Web site, answering questions about both its content and how to use it. If you provide a good one, your support time for users of the site may be greatly diminished.

Adding Interactive Elements

The most basic interactive element, which should be included on virtually all Web sites, is an e-mail link. When visitors click on the link, a preaddressed e-mail message window appears in the mail program of their choice. To send you mail, all they need to do is type a message and hit the SEND button. The link can be set to any e-mail address you specify. In PageMill, select some text (such as "send us mail") or a small graphic, go to the LINK TO area at the bottom of the PREVIEW window, type "mailto:" and then the e-mail address (an e-mail address always has @ in the middle). Hit the RETURN key, and the link is made. When you provide such a feedback link, be sure to answer any e-mails you receive!

Fill-out forms are little more complicated to set up. Creating the blank form is easy with any of the visual page-authoring tools that have been discussed, but getting forms to work requires that you tie them to a **script** that tells the Web server what to do with the information that comes back. Most of these scripts, written in languages such as Perl, are in a format known as **CGI**, or Common Gateway Interface. Your ISP may provide generic forms that use CGI scripts already on its server. Other ISPs will allow you to upload your own

CGI scripts to a folder within your private area on the server. If you are running your own server, your system administrator will know how to do this.

Microsoft's FrontPage offers an alternative to using scripts: the FrontPage server extensions, which add various kinds of functionality and interactivity to a Web site, including forms processing, search capability, and discussion areas. These features are invoked within FrontPage documents by commands inserted by the page designer, but as with CGIs, the extensions must be installed on the server for these features to work. If you use FrontPage, look for an ISP that provides these extensions for their customers.

Forms present their own design challenge: don't assume that they need only be blandly functional; strive for good page design, because filling out forms can be tedious.

Another useful interactive element is a search function. It is especially valuable on a text-rich Web site, such as one containing construction specifications, correspondence, or contracts. Search tools index every word on all the pages on the site; typically they are scheduled to do this every night. When a visitor enters a keyword, for example, *concrete*, a ranked list of pages is provided, with the page having the most instances of *concrete* at the top. Boolean searches allow the use of operators, such as AND or NOT. A search for *concrete AND reinforcing* returns pages containing both words.

E-commerce requires much more advanced kinds of interactivity. Web browsers can be made to interact with huge, enterprise-wide databases, such as product catalogs, using an intermediary layer of software known as middleware, because it resides in the middle, between browser clients and database servers. This three-tier system will be discussed in more detail in chapter 8.

Java

Do not confuse Java with JavaScript. The latter is a scripting language, rather than a programming language. JavaScript is used for Web site interface enhancements such as rollovers and mouse actions.

Java is a programming language developed by Sun Microsystems expressly for client-server networks such as the Internet. Java's unique property is that it is processor independent: Java works on all hardware platforms by invoking a Java Virtual Machine within any Wintel, Mac, or Unix computer.

Java applets are small programs that run within the Web browser—examples range from small animated enhancements that dance and sing to very useful items such as:

- Time-tracking and scheduling programs for project teams.
- Viewers that allow you to see and print documents within your Web browser without having the application that created the original. For example, there are Java-based viewers for viewing and marking up CAD drawings and GIS maps.

- Bridges to large databases of text, numeric, or graphical information.

Java applets are used to extend the functionality of Web browsers, turning them into amazingly versatile all-in-one applications that are virtually an entire operating system in themselves. Java can provide a user-friendly "front end" to large database functions, allowing, for example, architects to query a product manufacturer's database of prices, availability, or colors. Unlike plug-ins, which require the user to download and install extra software, Java applets reside on the server and are supplied to the browser "just in time" for each use. When the applet is updated, it is copied to the server only once and all clients are updated automatically, a tremendous convenience for systems administrators, who would otherwise have to install an application or plug-in on each computer within an organization. Java is a good fit for extranets, where outside consultants, subcontractors, and suppliers will be accessing information from a variety of hardware and software configurations beyond the control of the prime contractor. Recent versions of Netscape and Internet Explorer are Java-enabled, meaning they can call upon the Java Virtual Machine whenever they encounter a Web site with applets.

Java *applications*, by contrast, are standalone programs that run independently of the browser, in the same way as applications written in any other programming language.

Sun hopes that Java will become the glue that connects the diverse computing needs of far-flung enterprises; it is also a tool that may help connect the "islands of automation" so prevalent in the building industry. But Java is still a major performance drag on most systems. It is slow because the Java Virtual Machine runs in emulation mode on top of the computer's native operating system. If you do use Java, consider providing a non-Java (and perhaps a no-frames) version of your site as a quick-loading alternative for those on slow systems.

5 Graphics and

In previous chapters you have learned about the basics of planning Web sites, designing pages, using text, linking, formatting with tables and frames, and the rudiments of HTML. But the Web is a graphic medium—much of its power to communicate derives from its ability to present information in a visually compelling way. This chapter examines digital photography, raster and vector graphics, CAD and GIS imaging, and three-dimensional media.

Digital Imaging

One of the greatest strengths of the Web is its multimedia capabilities. Its greatest limitation, for the near future at least, is insufficient bandwidth. When designing Web sites, you must always keep in mind the time it takes to download a page. If your pages are text only, download time is not an issue, but graphic media inherently produce larger files, and larger files take longer to download. The time required to download and view a page is the sum of the time needed to download the underlying HTML file plus all the images and other media as separate files. Video and sound produce even larger files than photographs and illustrations. Since the time to download is directly proportional to file size, it is always an advantage, other things being equal, to reduce file sizes as much as possible.

The Web page designer must therefore strike a balance between graphic impact and speed. When working with media, many variables can affect the size of files. Fortunately, there are good techniques, discussed later in this chapter, for controlling the file size of media, or *optimizing* them. But first, let's review some basic concepts of computer graphics.

Three variables—color depth, resolution, and compression—affect both the quality and file size of digital photographs and illustrations.

Multimedia

Color depth (sometimes called bit depth) defines the number of colors that a computer screen can display at one time. It is a function of the amount of video memory, or **VRAM,** in a system. Greater color depth produces truer colors and larger files. In 8-bit color, eight bits of memory are devoted to each **pixel** in the display, so the number of colors possible is 2^8, or 256 colors. One-bit "color" produces only black and white. With 16-bit color, 65,000 colors are possible, and 24-bit color enables one to view 16.7 million colors at a time, exceeding the limit of what most human eyes can distinguish. With 24-bit color, each pixel has 8 bits of memory available for red, green, and blue. Images composed in 32-, 40-, and even 48-bit color are possible; they do not have more colors but include extra bits per pixel for transparency and other special effects.

Color depth is descriptive both of computer displays (figs. 5-1 and 5-2) and of individual image files. A monitor capable of only 8-bit color cannot display 24-bit images; conversely, a 24-bit display cannot add extra colors to an 8-bit image. When you include 24-bit images in a Web page, always check to see how they look in 8-bit color, because many people will view them that way.

The term *resolution* has different meanings, depending on context. In print media resolution refers to the number of dots per square inch of a **raster image.** Low resolution generally refers to a range of 72 to 100 dots per inch (dpi), which is approximately the resolution of images as they appear on a computer screen. High resolution is 300 to 1,200 dpi, the resolution of laser printers and high-quality inkjets. A high-resolution image has a larger file size than a low-resolution image.

Resolution also refers to the screen area, the physical size of an image as measured in pixels. Digital images are described in sizes of *X* by *Y* pixel dimensions. Most 14-inch screens have resolution of 640 by 480 pixels, many laptops have screens of 800 by 600 pixels, and larger monitors are 1,024 by 768 or higher.

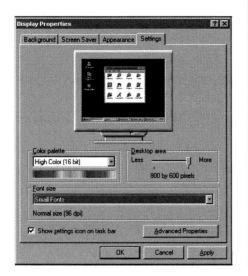

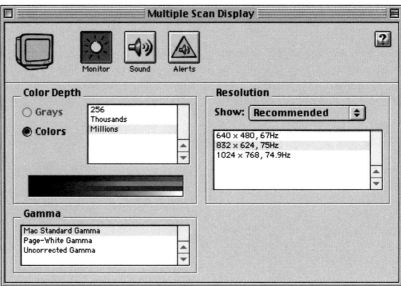

5-1. The Windows DISPLAY PROPERTIES panel.

5-2. The Macintosh MONITOR AND SOUND control panel.

Compression refers to the various "behind the scenes" techniques used to temporarily reduce the file size of an image (the ratio of the original file size to the new) so that it is transmitted more quickly. Some types of compression cause a permanent loss of image quality. **GIF** and **JPEG**, the predominant graphic file types used on the Web, both use compression. Since download time is directly proportional to file size, efficient compression is key to using images on the Web. Compression can reduce files to as little as 10 percent of their original size. When the Web browser loads the image, it expands it back to the original file size. This decompression can sometimes cause problems on systems with insufficient RAM.

Describing Color Numerically

The two principal systems for describing colors as combinations of numeric values (and thereby comprehensible to computers) are known as CMYK and RGB. RGB (red, green, blue) is *additive*; colors are formed by adding different amounts of red, green, and blue. CMYK (cyan, magenta, yellow, black), in contrast, is *subtractive*. The difference lies in the distinction between color as radiated by a luminous object such as a cathode ray tube, which is additive, and *pigment*, which is actually reflected light, that is, the colors that are *not* absorbed by an ink or paint. When red, green, and blue lights are combined, they form white. When cyan, magenta, and yellow pigments are combined, they absorb all colors and appear black. Any color can be described with either system by assigning a numeric value for each component. Thus, a particular teal green could be described as (R:66, G:176, B:154) or as (C:65%, M:1%, Y:42%, K:0%). RGB is used principally for graphics intended for viewing on computer displays, while CMYK is used for print media. Photoshop, CorelDraw, and the other major graphics applications support both color modes (fig. 5-3).

When working with images for the Web, remember that computer displays have resolutions of 72 to 96 dots per inch. Graphics saved at a higher resolution will not look any better on screens, but their file size will be larger and the time to download, longer. Of course, high-

5-3. The Macintosh allows colors to be selected using a variety of systems, including CMYK, RGB, and hexadecimal codes for the Web.

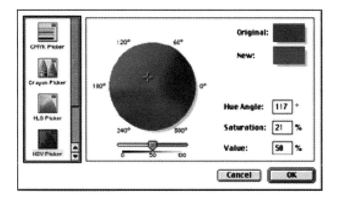

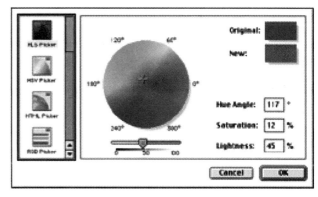

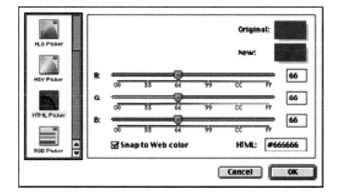

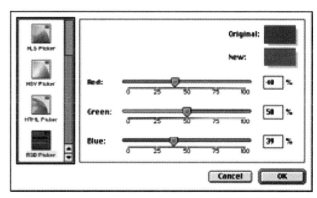

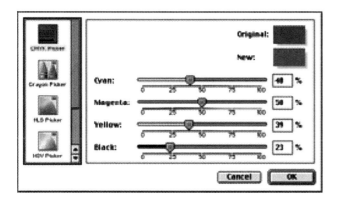

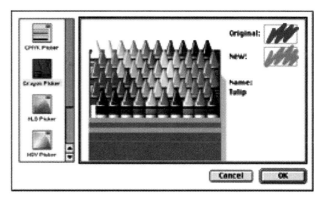

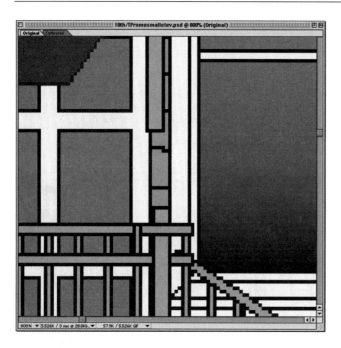
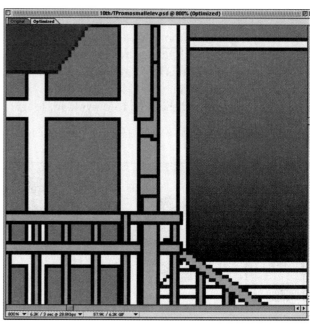

5-4. An original image saved as a TIFF with millions of colors. The file size is 58K.

5-5. The image saved as a GIF with 256 colors. Some dithering is visible in the gradient on the right. File size has been reduced to 6.3K.

resolution images can be made available on sites so that visitors can download and print them, but for images that are being used merely to illustrate pages, that higher resolution is wasted.

But even low-resolution images can look stunningly effective on Web pages because the high-quality color and the transmitted light of screens gives images more vibrancy than they have on paper. Don't hesitate to be liberal with color: high-quality color is very expensive in print media but costs nothing extra on the Web.

Using a few large graphics on a page is more efficient than using many small ones, because each separate file requires its own HTTP session between browser and server. For example, two 12-Kb files will appear on a page faster than six 4-Kb files will. Similarly, an imagemap that contains six links will load faster than six small single-link buttons.

When placing images in Web pages, always set a size tag (Web-authoring applications such as PageMill do this for you). Size tags establish a placeholder on the page that fills in when the image is downloaded. The HTML looks like this:

```
<IMG SRC="Jacket3.jpg "WIDTH="400" HEIGHT="500">
```

Without size tags, your pages will keep reformatting as each image appears, giving the visitor a disconcerting experience and making the page difficult to read.

Raster Image Formats

The late-nineteenth-century pointillist painter Georges Seurat created images using tiny dots of paint. From a distance, the colors blended into

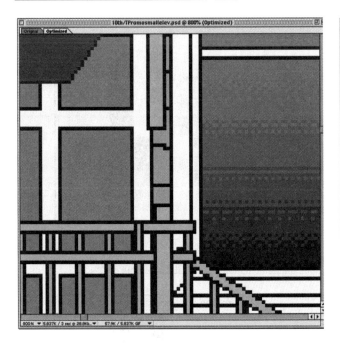 

recognizable shapes, but up close, one could easily distinguish the individual dots. In the same way, raster images, sometimes called *bitmaps*, are pictures composed of colored dots or pixels. The two most prevalent raster image file formats used on the Web are GIF and JPEG.

GIF: Graphic Interchange Format

GIF files are used for line art, illustrations, logos, and diagrams. A built-in compression scheme reduces the file size without lowering image quality. GIFs are limited to a maximum of 256 colors (although you can create them with many fewer), so they are not used for continuous-tone images such as photographs. Photographs saved as GIFs may suffer from *dithering*, in which the display tries to simulate a color it does not have by averaging adjacent pixels (figs. 5-4, 5-5, 5-6, and 5-7).

Standard GIF files load by displaying row after row of pixels until the image is complete. *Interlaced GIFs* show viewers a low-resolution version of the image quickly, instead of forcing them to wait for the entire file to download. In successive waves, the picture is filled in and becomes sharper, in a kind of venetian blind effect. Interlacing is most effective for large images, where the low-resolution placeholder delineates the image area while the full image loads. It should not be used when headline text is presented as a GIF, because the reader may miss the meaning of the paragraph.

Converting a GIF to an interlaced GIF is a one-click operation with PageMill (fig. 5-8). In the EDIT mode, insert a GIF into a page, select it, and choose OPEN SELECTION from the FILE menu. The image will appear in a new image-editing window. Select the MAKE INTERLACED tool from the toolbar on the left. Click the tool once to make the image interlaced.

5-6. The image saved as a GIF with 32 colors. Dithering is more severe.

5-7. The image saved as a GIF with 8 colors. Dithering is extreme.

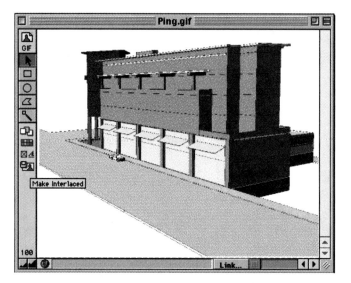

5-8. PageMill's image-editing tools include a MAKE INTERLACED command.

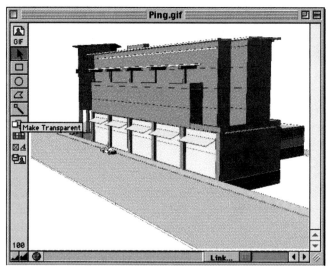

5-9. The MAKE TRANSPARENT tool is selected.

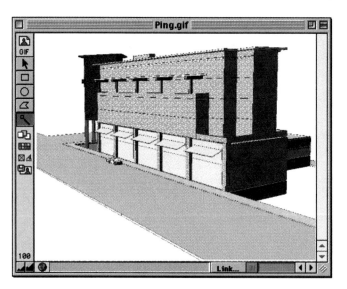

5-10. Clicking on any solid color in the image makes it transparent.

Transparent GIFs allow you to make a single color in the image transparent, effectively causing that color to disappear when displayed on a Web page. By making the background color of a GIF transparent, one can add the illusion of depth: the image will appear to float on the page instead of being defined by a rectangular border. To add transparency in PageMill, select a GIF while in the EDIT mode, and choose OPEN SELECTION from the FILE menu. The image will appear in an editing window. Select the MAKE TRANSPARENT tool from the toolbar on the left and click on any solid color in the image to make it transparent (figs. 5-9 and 5-10). Essentially the same effect can be achieved by giving an image the same background color as the Web page on which it will be shown.

Imagemaps are GIFs with clickable links mapped to different parts of the image. They are widely used as navigational graphics (navbars) that link visitors to parts of a Web site, replacing linked text or buttons. Any GIF can be turned into an imagemap by first placing it into a Web page, and then using a Web-authoring application to map links to it. This mapping does not alter the image itself; it is written in HTML on the page that contains it.

To create an imagemap in PageMill, select any GIF on a page while in the EDIT mode. From the FILE menu, choose OPEN SELECTION. Use the drawing tools in the toolbar to create hot spots in the image (fig. 5-11). You can make local links to a hot spot by dragging and dropping any file in your Web site over it; create remote links to a hot spot by selecting it and then entering a URL next to the globe icon at the bottom of the image-editing window. When creating imagemaps, remember that the clickable areas of the image may not be intuitively obvious to visitors. Use clearly defined regions of the graphic, with obvious boundaries between different hot spots. Remember that you are using imagemaps as a substitute for discrete buttons, so try not to overlap the boundaries.

Imagemaps are often made up of a combination of text and illustration. To get the best-looking type, compose the text in an illustra-

5-11. An image containing text is being converted to an imagemap in PageMill. Drawing tools allow hot spots to be made in different shapes.

5-12 and 5-13. Anti-aliasing smooths type by averaging adjacent pixels (enlarged 800 percent).

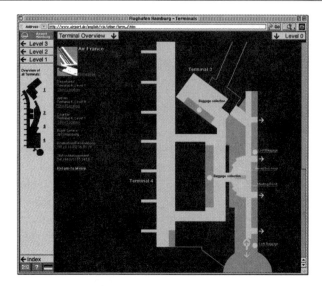

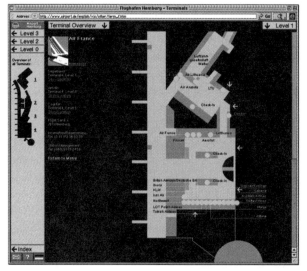

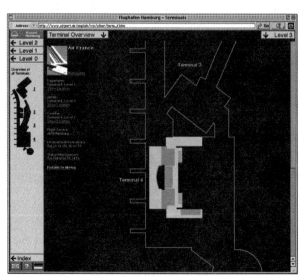

5-14, 5-15, and 5-16. A complex environment such as Hamburg's airport is made comprehensible in this Web site by ViceVersa. Arrivals and departures are updated every two minutes. Shops, restaurants, car rental, hotels—all are shown on clickable multilevel floor-plan imagemaps.

tion or word-processing program and bring it into Photoshop for conversion to GIF. Figure 5-11 shows a navbar saved as a GIF in Photoshop and turned into an imagemap in PageMill. When text is saved as a raster image, it is no longer really text but a picture of text. To avoid a jagged stairstep effect with type, use **anti-aliasing**. This smoothing effect is achieved by adding intermediate colors around the edges (figs. 5-12 and 5-13).

Architects, planners, and engineers can use this kind of spatial referencing of images in creative ways: to key a floor plan to other drawings or Web pages, for example, or by linking zoning maps to zoning tables, census data, or assessors' information (figs. 5-14, 5-15, and 5-16).

Text saved as GIFs for headlines and navbars can be given special effects in Photoshop. For example, in figures 5-17, 5-18, and 5-19, a drop shadow has been added to anti-aliased text.

Animated GIFs are sequences of two or more still GIFs that become "flip-book" animations. Tools such as ImageReady and GIFBuilder enable designers to vary the delay between frames and determine whether the animation will play once and stop or will loop endlessly. Animated GIF is the simplest method for creating animations that can be seen in Web browsers without plug-ins. Used well, it can be an effective means of presentation, especially when used for "slide shows" of sequenced images (fig. 5-20). More sophisticated Web animations can be made with Macromedia's Shockwave software.

The future of GIF is clouded by a patent dispute that has roiled the Internet community. In December 1997, CompuServe and Unisys Corporation suddenly announced that GIF was a proprietary format and that software developers designing programs to read or write GIF would have to pay license fees. By this time, GIF had been in wide use for ten years and was assumed to be public. In fact, the underlying compression technology had been widely published in technical journals with no mention of the fact that Unisys had quietly obtained a patent for it in 1993. Although the legal issues are complex and far from settled, commercial Web sites using GIFs created with unlicensed software (such as most freeware and shareware graphics applications) are potentially at risk. A new file format, PNG (for Portable Network Graphics), is being advanced as an eventual replacement for GIF. PNG is nonproprietary and offers the significant advantage of supporting 24-bit color. As of this writing, however, adoption of PNG has been scant.

5-17 and 5-18. Drop shadows give an impression of depth to headlines.

5-19. A portion of the drop shadow enlarged 800 percent. Note that the type is anti-aliased.

5-20. A sequence of GIFs is combined into an animation. Each frame can be timed separately. Adobe ImageReady can "tween" between two images, creating transitional images that smooth the animation.

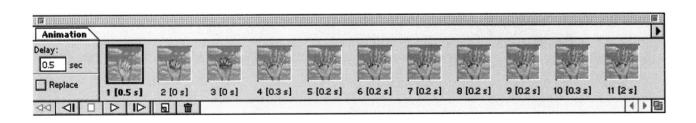

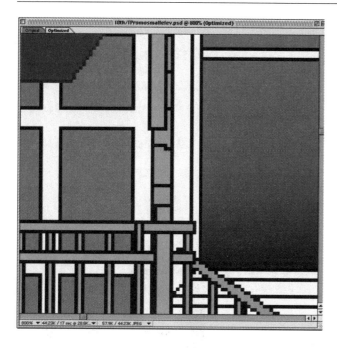

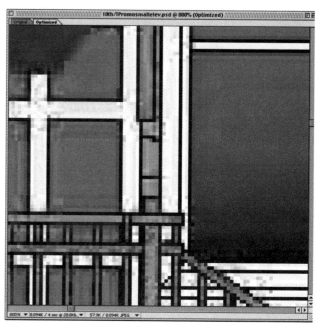

5-21. (Above left) The same image as figure 5-4, saved as a high-quality JPEG with millions of colors. File size has been reduced from 58K to 44K.

5-22. (Above right) The same image saved as a low-quality JPEG. "Artifacts" have appeared in solid color areas. File size has been reduced to 8K.

5-23. Illustrations with broad areas of solid color should be saved as GIFs.

5-24. The image saved as a JPEG. Note the blotchy "artifacts" in areas of solid color (enlarged 16 times).

JPEG: Joint Photographic Experts Group

JPEG is the other commonly supported Web graphics file format. JPEG images display in 24-bit "true color," making it the appropriate choice for photography and illustrations with continuous tones and gradients.

With JPEG, the trade-off between quality and file size is easy to control. Because JPEG increases compression by eliminating data (known as "lossy" compression), the greater the compression, the lower the resulting quality of the image will be. JPEG settings range from 1 (highest compression, lowest quality) to 10 (lowest compression, highest quality). The difference in file size can be dramatic, but so can the loss of image quality if too low a setting is used. There is no rule of thumb about which setting to use; to optimize an image, you must preview it at different settings and consider the trade-off between image quality and size in each case (figs. 5-21 and 5-22). Be aware that once you have created a low-quality JPEG, you have permanently lost some of the data, and you cannot add it back later. Always work with a copy of the original image.

JPEG is the native file format of most digital cameras; its high compressibility enables more images to be stored in the magnetic cards such devices use. These images can go directly onto the Web unaltered, but most designers will want to use Photoshop to adjust their compression, crop them, digitally sharpen them, and perhaps manipulate them with filters. When an image has been scanned from a photographic print or slide, it is typically saved in the **TIFF** file format and kept as an original. That way, the maximum image quality is preserved. It is easy to convert TIFFs to JPEGs with Photoshop.

Progressive scanning of JPEGs is analogous to interlacing GIFs: the image takes several passes to load completely, becoming sharper with each pass. As with interlaced GIF, this technique is used to create a fast-loading placeholder for an image while the full file is downloading. Photoshop offers a progressive checkbox when saving JPEGs.

Although JPEG would appear to be a higher-quality format than GIF, because of its support for 24-bit color, it actually produces very poor results with hard-edged, brightly colored illustrations (figs. 5-23 and 5-24). Such images should always be saved as GIFs.

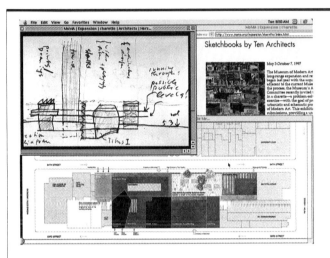
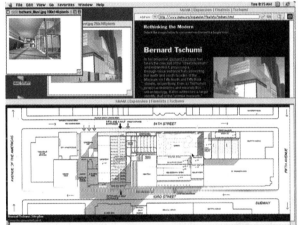
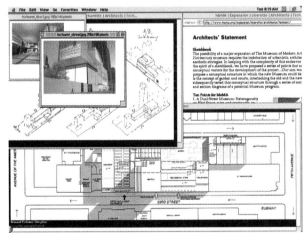
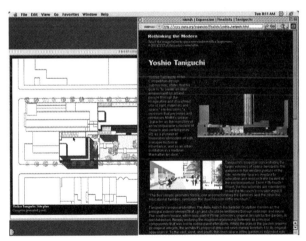

The MoMA Reconstruction Charette

A superb example of an on-line architectural presentation, using nothing more than standard Web technology, can be found on the Museum of Modern Art Web site (www.moma.org). In 1997 the museum invited ten international architects to participate in a charette to produce ideas for the expansion of the museum's 1939 facilities, exploring "basic urbanistic and conceptual strategies for the redevelopment of the entire Museum." Through a variety of media,

5-25 through 5-28. The Museum of Modern Art's expansion project. (©2000, The Museum of Modern Art, New York; Art Direction: Greg Van Alstyne, The Museum of Modern Art; Design and Programming: OVEN, New York)

including hand sketches, plans, computer-generated renderings, and collage, the on-line exhibit shows the power of the Web in presenting architectural ideas for a complex proposal in a stimulating and informative way (figs. 5-25, 5-26, 5-27, and 5-28).

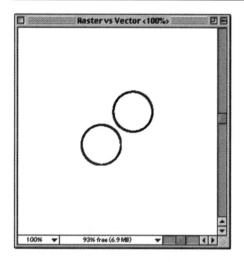

5-29. The circle on the left is a raster image; the circle on the right is a vector graphic. At 100 percent, they look the same.

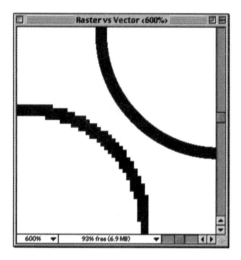

5-30. The same two circles enlarged to 600 percent. The raster image on the left is pixilated, while the vector graphic on the right is smooth at any magnification.

Vector Graphics

Because GIF and JPEG are raster image formats, the image is a picture, consisting of colored dots or pixels, rather than a drawing, consisting of lines and shapes with geometric attributes. In computer parlance, the term *drawing* usually denotes a vector graphic, such as a CAD file or an illustration made with such programs as Adobe Illustrator, Macromedia Freehand, or CorelDraw. In a vector graphic, drawing elements have properties such as thickness and length. A circle is a circle, described by a formula, not the picture of a circle made up of pixels. A vector graphic is scalable and can be printed at high resolution (figs. 5-29 and 5-30). Even colors are more accurate.

Both types of graphics may look the same on a computer display (which is a kind of bitmap itself), but a raster image is nothing more than an ephemeral pattern of dots, whereas a vector graphic can be scaled, edited, and rotated. Because vector graphics are numeric descriptions, they are inherently more efficient in terms of file size than equivalent raster images.

At present, the vast majority of graphics displayed on Web pages are raster images, in part because there has been no standard vector file format that browsers can understand. Proprietary solutions have appeared, such as Macromedia's Flash and Corel's Xara, but these require plug-ins to view. They are intended for simple Web animations rather than the complex, precise graphics used by design professionals. The need for vector graphics on the Internet is being addressed by the World Wide Web Consortium (W3C), an industry group that proposes new, vendor-neutral standards for Web technology. A new format called SVG, for Scalable Vector Graphics, will enable graphics created by a wide variety of vector-drawing applications to be used on Web pages. SVG will have the advantages of smaller file size, scalability, high resolution, and the capacity to be altered on the fly with style sheets. Text within SVG graphics will be visible to search engines, whereas text in raster images is converted to unsearchable pixels.

SVG grew out of a compromise between two earlier candidates, PGML (Precision Graphics Markup Language), developed by Adobe and based on Postscript, and VML (Vector Markup Language), proposed by Microsoft. All three are applications of XML (Extensible Markup Language), which is discussed in detail in chapter 11.

For design professionals, the ability to place vector graphics such as CAD documents and GIS maps on Web pages, capable of being viewed without plug-ins, will obviously be of great value. With SVG, vector graphics could be served "live," with Web pages dynamically linked to CAD files in progress. Used together with XML for industry-specific tagging of data, it could transform the way construction documents are created and used.

Until then, the solutions available for viewing vector graphics on the Web are proprietary and mostly require plug-ins to work; as a result none has achieved wide adoption.

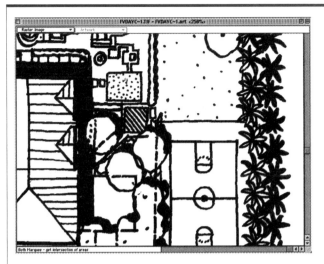

5-31. A portion of a felt-tip marker drawing has been scanned and digitized. The image consists of pixels. (Sketch by Cliff Lowe)

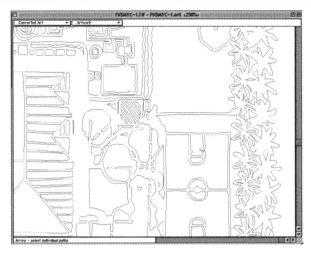

5-32. Using Adobe Streamline, the drawing has been converted to a vector graphic.

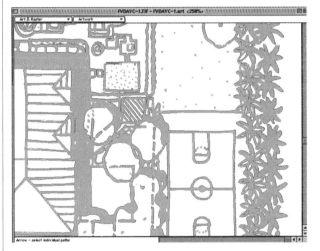

5-33. The vector and raster images saved as layers and displayed together.

Raster-to-Vector Conversion

In my seminars, people frequently ask: "My most brilliant ideas are drawn on the back of cocktail napkins. I can fax them to my client, but how do I get these gems into my computer?"

It is possible to convert a raster image (such as a scanned cocktail napkin) into a vector image which can then be manipulated with a drawing program, using Adobe Streamline (figs. 5-31, 5-32, and 5-33).

Many CAD programs also include this feature, usually called something like TRACE BITMAP. Architects use it to convert scanned photos or sketches into base layers for CAD drawings. The results of converting a hand drawing are not always very satisfying, however. Straight lines become jagged, unless they are exactly aligned with the dot pattern. To preserve the hand-drawn charm of your sketches, try scanning into a PDF file with Acrobat.

The DWF (Drawing Web Format) format was developed by Autodesk to allow versions of DWG files (AutoCAD's native format) to be published on the Web. These files are compressed subsets of the original CAD file that retain their two-dimensional vector data and therefore the precision of their drawing properties. Files can be zoomed, panned, and printed by the viewer but cannot be altered. They are analogous to Adobe's PDF in that they are essentially electronic plots. With AutoCAD Release 14 or higher, users can:

- Export drawings as DWF files for placement on Web pages. Three levels of precision are offered, with varying rates of compression. The current view is exported as a two-dimensional drawing.

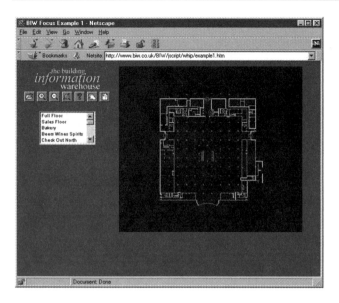
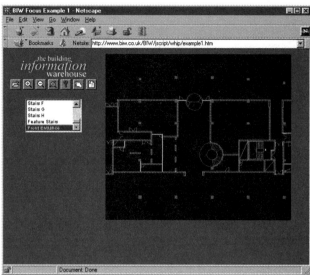

5-34 and 5-35. The WHIP plug-in allows viewing of AutoCAD files in Web browsers. (Courtesy Advanced Visual Technology)

- Embed hyperlinks to associate all or part of a drawing to other drawings or Web pages. Hyperlinks can be relative, referring to other, related drawings or views within the same file directory. Although DWF files have fixed viewpoints, users can link together several views of the same design. DWF files can also be saved with multiple, named views.
- Associate DWF files with the original DWG file. Remote AutoCAD users can access it by dragging and dropping a DWF from a Web browser into AutoCAD.
- View the hyperlinks in a drawing, and launch a Web browser to access them.

Curiously, AutoCAD can write but cannot read DWF files.

Several options are available for viewing DWF drawings in a Web browser without requiring that AutoCAD be present:

5-36 and 5-37. CADviewer is a Java-based solution for viewing DWG files in Web browsers. (Courtesy Arnona Software and Cephren)

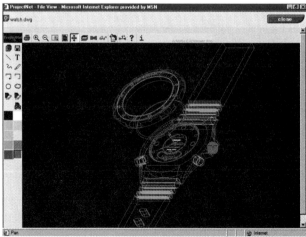

- Autodesk's WHIP plug-in enables users to view DWF files with zoom, pan, and mark-up functions (figs. 5-34 and 5-35). Visitors to a Web site with DWF files must download and install WHIP (it is large—about 3 MB), which is currently available only for the Windows platform. As with all browser plug-ins, the server software must also be configured to identify the MIME type. In March 1999 Autodesk announced a new product, Volo View, which will permit viewing, printing, scaling, and markup of DWG, DWF, and DXF files, along with MicroStation DGN files and HPGL plot files.

- CADviewer is a server product from Arnona Software that presents vector drawings for display in Web browsers (figs. 5-36 and 5-37). Because it is Java based, it runs on any hardware platform with no download required. Viewers can zoom, pan, print, add URLs, and leave redlined markups on the drawing, which are saved to a separate file linked to the original. The original drawing remains on the server and is not modified.

- WebDGN, from Pangaea CAD Solutions, allows remote viewing of MicroStation DGN and AutoCAD Release 14 files in a browser using a free plug-in (figs. 5-38 and 5-39). Unlike WHIP, the original file is used, and no translation to DWF is necessary, thus eliminating a time-consuming step and avoiding possible problems of version control. As with CADviewer, redlining is supported without altering the original.

- Other CAD viewers include Dr. DWG NetView and AutoManager View from Cyco Software (figs. 5-40 and 5-41).

- Adobe Acrobat can be used to "print" CAD and GIS graphics to high-resolution PDF files. It works equally well from within any drawing application and on all hardware platforms.

Developments in GIS imaging have paralleled those in CAD. It is now widely recognized that the Web will dramatically increase the demand for GIS, by offering the ideal vehicle for delivering GIS map-

5-38. A MicroStation file shown in a browser window, served by Pangaea's WebDGN. (©1999 Pangaea CAD Solutions, Inc.)

5-39. WebDGN also handles AutoCAD DWG files. (©1999 Pangaea CAD Solutions, Inc.)

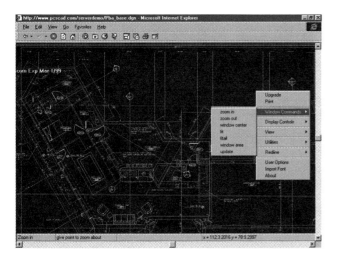

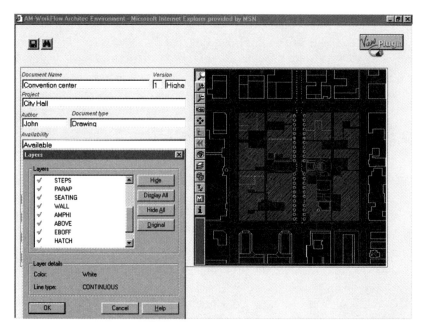

5-40. AutoManager View CAD viewer, with control over layer visibility.

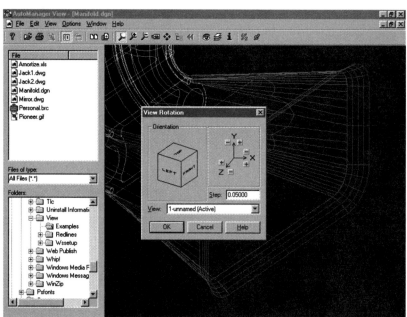

5-41. The standalone AutoManager View browser displaying a MicroStation DGN file.

ping inexpensively to businesses and the public. Software developers have scrambled to create view-only file formats for GIS data so that information can be widely shared on the Web.

As with CAD, there is no open, standard technology for viewing GIS maps on-line. Proprietary solutions include the following:

■ Autodesk's MapGuide, a client application for viewing map databases in the SDF format dynamically within Web browsers (figs. 5-42, 5-43, and 5-44). MapGuide is also available in a platform-independent Java version.

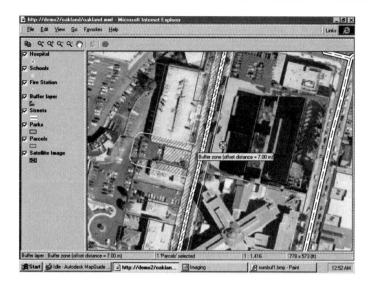

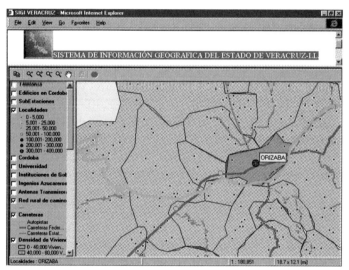

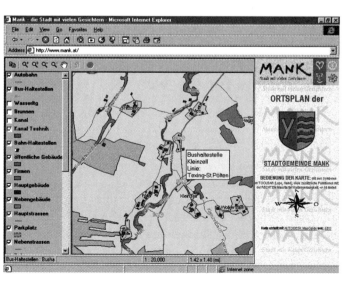

CAD Esperanto?

A question I often hear from colleagues is, "Why are we talking about design process data integration when we cannot even read each others' CAD files?" Autodesk has championed its own DXF format as the Esperanto that allows CAD programs to work together, yet rivals are suspicious that Autodesk deliberately crippled DXF to limit its utility:

- There is no batch processing within AutoCAD to generate DXFs from an entire folder of DWG files, making it a needlessly cumbersome process for an AutoCAD user to prepare a set of drawings for a non-AutoCAD colleague.
- There is no linking of DXF files to the DWG original, requiring a new export each time the original is changed.
- DXF files are much larger than DWF, making storage and transmission difficult and costly. Because they are so large, they take much longer to load and save, even from within AutoCAD.
- Some information from DWG files is not translated into DXF at all, or it is encrypted, making it inaccessible to other programs.
- DXF files are inherently less precise than their DWG "parents."

In February 1998 a group of the "other" CAD companies, led by Visio, organized the OpenDWG Alliance to pressure Autodesk into opening its native DWG format. These companies want access to the source code for DWG so that better interoperability between CAD platforms can be achieved. So far, these companies have had to laboriously reverse-engineer DWG to allow their programs to read and write to this format. Each time Autodesk releases a new version, they have to go through this process again. They know that users will not accept the less-than-perfect translations offered by DXF.

In 1996 Autodesk published a set of programming tool kits called DWG Unplugged to aid developers of add-on programs for AutoCAD, but it still refuses to license its technology to competitors. The strategy of positioning AutoCAD as the de facto standard in the AEC industry has been a successful one for Autodesk, but it has cost the industry dearly by limiting choices and hindering collaboration and data sharing. As many as 2 billion DWG files are in existence worldwide, representing an astounding information investment under the control of one company's technology.

Visio was acquired by Microsoft in 1999. It will be interesting to see how that might change the equation in CAD software.

5-42, 5-43, and 5-44. Autodesk's MapGuide browser plug-in.

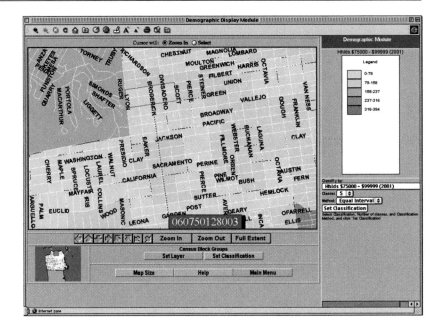

5-45. ArcExplorer from ESRI is a free GIS viewer.

- ESRI, another leader in GIS, offers ArcExplorer, a free, downloadable GIS browser for viewing information created with ESRI's flagship GIS products, Arc/Info and ArcView. ArcExplorer is a standalone program rather than a browser plug-in (fig. 5-45).
- GIS software, like CAD, is not very good at producing presentation-quality output. To remedy that, Avenza Software developed Map-Publisher, which exports GIS data to widely used vector graphics programs such as Adobe Illustrator or Macromedia Freehand. The underlying GIS data is not lost, as is the case when maps are converted to raster images. The software can take scanned images, such as aerial photographs, and scale them to correspond to the spatial information on a map. With the sophisticated graphic and text tools provided by Illustrator and Freehand, GIS mapping can be handsomely rendered for use in reports and on Web sites (figs. 5-46 and 5-47).

Photographic Images for the Web

You can choose from three approaches to generate photographic images for the Web.

1. Scan your conventional negatives, prints, or slides. For Web page illustrations, images taken with a high-quality 35mm camera and scanned are still likely to be better than those taken with all but the most expensive digital cameras. Best results can usually be obtained by using a slide scanner (which can also scan 35mm negatives), rather than by scanning prints in a flatbed scanner. Most scanners are bundled with a version of Photoshop so that you can import your scans, manipulate them, and convert them to JPEGs (fig. 5-48).

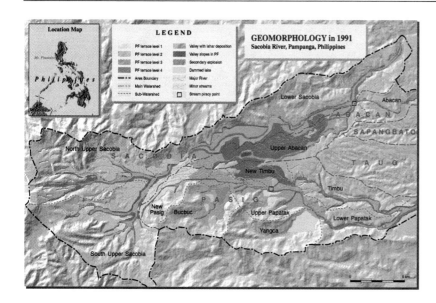

5-46. Geomorphology after the rainy season of 1991, Upper Sacobia Catchment, Pampanga, the Philippines. (Cartography and Visualization, ITC, Enschede, The Netherlands)

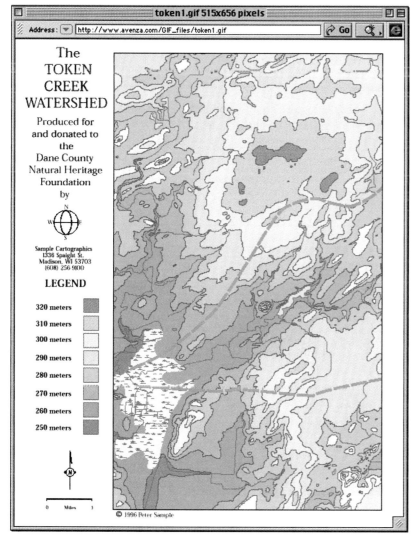

5-47. Avenza MapPublisher exports GIS data to illustration applications. (©1996 Sample Cartographics)

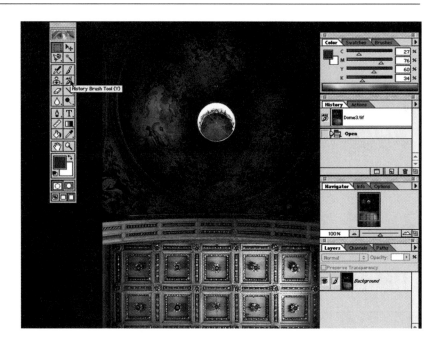

5-48. Photoshop offers a powerful array of image-editing tools.

2. Take photographs with conventional slide or print film, and have your photo finisher or service bureau place them on Kodak Photo CDs. After conventional processing, the film is scanned and digitally written to a CD. This is undoubtedly the most convenient way to store and catalog a large collection of images. Each disk holds approximately one hundred images, in five resolutions each—higher resolution for printing, lower for illustrating Web pages. New images can be added until the disk is full. The cost is reasonable—a dollar or two per image—and each CD comes with a printed catalog of all the images it contains. Kodak uses its own file format, which can be opened by Photoshop and saved to TIFF or JPEG.

3. Shoot with a digital camera. Obviously, this is the most direct approach to digital imaging. For highest image quality, the key factor to look for in a digital camera is the maximum resolution, expressed in megapixels: the higher, the better. This number is the product of the X by Y pixel dimensions of the largest image the camera can produce. For example, a 1,200- by 900-pixel image yields just over 1 megapixel (one million pixels). As of this writing, several cameras selling for under $1,000 are capable of capturing 3-megapixel images. Make sure any camera you buy has an optical viewfinder in addition to an LCD screen. Many digital photographers who try out cameras in a store discover too late that LCDs tend to wash out completely in bright light, making the camera nearly useless for exterior photography. Consider also how you will get the images into your computer. Some cameras use removable media such as magnetic cards; tiny PCMCIA hard drives that fit in laptop slots; or SCSI, USB, or FireWire ports to move data on to your computer via cables. You may need to buy extra equipment for your computer to take advantage of these technologies.

Digital cameras are ideal for documentation purposes, such as construction observation and site reconnaissance, and for creating images for the Web. For presentation purposes, especially when photographs will be used in printed brochures and portfolios, the quality is still well below what is attainable by digitizing professionally made conventional photographs. In addition, digital cameras have a more limited range of accessories—interchangeable lenses, filters, and the like—than do conventional film cameras. But they are improving rapidly.

Optimizing Images for the Web

Optimizing is the art of reducing images to the smallest file size possible without losing an acceptable level of quality. Optimization may entail reducing the number of colors actually used in the image, because this factor is directly related to file size.

When manipulating any kind of digital image, always save the highest-quality version of it as a reference file, or "original." You can never restore image quality that you throw away, but you can return to the original if you saved it. Storage on CD-ROMs and zip disks has become so economical that there is no reason ever to delete an original image. The reference file may be a high-quality scan of a conventional analog photograph or an image file taken directly from a digital camera. From this original you can make any number of different versions of the image for different purposes. The highest-quality version might be used for color printing; lower-quality, smaller-sized versions, for Web pages.

Dither is the computer's attempt to approximate colors not in its palette by averaging adjacent pixels with colors it does have. Dithering can result from several causes. For example, when two or more GIF images are displayed on a Web page, an 8-bit display must choose the 256 colors to use for both of them. Unless the two files use the same palette, dithering occurs.

In addition, Web browsers try to resolve colors into the standard palette of their underlying operating system. Unfortunately, different operating systems do not use the same standard palette of 256 colors. The Windows and Macintosh system palettes, for example, have only 216 colors in common. This subset of 216 colors is referred to as Web-safe; GIF images that limit themselves to the Web-safe palette will look fine on both platforms (fig. 5-49). Colors that do not conform may dither under some conditions, with unpredictable and sometimes hideous results. Image-editing tools such as Photoshop enable you to choose Web-safe colors easily (fig. 5-50). If it is likely that your most important visitors will be using 16- or 24-bit systems and you do not care that the others will see dithered images, then choose a palette that most enhances the quality of your images.

An excellent tool created especially for optimizing Web images is Adobe's ImageReady. ImageReady is a subset of Photoshop; the menus and toolbars will be very familiar to experienced Photoshop users. Its

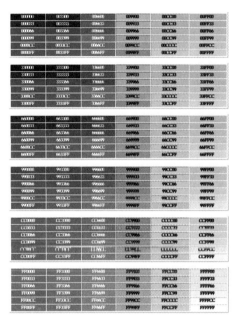

5-49. The Web-safe palette with hexadecimal codes.

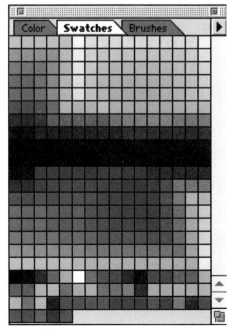

5-50. Photoshop's Web palette.

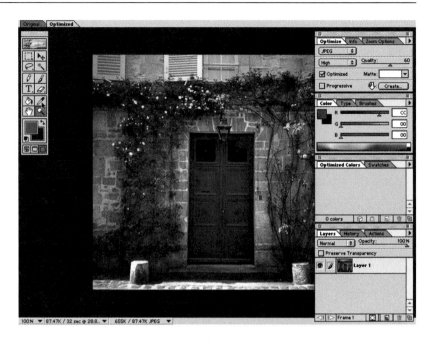

5-51. The original photograph as a 655K TIFF.

5-52. The photograph optimized as a JPEG in ImageReady. File size has been reduced to 87K.

best trick is the ability to show original and optimized image versions side by side, so that one can see the effects of each tweak on image quality and file size (figs. 5-51 and 5-52). ImageReady enables you to systematically reduce colors (and thereby lower file size) until you begin to lose image quality noticeably. It also allows you to compare GIF and JPEG versions of an image side by side.

Black-and-white images, such as most aerial photographs, GIS images, and architectural drawings, will display beautifully as gray-scale images saved as GIFs. In this case, 256 colors become 256 shades of gray (fig. 5-53).

5-53. Gray-scale images can display beautifully in browsers. (Courtesy Stephen Lauf, Quondam)

Adobe Portable Document Format (PDF)

An alternative and supplement to HTML is provided by Adobe's PDF technology. The Acrobat program creates PDF files that capture all the attributes of a printed page, including fonts, layout, resolution, page size, and margins. In contrast to HTML, PDF files use high-resolution graphics and typography and can be viewed and printed on any computer with the free, downloadable Acrobat Reader application. PDF is a good alternative to paper publishing for technical documents of all kinds, because of the ability it offers to mark up files, create links, and print at high quality. PDF files can contain scalable vector graphics, making them excellent vehicles for cross-platform sharing of CAD and GIS graphics. PDF is a good way to distribute high-impact documents such as a firm portfolio, a catalog, or a statement of qualifications, which the remote recipient can view and print but not modify unless the author allows it. Fonts are embedded in the document itself, so it does not matter if the recipient has them installed. Instead of printing multiple copies of a document and shipping by overnight mail, consider creating PDF files and sending them as e-mail attachments or making them available via FTP.

The Acrobat Reader application permits viewing within its own windows or inside a browser window with a plug-in. PDF files are larger than the equivalent material in HTML and therefore take somewhat longer to download and display. And because they have a fixed dimensional format suitable for printing, they may not be comfortable

5-54. (Left) A page from a report saved as a PDF file and viewed in Acrobat Reader.

5-55. (Right) A portion of the page enlarged 600 percent. PDF files preserve all the formatting and high resolution of printed pages.

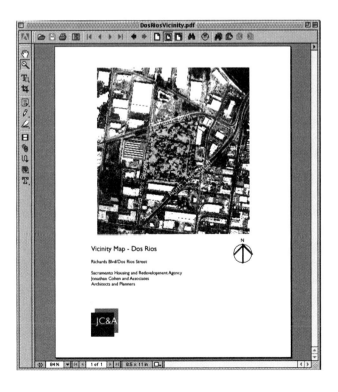

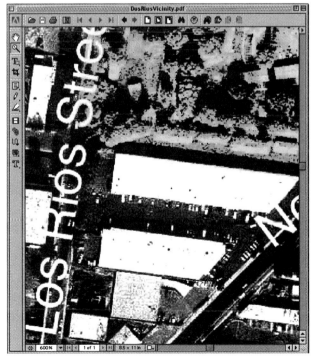

On-line Project Manuals

Lessons can be learned from the technology industries that may have application for AEC professionals as well. For example, the computer industry has fully embraced the Internet for product support. Almost all hardware and software products now come with little or no printed documentation; all the information is on-line, saving the cost of publication and enabling manuals to be frequently updated. Similarly, building project manuals could easily be produced in on-line form, using PDF or HTML format. Such project manuals would always be available to facilities managers, maintenance personnel, and repair crews. Currently, a facilities manager must hunt for information from among a variety of disconnected sources, including as-built drawings, product manuals, catalog cuts, maintenance records, and shop drawings.

A well-designed on-line project manual would have hyperlinks to manufacturers' Web sites, specifications, maintenance information, e-mail addresses, and relevant drawing details. A basic manual could be produced as a CD-ROM but be navigable with a Web browser, so that links to on-line resources would be just a click away.

for users to read onscreen, particularly those with small monitors (figs. 5-54 and 5-55, page 119).

With Acrobat, any document can be converted on the fly to a PDF file from within any application by simply sending a print command, with PDFWriter selected as your "printer." This allows you to reuse materials that have already been prepared in a page-layout application or in a word processor. Adobe PDF files can be associated with a searchable index using Adobe's Catalog add-on. Hyperlinks can be added to documents so that onscreen readers can jump to other sections of the document or to URLs on the Internet. The author of a PDF document has the option of allowing alteration by others, so that it can be used collaboratively, or write-protecting it so that it cannot be modified. Text in PDF files is fully searchable.

In the software industry, PDF has become the de facto standard for publishing manuals and documentation, because of its low cost and ease of updating compared to printed materials. PDF files can be distributed on disk or the Web. Andersen Windows, for example, publishes its entire catalog with high-resolution architectural details and specifications in PDF and distributes them on a cross-platform CD-ROM. Embedded hyperlinks enable users to jump from an index to a detail much more easily than with a printed catalog. Updates to the catalog are published on Andersen's Web site.

Multimedia: Video and Sound

Architecture is the most public of art forms. As project stakeholders and the lay public become increasingly involved in design and planning, design professionals are challenged to make complex spatial and visual ideas comprehensible to this larger audience of nonexperts. There has never been a greater need, nor a better opportunity, for architects to communicate effectively with diverse groups. Architects and planners can harness multimedia tools to broaden and inform the public debate and influence its outcome. Practitioners must learn to do a better job than they have of explaining in lay terms what they do, to the public and to their clients.

Movies, television, and video games have made ordinary people quite sophisticated about multimedia and three-dimensional computer visualization. Design professionals should not expect to communicate very effectively with this audience using static means of representation, such as traditional orthographic architectural views. Despite advances in CAD, computer-based virtual reality modeling and visualization are still not mainstream skills.

Fortunately, the tools of multimedia production have become far more accessible, cheaper, and easier to use. More powerful computers with video capture, large, fast hard drives and removable media, and low-cost digital video cameras with powerful, easy-to-use software put multimedia production within reach of most small businesses.

Digital Video

For now, insufficient bandwidth forces severe limitations on the ability of Web site designers to make full use of multimedia. Digital video, in particular, requires large files. But as broadband Internet connectivity becomes more widespread throughout the world in the next few years, there is great potential for using multimedia on the Web for a variety of purposes, including construction documentation, site reconnaissance, and presentation.

If your computer has a video capture card, you can make movie clips that you can place in Web pages just as you do still-image files. Video is captured by attaching a video camera or VCR directly to the computer's video input ports or by recording onto magnetic media with a digital video camera and then transferring files to your hard drive. Software packages, including Adobe Premiere and Apple's Final Cut Pro, allow you to edit and mix your shots, add soundtracks and special effects, make titles, and so on. Movie clips are saved as QuickTime MOV or MPEG files. With PageMill or any of the other visual Web-authoring software, you can drag and drop these files into Web pages just as you can GIFs and JPEGs. Some Web browsers require appropriate plug-ins for video, such as Apple's QuickTime and Windows Media Player. If you use video on Web pages, provide a download link so that visitors can get what they need easily.

The size of video files is a function of several variables, just as it is with still images. The physical size of the display window in pixels, the length of the clip, and the frame rate all have a proportional impact on file size. A soundtrack adds still more. Since a video is made up of twenty-four or thirty still images per second, file size grows very quickly into the multi-megabyte range.

If visitors to your site are on a high-speed network or broadband connection, using video makes sense right now. But if your visitors are using dial-up connections, you will strain their patience if you make them wait a very long time to view a jerky, low-resolution movie in a tiny window. As a partial near-term solution, *streaming* video permits sound and video files to begin playing back before they are completely downloaded. The download continues as the first part begins playing on the viewer's screen. As in broadcasting, media are presented as they come over the wire and need not be stored in the viewer's memory. Streaming technology can be used to present content that is live or prerecorded. Browser plug-ins are required to view the material, and hosting a site with streaming media also requires special server software, although your ISP may provide it. RealMedia and QuickTime are currently the leading players in streaming media technology.

Audio

A narrated slide show can be an effective alternative to video at a small fraction of the bandwidth requirement. To create a Web slide show, simply arrange a sequence of pages containing text and images and record your narration into a corresponding sequence of audio files. Most PCs with sound capability come with a microphone jack or a built-in microphone and basic sound-recording software, such as Windows' Sound Recorder or SimpleSound for Macintosh. Many other shareware and commercial sound-recording software packages are available at low cost for both platforms. Once you have completed your sound recordings, you can drag and drop the individual files (in Windows Wave, AIFF, or QuickTime formats) into your Web pages just as you would image files.

There are two types of Internet sound: sound that is recorded and then digitized, such as a voice-over narration or recorded music, and sound that is synthesized. The latter, typically in the form of MIDI files, is a way to add a soundtrack to a Web site with a tiny amount of overhead. MIDI (Musical Instrument Digital Interface) is the digital equivalent of sheet music. Only the notes are contained in the file; the recipient's computer does the heavy lifting by playing the music, calling upon the software music synthesizer built into the operating system. The difference between MIDI and recorded sound, such as a Wave or AIFF file, is analogous to the distinction between vector and raster images: MIDI files contain only the numeric description of the music, rather than the sound itself, and are therefore much smaller files. Public-domain MIDI files are available for download on Internet music sites, or you can make your own with a music synthesizer.

Recorded sound files, for which there are a bewildering array of file types, are much larger than MIDI files, but they can be squeezed down with compression and *downsampling*. When recorded sound is digitized, samples of the sound are taken at very close intervals of time. The more samples taken per second, the more accurate the sound will be. For example, CD-quality music is sampled 44,100 times per second, which ensures that the full range of human hearing is covered, from deepest bass to highest treble. A narrated presentation doesn't need this level of quality, and by recording it at a low sample rate, file size is greatly reduced. As with video, audio can also be streamed, so that only a small portion of the total file need be downloaded before play begins.

Photography-based Virtual Reality

In order for a visualization technique to be considered virtual reality, as opposed to mere simulation, it must have three qualities: it must be *immersive*, *navigable*, and *interactive*. Montages of two-dimensional images do not qualify, nor do static views of three-dimensional models, nor video clips of fly-overs or walk-throughs, although all of these are potentially valuable presentation formats. Obviously, a flat image on a computer screen, no matter how large it may be, cannot be truly immersive. But the state of the art in flight simulators, industrial robotics, and even sophisticated arcade games demonstrates that a feeling of immersion can be achieved in the mind if not the body. The problem with these kinds of virtual-reality experiences is that the hardware required is very expensive and certainly not portable. But several surprisingly effective options can enable you to convey something like a virtual-reality experience on the Web.

QuickTime VR is an extension of Apple's QuickTime multimedia software for creating and viewing sound and video. Unlike true three-dimensional modeling, QTVR is based on still images that are stitched together by the software into a seamless virtual environment. The visitor cannot roam at will through a model or scene but must follow a predetermined path to fixed vantage points. But because the scene is created from real photographs or from highly rendered model views, the effect is of considerable realism. Visitors use the mouse or keyboard to pan around, look up or down, and zoom the image. This level of interactivity lends a seductive quality to these panoramas that approximates the pleasure one gets from examining a physical model.

The still images used can be photographs of an actual scene, saved views of a computer model, or a combination of the two. In any case, there is no limit on the complexity of the image. You can make a panorama of an existing site and then insert matching views of a model into it to simulate very effectively how a building will look within its actual setting (figs. 5-56 and 5-57). QTVR files are relative-

5-56 and 5-57. A QuickTime VR scene showing the modeled reconstruction of a Roman peristyle superimposed on the actual site in Portugal. A plan shows the viewpoint. (Courtesy Santiago Ribas)

5-58. These twelve photographs will be used to create a QuickTime VR panorama.

ly small, particularly in comparison to CAD models or digital video, and therefore highly appropriate for use on Web sites, even when accessed by low-bandwidth visitors.

Just as with imagemaps, hyperlinks can be mapped to hot spots within in a scene to jump the visitor to another Web page. A scene of an office interior, for example, might link a chair to a Web page describing the chair, its finish options, alternative chairs, or a spreadsheet showing the number of such chairs in a building. Or by clicking on a window, one might be shown the view from that window. Scenes can be connected together in a "multi-node" panorama, so that a sequence of spaces can be interactively explored by the viewer. Each room in a structure can be represented as a separate node, and these can be keyed to floor plans. The transition between nodes can even be shown as a short video clip of the path between two vantage points. It is a very effective way to present both interior and exterior spaces. You can even add a soundtrack to QTVR scenes, and with add-on products such as SoundsaVR from Squamish Media Group, you can map directional sounds to specific locations within a scene. Such technology could be used to model directional sound effects in an auditorium, for example, or to simulate traffic or airplane noise in urban environments.

Figure 5-58 shows a series of twelve still images that will be converted to a QTVR panorama with Apple's QuickTime VR Authoring Studio. Twelve to eighteen images are needed to generate a panorama, depending on the focal length of the lens used to shoot them. Generally, a wide-angle lens in the range of 18mm to 28mm (for a 35mm camera) is best, with exposures taken in a vertical format. Special tripod mounts, such as the Kaidan Kiwi, have click stops at set intervals to make this process easier. A digital camera can also be used, but for highest quality, use a good single lens reflex camera, shooting conventional slide or print film. After processing, the photographs are digitized and placed on a Kodak PhotoCD. Figure 5-59 shows two adjacent images and the controls for correcting any misalignment between them. Adjacent images overlap each other considerably. The software first stitches the photographs into a flat panoramic image (fig. 5-60) and then into an interactive QuickTime VR scene, which can be placed directly into Web pages (fig. 5-70, page 128).

5-59. Adjacent images can be adjusted for alignment. The blurred region in the center is the overlap between two adjacent photographs.

5-60. The first stage is a panoramic image combining all twelve photographs.

Reconstructing History

A fascinating application of computer-based architectural visualization is the modeling of buildings that have been demolished or were never built. Examples include the detailed reconstruction of German synagogues lost to the Holocaust (figs. 5-61, 5-62, and 5-63), three-dimensional simulations of the twelfth-century B.C. temple palace of Ramses III (figs. 5-64 and 5-65), and a QuickTime VR rebuilding of Ludwig Mies van der Rohe's Barcelona Exposition pavilion (figs. 5-66, 5-67, 5-68, and 5-69).

5-61, 5-62, and 5-63. Students at the Technical University at Darmstadt, Germany, are using computer modeling to reconstruct synagogues lost to the Holocaust.(©1999 Prof. Dipl-Ing. Manfred Koob, Department CAD in Architecture, Darmstadt University of Technology)

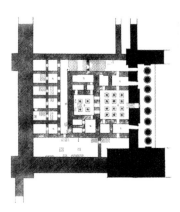

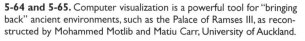

5-64 and 5-65. Computer visualization is a powerful tool for "bringing back" ancient environments, such as the Palace of Ramses III, as reconstructed by Mohammed Motlib and Matiu Carr, University of Auckland.

5-66 through 5-69. A computer reconstruction of Mies van der Rohe's German Pavilion for the 1929 Barcelona Exposition, presented with QuickTime VR by Matiu Carr, University of Auckland.

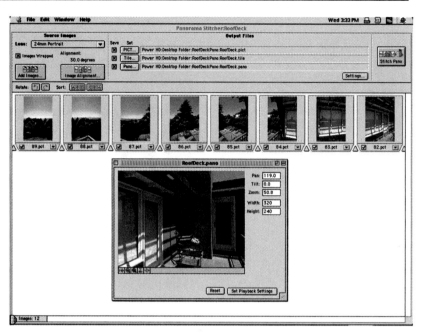

5-70. Apple's QuickTime VR Authoring Studio makes it easy to create panoramic, navigable scenes that can be viewed in Web browsers.

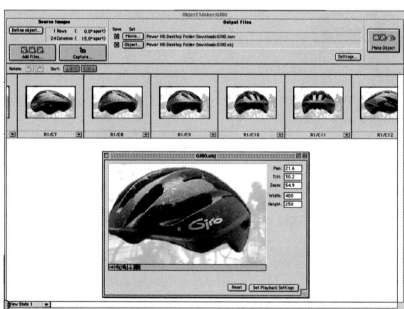

5-71. QuickTime VR objects are also created from a sequence of still images. (Courtesy Don Taylor Studio 360)

A variant is the QuickTime VR *object*. Instead of being inside a room or space looking out, the viewer is outside looking in, holding and manipulating a photorealistic object. Figure 5-71 shows a sequence of images being prepared for stitching. Unlike the QTVR panorama, which can be easily made without special equipment, QTVR object photography requires a rig that can either rotate the object from side to side and forward and back, or spin the camera completely around the object being photographed. The two QTVR modes can be combined; one can enter a room, for example, look around, and pick up an object. The Scene Maker component of QuickTime VR Authoring Studio lets

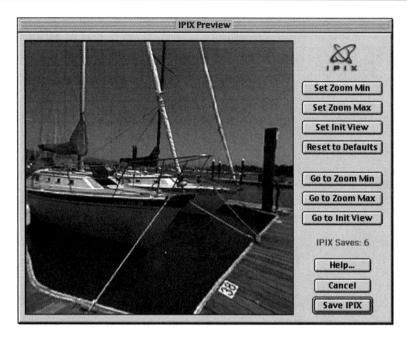

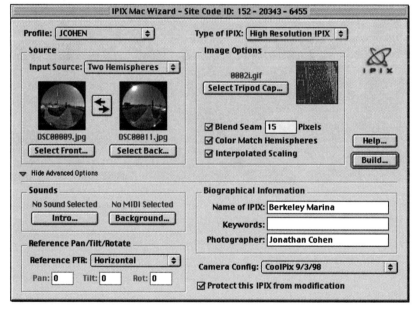

5-72 through 5-75. IPIX panoramas are made from hemispheric fish-eye images. (Interactive Pictures and IPIX are trademarks of Interactive Pictures Corporation)

you combine objects and panoramas into multi-node scenes, which you can key to a floor plan or map.

IPIX, from Interactive Pictures, gives a completely unbounded floor-to-ceiling view that is particularly effective for presenting interior space. With IPIX, only two photographic images are needed to generate a panorama, but they must be taken with a fish-eye lens capable of shooting a full 180-degree hemisphere. Figures 5-72 and 5-73 (above right) show two fish-eye images that will be melded into an IPIX file (fig. 5-74). Images can be viewed in Web browsers with either the free IPIX plug-in or a Java viewer (fig. 5-75).

5-76. VRML model of the Tiffany Fountain at the Metropolitan Museum of Art, New York. (Mark Lawton, Construct Internet Design)

Three-Dimensional Imaging

The only Web standard for true 3D is VRML, Virtual-Reality Modeling Language, which grew out of the first World Wide Web conference held in Geneva in May 1994. It sought to do for three-dimensional modeling what HTML did for text and two-dimensional media: to introduce a public-domain, cross-platform file format that would standardize three-dimensional imaging on the Internet. Unlike the photographic VR media discussed above, VRML supports true immersive 3D: viewers can enter a scene and move about completely at will. VRML supports three-dimensional geometry, lighting, and materials in the form of bitmapped graphic textures that are wrapped over modeled surfaces (fig. 5-76).

Most commercially available CAD software can export a model as a VRML file (with the suffix .wrl), and these files can be placed in Web pages like other media. When a Web browser enounters a

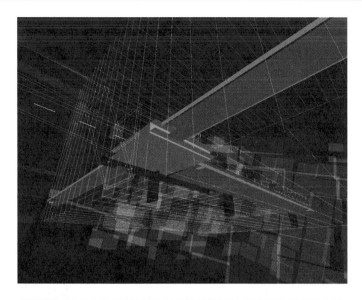

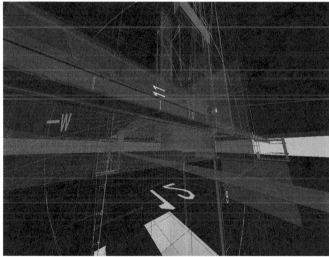

5-77, 5-78, and 5-79. VRML models are fully inter-active on the Web: visitors can move through them at will. (Mark Lawton, Construct Internet Design)

5-80. Part of the VRML model of Bath, England. (Courtesy of The Centre for Advanced Studies in Architecture, University of Bath, United Kingdom)

VRML model, either within a Web page or as a standalone file, it hands it off to a VRML plug-in, such as CosmoPlayer, which then renders it on the screen and allows the viewer to move freely in *X*, *Y*, and *Z* axes. The model's creator can save an unlimited number of preset views from which visitors can begin to explore. Surfaces within the model can be wrapped with textures, either embedded in the VRML file itself or as separate image files, which are downloaded as needed when relevant portions of the model are viewed (figs. 5-77, 5-78, and 5-79, page 131).

VRML has not yet been the commercial success its adherents had hoped it would be, in part because the browser plug-ins have been somewhat unstable; moreover, moving about smoothly within models calls for a relatively high-end computer. VRML is composed of text, like HTML, rather than binary 1s and 0s, and this creates rather large files. But VRML offers the great advantage of allowing true, three-dimensional models to be navigated on the Internet with free, widely available software.

One of the most ambitious VRML projects for urban visualization is the three-dimensional model of the city of Bath, England, undertaken by Vassilis Bourdakis and Alan Day of the Centre for Advanced Studies in Architecture (CASA) at Bath University (fig. 5-80 and fig. 1-2). The model was intended to be a working tool to enable planners to consider a wide range of views of proposed buildings by accurately modeling development schemes within their simulated context. It has spurred public discussion about long-range planning for the historic city. The model was constructed entirely on PCs using AutoCAD, 3DStudio, and street-level photographs, which were exported as DXF files and translated to VRML. The model is capable of displaying four distinct levels of architectural detail, depending on the distance from an object being viewed. It includes 160 sub-models representing individual city blocks, each small enough to fit on a floppy disk. These submodels are freely distributed to architects working on proposals for new or remodeled buildings. Their schemes can then be easily reimported into the full city model.

The Bath model developers intend to extend its functionality by adding data mapping of pollution, crime statistics, land use, and property value, as well as by integrating traffic-modeling software and simulating plant growth with accurate seasonal variation.

An earlier CASA experiment, a model of London's West End, was originally created to study the location of cellular telephone transmitters. That model has now evolved into a "map of the future," in which embedded links provide information about entertainment, transportation, and other services.

Another Web-based VRML experiment is unfolding in Finland. A joint venture between the city of Helsinki and its principal telecommunications provider, the Helsinki Telephone Company, aims to turn the Finnish capital into the world's first totally connected city in time for its 450th anniversary in the year 2000. The centerpiece of this ambitious effort is a large-scale VRML model of the city that will be available on-line to city residents (figs. 5-81, 5-82, and 5-83). The model will contain hyperlinks to city services, cultural institutions, and commercial enterprises, and it will be augmented with QuickTime VR panoramas and two-way live video. City residents will be able to move interactively through the model and make purchases, obtain real-time information about events, and use government services.

At UCLA, the Urban Simulation Team, led by Bill Jepson, is building an electronic model of the entire Los Angeles basin, comprising thousands of square miles. This model, called Virtual LA, is accurate to the level of graffiti on the walls and signs in the windows. It is being constructed by combining aerial photographs with street-level imagery, city engineering maps, and CAD modeling to create a highly realistic three-dimensional database. More than a dozen separate area models have been built, ranging in size from 1 to 15 square miles, to study specific areas of Los Angeles. After creation, these individual urban models are inserted into a large-area-terrain database. Jepson's team is currently working with the city to create virtual models of the Hollywood Boulevard and MacArthur Park neighborhoods, each about thirty-five blocks in size.

As new areas are studied in detail, the model will continue to grow incrementally over time. Each virtual neighborhood can be used for interactive fly-over and walk-through demonstrations, enabling close inspection of proposed developments and highway structures. All movement is in real time, giving an effect similar to playing shoot-em-up video games, except that all the landmarks are familiar.

5-81, 5-82, and 5-83. The VRML model of Helsinki, which aims to be an electronic citizens' forum. (© Helsinki Telephone Corporation)

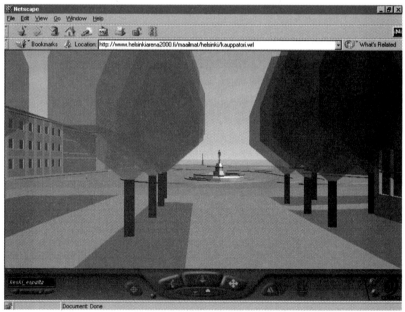

Changes over time can also be simulated: the database includes tree models, for example, that accurately "grow." The model can link every parcel and storefront to a URL, pointing to Web pages maintained by the individual business or property owner.

Mike Hernandez, a Los Angeles city councilman, said this about Virtual LA: "The real value is to allow citizens to participate in the planning process. It really benefits in developing large projects and in looking at the impacts of those projects on communities. You can actually see it before you build it."

6 Web Site

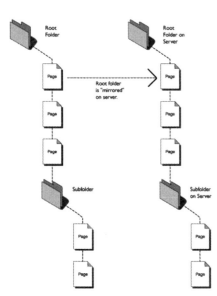

6-1. Web administrators maintain mirrored copies of the Web site files and directories between the local computer used for Web authoring and the server that hosts the site.

A Web site is not a short-term commitment. Maintaining your site, keeping it current, and managing the information that comes back from visitors are all part of the job.

Previous chapters provided an overview of the process of creating Web sites and preparing media for them. The next step is to mount the Web site on a server, which entails transferring all of the HTML pages, linked files, subsidiary folders, and graphics together, maintaining them in the same relationship to one other (fig. 6-1). If the server is physically within your organization, it is probably on a network that allows you simply to place files in the appropriate directory. If not, then you will connect to the server using FTP and transfer the files over the Internet. Most of the current Web-authoring applications have an FTP function built into them (fig. 6-2), or you can use a standalone FTP application such as FTP Control Pro, Bullet Proof FTP, or Fetch (fig. 6-3).

On the Web, every file type must be identified by a three- or four-letter suffix, such as .gif or .html. Most of the applications you will use to create content for the Web add these suffixes to the file name automatically, but it's a good idea to check them before uploading. On Unix servers, the file name is case sensitive: picture.gif will not be recognized to be the same file as Picture.GIF, PICTURE.gif, or PICTURE.GIF, although any of these forms can be used. Do not use blank spaces, slashes, tildes, or other special characters in file names; it's safest to stick to lowercase letters, numerals, and perhaps underscores or dashes. Decide in advance on a consistent method of naming files, and stick with it. File-naming conventions vary depending on the operating system of the server, so check in advance with your Webmaster or Internet Service Provider.

Management

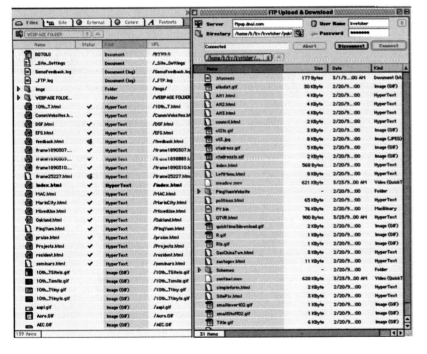

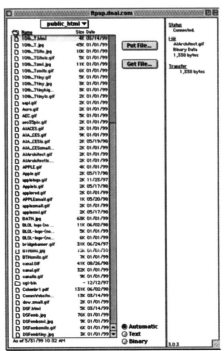

6-2. Adobe GoLive has FTP built in, allowing site designers to synchronize folders between the server and the computer used for design. (Used with permission of Adobe Systems, Inc.)

6-3. Fetch is a shareware FTP client for the Macintosh. (Courtesy of Dartmouth College)

Should You Have Your Own Server?

A key question for every organization planning to use the Internet is whether to operate its own Web server or to opt for outsourcing to an ISP or other provider. Several options are available:

Web hosting refers to the practice of renting space on an outside server (usually from an ISP) that you share with other users and organizations. You will be given access to your own directory on the server for uploading and downloading material to your Web site via FTP. When you register a domain name, such as www.abcdesign.com, the Web hosting service will arrange to have visitors directed to your site on their server.

The principal advantages of Web hosting are that you avoid the expense of purchasing and maintaining a server and of bringing a high-speed Internet connection to your location. The primary disadvantage is that you will not have the same degree of control and security that operating your own server provides. If you plan on using interactive features in your Web site, you may be limited in what you can offer by the policies of the ISP. For example, if you are providing fill-out forms, threaded discussion lists, or password authentication, you will require the ability to upload **scripts** to the server. Usually the ISP will require that scripts be placed in a designated subdirectory on the server to which you may or may not have direct access. Your ISP may require that you use only standard scripts that it provides, or it may require prior review and authorization of custom scripts. Some ISPs will not allow scripting functions at all, while others allow unlimited upload of custom scripts without review. Moreover, an ISP may or may not provide a searching/indexing function for your Web site. If your site contains information that you want users to be able to search, such as specifications, correspondence, or product data, lack of such a function would be a significant loss.

A limited degree of Web hosting is offered by most ISPs as part of the basic subscriber package. Most ISPs will limit the size of the Web site that can be placed on their servers, and their limits vary widely, from 2MB to 50MB or more. ISPs may also place upper limits on the *activity* of the Web site, defined, perhaps, as a specified number of hits per month, or just a volume of traffic expressed in megabytes. A larger Web site or more monthly activity may result in a higher monthly fee. The reporting or logging of activity on your Web site will also vary, depending on the policy of the ISP.

An alternative to Web hosting is *co-hosting* or *co-location*, which refers to the practice of owning and operating your own server but physically locating it at your ISP, where it can be attached to a high-speed connection and kept in a secure location. In this case, you have the same degree of control that you would have if the server were located on your premises, without the physical security concerns or the need to bring expensive high-speed dedicated lines into your offices. Most of the administrative functions that are required to keep the server operational can be done remotely, usually through a browser interface. The advantages of co-hosting over having your own server include:

- Reduced cost—leased lines to your facility are expensive.
- Physical security is the responsibility of the ISP. Usually your server will be placed in a open-mesh cage in a secure room. Battery back-up power supply should be provided.
- Increased reliability, because the server is connected more directly to the Internet than if it is at the end of a leased line in your office.

If you have decided to operate your own server, the next set of choices involves the hardware and software required. Configuring and maintaining a server require more than the minimum amount of in-house computer expertise. You will need one of the advanced network operating systems, such as Windows NT/2000, Novell Netware, Mac OS X, or Unix (which includes such versions as Sun's Solaris, SGI's IRIX, and the freeware Linux). Considerations here include security, ease of setup, capacity, and cost. A low-traffic site where ease-of-use and security are primary concerns might use the Mac OS, which was rated by the World Wide Web Consortium as least susceptible to hacker break-ins. A high-traffic e-commerce site with trained support personnel will probably use Unix.

Your server must run continuously and unattended for long periods of time. The requirements of a server are very different from those of a desktop PC or workstation, and it usually makes sense to purchase hardware and software specifically for this purpose. Your server hardware and operating system must run unattended twenty-four hours a day.

With a client-server system, all of your files are in one central location, but if the server goes down, you are out of business. Frequent backup of all data is critical. Some features that enhance hardware reliability include: redundant and/or quickly replaceable power supplies, redundant cooling fans, error-correcting memory, and multiple, hot-swappable hard drives which can be replaced without shutting down the computer. Your system must also be scalable; its capacity can increase as the company grows. A scalable server might include easily replaceable CPUs, a capacity to support multiple processors, and room for lots of RAM. Technical support for the system is also critical. Firms without a dedicated Unix or NT/2000 support expert should consider contracting for service with a support company that can guarantee on-site response within a few hours.

Security and Access Control

If you are hosting your own server, physical security becomes an issue. You must protect the server from theft and vandalism, power outages, and voltage fluctuations. Keeping it in a locked room usually provides adequate physical protection, while the use of surge protection, an uninterruptible power supply, and/or battery backup take care of the latter concerns. You must back up your data on a regular basis, preferably daily; back-up tapes or other media should be stored in a secure location away from the server. The best strategy is to have at least two complete back-up archives, with one kept in another building under lock and key.

Protecting your data and ensuring confidentiality require that you limit access to the Web server. Usually access control is attained through **authentication**: establishing, through the use of such devices as digital signatures, the identity of users on the system and their level of permission.

If an Internet site is intended for public consumption, security is usually not an issue. For extranets and intranets, however, it may be critical. Obviously, security is a matter of degree, and achieving a comfortable level of protection will vary from firm to firm. The security measures required to ensure confidentiality, for example, may be quite different from those needed to protect electronic transactions. There, authentication may have to be augmented by *nonrepudiation*, which means that a particular act can be attributed to a specific person, for example, an architect signing off on a change order request or a subcontractor submitting a bid. With nonrepudiation, once a person enters into an agreement, they cannot cancel it by claiming someone else authorized it.

A secure Web site requires an access plan. You will likely want to allow different levels of access to the site for different categories of visitors, including employees, clients, consultants, agencies, and contractors. You might provide read-only access to some classes of users, while others will be allowed to upload and download material. You might also organize the site into functional areas that allow users access to appropriate parts while restricting access to others. (You may not want that roofing contractor to read the owner-architect agreement.)

Ken Sanders, of Zimmer Gunsel Frasca, said this about access control: "One thing we learned was: don't reveal to people the information they *can't* have access to. They should only see what they *can* have and not get a glimpse of what they're not getting." Otherwise, they may feel slighted by their exclusion.

Password Protection

A reasonable level of security can be obtained with a user name and password system. This system can be implemented with a simple CGI script and is available to you even if you are not operating your own server, provided your ISP gives you this privilege. Under this system, you generate a small access file setting a user name and password for any folder or subfolder within your site. The file is then placed in the designated location on the server. Whenever someone tries to access a protected folder within your Web site, they are presented with a dialogue box requiring this user name and password. Unless you are dealing with highly sensitive projects involving government or industrial secrecy, this level of security is probably adequate. Access levels might be nested, that is, access to a deeper level of the Web site requires a second password. Such control is accomplished simply by creating a subfolder with another access file. You can change the user names and passwords whenever you wish or have reason to suspect that unauthorized users are attempting to access the protected area of the site. Password protection can be used to limit access to Web pages and FTP directories. You may allow partners to upload files directly to FTP directories; in this case the system must be designed so that such users are limited to particular directories and can have no access to higher-level directories.

Access to the Web site is one thing; access to the server itself is another. When you upload files to your Web site via FTP, you will require a different password; this one should be well guarded from unauthorized use. Since your Web site and your FTP site are on different areas of the server (or on different servers), you can allow partners to directly upload to the FTP site without compromising the security of the Web site.

SSL Protocol, or HTTPS, is the secure version of HTTP. It uses **encryption** to hide sensitive data and is the basis of e-commerce, online securities trading, and banking transactions. It enables server and client to negotiate a secure "handshake" relationship with each other before sensitive information (such as a credit card account number) is exchanged.

Some reasonable measures should be taken even when a relatively low level of security is adequate:

- Don't use obvious passwords, such as initials, names of children, phone numbers, or addresses. Passwords should be at least six digits, a mixture of upper and lower case, letters and numerals.
- Passwords should be changed every thirty days.
- All password-protected transactions should be logged.
- Session IDs provide a somewhat higher degree of security than passwords alone. When a user logs in to the system, a unique time stamp and identifier, which expires after a set period of time, are automatically issued. Session ID is most useful for providing an audit trail to track site usage. It is provided by the subscription-based project-specific Web site services such as ProjectNet and Evolv.
- Dynamic passwords is a system that generates a password on the fly for a particular session, in combination with a more permanent password issued to the user.

If you or your clients or partners are possible targets of sophisticated industrial espionage, you may need a higher level of security, such as is provided by card readers, encrypted certificates, or even biometric authentication.

Firewalls

Firewalls (another term borrowed from architecture!) are systems that protect your internal network from unauthorized outsiders. The term is used loosely and can refer to both hardware and software barriers to intrusion. A managed firewall is an integrated security system consisting of hardware, software, and monitoring and management tools that actively analyze and protect your internal network from potential break-ins.

The issue arises when you build a bridge between your intranet and the larger Internet. If you are using the Internet strictly for external operations, then it may make sense to isolate it physically from your intranet by running two independent servers with no connection between them. The Internet server might be outside of the office at a Web hosting service. However, most companies that have invested in an intranet want employees, clients, and colleagues to be able to access it from outside of the office, and they also want to reach Internet resources from within the intranet. The interface between Internet and intranet is where the security problem arises. How do you let the "friendlies" in while locking out the bad guys? That's where the firewall comes in.

One kind of firewall uses packet filters to check the IP address of all external computers attempting to access the intranet. Generally companies will have decided what kind of external access they want to provide, and if a request is made from a computer that does not fit the profile, it is turned away. Configuring a packet filter entails deciding what kinds of access will be allowed and writing rules that enforce it. For example, a company may want to let traveling employees check their e-mail and access their project files but not view financial data. Restrictions can be written for internal Web sites, e-mail, FTP sites, and all other services.

Proxy servers act as intermediaries between the intranet and those outside. These more sophisticated systems look not only at the identity of the outside computer but the content of messages and requests. These systems provide the highest level of security but are quite expensive and can noticeably slow access from outside.

Higher levels of security depend on encryption. With public key encryption, a message is scrambled into unreadable gobbledygook that must be decoded using a digital key, essentially a series of numbers. Public key encryption uses pairs of keys, one public, one private. Both keys are required to decipher a message. If Company A wishes to receive encrypted messages, it would freely distribute its public key to business partners B, C, and D. When any of these companies need to send private messages to Company A, they encrypt them with Company A's public key. These messages are now unreadable by anyone except Company A, which uses its private key to decrypt them.

The longer the key (in bits), the stronger the encryption, that is, the harder it is to break. The federal government has been wrangling with Internet companies for years over 40-bit versus 128-bit encryption. The FBI and other agencies do not want drug lords and spies to have access to strong encryption without a back-door key available to government watchdogs, so export controls have been placed on 128-bit encryption technology. These limits have been vociferously opposed by an alliance of civil libertarians and e-business promoters, who see security as the key to wide public acceptance of electronic commerce. At the time of this writing, it looks as if the government is backing off to some degree.

Technologies used to support Internet security include certificates, digital signatures, and Virtual Private Networks. *Certificates* (also known as digital IDs) vouch for the identity of the user, much like a digital passport. They are purchased from a so-called trusted authority (companies such as Verisign, AT&T, and Entrust). The browser or e-mail client looks for a certificate from the sender and must be configured to receive it. Different classes of certificates reflect the level of investigation that the trusted authority has made of the certificate holder.

Digital signatures are the inverse of the public key encryption system described above. Now, the private key is used to authenticate a message, which can then be opened with the public key. In this case the private key serves to authenticate the sender, rather than hide the message. Certificates and digital signatures enable secure e-mail; recent mail programs such as Microsoft Outlook Express keep track of digital IDs and perform encryption and decryption automatically.

A *Virtual Private Network* (VPN, also known as *tunneling*) takes a global, rather than per-message, approach to security. It allows you to gain the benefits of a secure extranet without forcing individual users to fiddle around with settings and certificates. All network traffic between the intranet gateway and partner sites (or individual remote users) is encrypted, then sent over the public network. Instead of requiring each user to authenticate each transaction, *all* traffic is secure, much as if you were using your own private lines. VPNs are typically proprietary solutions, meaning you must have compatible hardware at both ends, which may be a problem for VPNs set up on the fly to support a particular project, or even for a permanent extranet that must accommodate a variety of client systems and a changing cast of players.

Tracking Your Site

You may be interested in tracking usage of your Web site. If you are running your own server, your Web server application can generate a log file for your site. Most ISPs offering Web hosting will let you

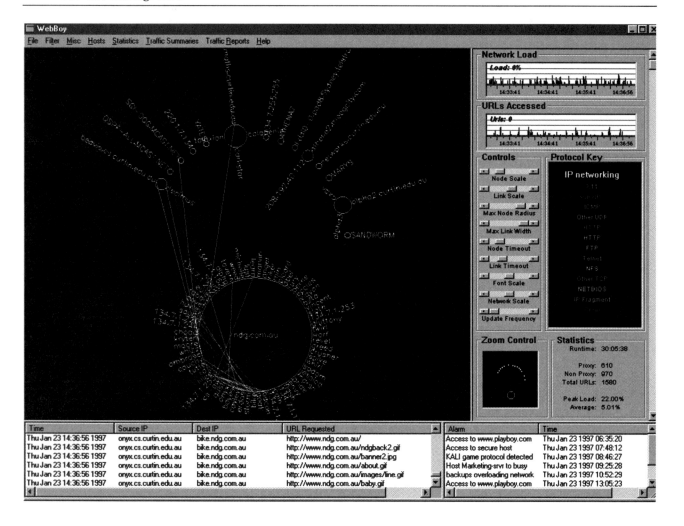

6-4. WebBoy monitors Internet and intranet traffic flow. It provides statistics on URLs accessed within sites. (WebBoy and GeoBoy are trademarks of NDG Software, Inc.)

download the file from their server. You can then use a log analysis utility, which will allow you to sift through the information and determine who is visiting your site, when and for how long, which pages were visited, and so on (fig. 6-4). Done on a large scale, such analysis is called *data mining*.

Be wary of inflated claims of site usage from Internet promoters who boast of a million hits per month on their sites. *Hits* is a measure of the number of file accesses to a Web site. If the home page has ten small graphics, one visit to that page will generate eleven hits, because eleven different files were accessed, assuming that the visitor didn't leave impatiently before loading all the images. If a large number of small buttons are used for navigation instead of one large imagemap, for example, the number of hits will be much larger, without revealing anything useful about how intensively the site is being used. The number of visitors is a more meaningful figure, but even that does not reveal much about how deep into a site those visitors went. Did they all look at the first screen and leave?

Making Your Pages Searchable

Potential visitors will find your site more easily if you make it friendly to the Internet search engines. One of the limitations of these Web crawlers is that they are text based, that is, they search for pages containing keywords or phrases and therefore sometimes miss the real meaning of pages that are primarily graphic. For example, an architectural firm may have a publicity page about all the elementary schools it has designed. The page is illustrated with pictures of completed designs, and it conveys much information to the intended audience of school boards and administrators looking for a good architect. The search engine, however, misses the meaning entirely, since the text "elementary school" does not appear on the page. The use of *meta tags* corrects this problem, allowing you to embed keywords describing the page in a hidden header section of the HTML that is invisible to the user but discernible by a search engine. Metadata is roughly equivalent to a library catalog record. If it were widely adopted, it would make Internet searching more efficient, particularly if an industry-specific system of keywords were developed and implemented. Future versions of Web-authoring and word processing software may have the ability to extract standard keywords from a document (including notes attached to or embedded in graphics files) and place them in metadata format. An HTML meta tag looks like this:

```
<META NAME ="keywords" content="architecture, city planning, interior
design, structural engineering, construction">
```

Meta tags can be seen in Web pages in the VIEW SOURCE mode. You can add them to your pages by hand, using a text editor such as Windows NotePad or Macintosh SimpleText. Place them between the <HEAD> and </HEAD> tags, and they won't be visible on the page. Search engines sometimes have trouble with framed pages, because the primary link is to the frame set page, which has no information in it beyond the arrangement of the frames. If your site uses frames and you want search engines to find you, place meta tags with keywords in the header section of the frame set page.

HTML's sophisticated cousin, XML, improves upon meta tags by using declarations that tell a Web browser about the kind of information that will be presented on the page, using terms specific to an industry or discipline. XML is discussed in more detail in chapter 11.

In addition to making your pages searchable, you can add your own search function to your Web site. All of the popular Web servers, including Apache, Netscape and Microsoft, have a built-in search capability. Even if you are not running your own server, your ISP may allow subscribers to add indexing and search functions to their Web sites. You may need to trigger the search func-

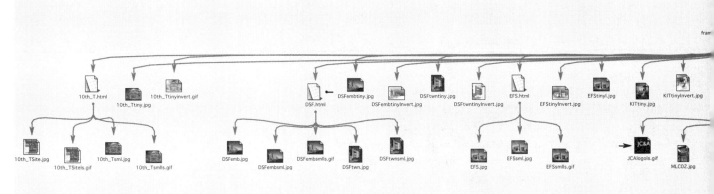

6-5. The larger the Web site, the bigger the task of managing it.

tion by invoking a CGI script. Microsoft FrontPage 2000 includes a built-in indexing and search function for sites it creates, but the FrontPage extensions must be installed on the server. Customized search forms can be dropped into Web pages for word searches of the entire site.

Managing Your Media Assets

Desktop publishing has accustomed many people to arranging formatted text and graphics into publications to be printed on paper. With the arrival of interactive media such as CD-ROM and the Internet, these printed materials must be adapted for the new formats. More and more information will be published simultaneously on the Web and as printed documents, presenting the same material in ways appropriate to their respective formats.

How can you efficiently make use of your assets—text and media—without duplicating your efforts? One approach is to create a publishing database. Keep all text and media as separate files in a central repository from which you can *place* them in desktop-publishing applications such as QuarkXpress for printed publications, and *link* them to Web-authoring applications such as PageMill or FrontPage. Such a database makes synchronizing printed, CD-ROM, and Web versions of related material much easier. Database publishing also helps with version control, easing the task of making corrections and updates simultaneously to all publishing formats. Whenever a text or graphic file is updated, all print- and Web-based documents that make use of it are automatically updated as well. Some form of database publishing is needed for tracking the large number of CAD drawings in a typical architectural project. As firms

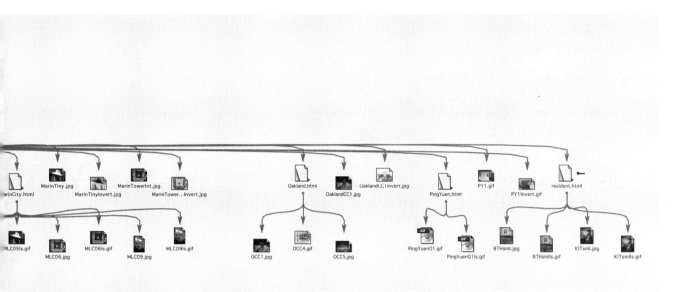

transition from paper-based to Web-based project management systems, making sure the various versions of files are coordinated during the overlap period is critical.

One of the strengths of Web publishing over paper is the ease with which you can customize publications for specific purposes. For example, most subcontractors don't need an entire set of drawings and specifications. But because specification sections typically make reference to other sections, giving subcontractors just one or two sections is risky—a roofing section may refer to a flashing section and a waterproofing section, and they may all refer to the general conditions and other boilerplate material. By using hyperlinks, spec sections can carry links to other material that physically resides elsewhere. You can give subcontractors a URL that points to a specific spec section on your server, for example. All necessary references will be a click away, including links to related documents such as industry standards, building code, and manufacturers' Web sites. When sections are revised, you need not reissue new paper versions.

7 Expanding Your

Now that you have been introduced to Web terms and techniques, let's turn to a consideration of how designers, planners, and building professionals are using the Internet to expand their capabilities and broaden their practices. This chapter will explore a variety of ways that AEC firms are using the Internet for programming, marketing, product research, permitting, and project management. Chapter 8 examines how intranets and extranets are being used to manage and improve communication within firms and project teams.

Programming and Problem Definition

Architects are trained in an iterative design process. The idea is to solve the big problems first, then smaller and smaller ones, circling around in tighter and tighter loops until arriving at a elegant and responsive solution to the design problem. They gather knowledge—from a client, from a group of end users—and attempt to synthesize that knowledge into a program and then a drawing. Over the life of a design project, all of these iterations are captured on many pieces of paper, but too much of that careful thought and reasoning gets lost or forgotten. By the time a project is completed, it is frequently very difficult to reconstruct the rationale for early decisions.

Programming for the built environment can be greatly enriched with the active participation of all stakeholders during the problem definition phase. Documenting a programming process can become the foundation of a knowledge base that is used throughout a project, instead of a static report that gathers dust on a shelf. Too often, the knowledge and insights gained in programming and early design are forgotten in the long slow march toward a completed building. Often the design intent behind important early decisions is not adequately preserved. It is virtually impossible for anyone to keep in mind the

Practice with the Internet

comprehensive history of even a simple design problem—all the trade-offs between conflicting goals, all the reasons behind each decision. Often, when they are called upon to reconstruct a decision (or even just to respond to a substitution request during construction), architects often cannot recall in detail why they chose a particular direction. People who made crucial decisions during programming are often not around when a building is finished. A comprehensive record of any project should allow decisions made during the early phases of design to be played back when needed.

With the Internet, programming can include increased interaction between designer and client or end user, and it can enable the results of such interaction to be retained in a format that is easily accessed throughout the project. A Web site can act as a group repository of issues discussed and decisions made. Technical information, photographic documentation, group meetings with whiteboard—all are tools that can be used in the programming stage. In so doing, the relationships among pieces of information become clearer; information gathering and sharing become easier.

Creating a comment-and-information Web site at the earliest stage of programming may go a long way toward catching problems and realizing design opportunities that might have been overlooked. New York–based Hardy Holzman Pfeiffer Associates is using the Web to supplement live programming workshops with clients and user groups. Collaborative programming has long been a hallmark for this firm, and now the Web is part of the tool kit. For a recent project at Northwestern University, a Web site helped prepare participants for programming workshops and allowed students and faculty who could not physically be present to participate (figs. 7-1 and 7-2). "Schools are really interested in collaborative design," said James R. Brogan, HHPA Director of Information Technology. "They want the students

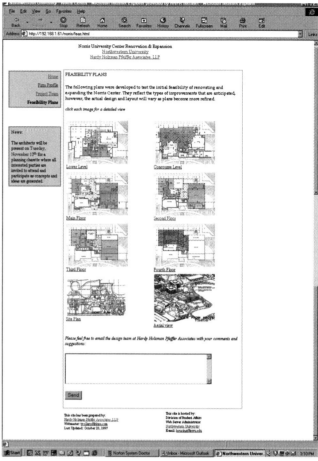

7-1 and 7-2. The New York architectural firm Hardy Holzman Pfeiffer Associates uses interactive Web sites to solicit comments from project stakeholders. These pages display schematic drawings and provide e-mail links and comment blocks. (©1999, Hardy Holzman Pfeiffer Associates; all rights reserved)

and faculty to have real input into the project. With the Web, we can have fewer live meetings and less travel—it's the perfect supplement to what we do, and I can easily imagine that for some projects it could substitute for the workshops completely."

Marketing

Everyone, it seems, has a Web site, but how effective are they as marketing tools? It depends how you use them. During the 1990s many firms placed their billboards on the information highway by setting up a promotional Web site. It might have included a portfolio of work, some high-sounding statements of design philosophy, perhaps a client list and news of current projects. Then they waited for the phone to ring, and sometimes they were disappointed. Just like other forms of unfocused advertising, a splashy Web site probably is not a very effective way to generate new work. Good marketing is targeted to specific groups or individuals that you have identified as potential clients of your firm. Just as with a paper brochure, a Web site is only effective as a marketing device if you have placed it in front of an appropriate audience.

But Web sites do have a place as part of a comprehensive marketing program. They are inexpensive to create, cost nothing to distribute, and can be updated very easily. Promotional material such as photography and renderings that you may have created for a paper portfolio can be reused on the Internet at almost no cost, and you can also use media such as video and QuickTime VR, which don't work on paper at all. Using templates, frames, and the other devices discussed in chapter 4, you can easily recombine your collection of marketing materials

7-3 through 7-6. Foster and Partners' Web site, which includes their work on the Great Court of the British Museum. (Courtesy of Foster and Partners)

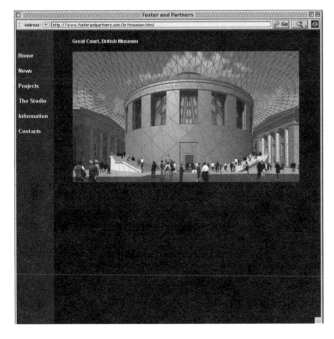

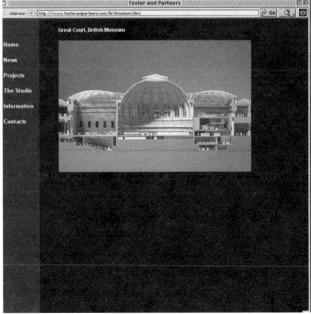

into a series of interlinked subsites directed at specific types of potential clients.

A Web site is an excellent way to educate potential clients about your capabilities. It's also a wonderful platform for displaying your particular expertise and sharing some of your knowledge with the world at large. If you have written an article or white paper that might be of interest to others, by all means put it on your Web site or make it available for download. A potential client who is browsing the Web in search of help with a particular problem will likely appreciate a well-designed site that provides detailed information, not just sales fluff. Such a client might be in the earliest stage of project definition and looking for help in understanding the problem and formulating a possible solution. When that client is ready to select a designer or builder, your name will come readily to mind (figs. 7-3, 7-4, 7-5, and 7-6, page 151).

Just as architects are comparing faucets and roof drains on the Internet, clients are researching design firms. They are finding it a useful means of gathering information, instead of having to rely entirely on referrals and recommendations from their professional networks. Like it or not, professional service firms have become part of the global electronic marketplace along with all other providers of goods and services. Intelligent Web agents that find sites based on user-established search criteria will become more sophisticated tools for collecting information. Clients will evaluate potential service providers from among all those whose past work and references are available on the Internet. They will look for sites with substantive information, not just gorgeous photography. Every published fact about your firm, good and bad, will become available to all potential clients on the Web, whether you provide it yourself or it is gathered from other sources. Clients will certainly be better informed about firms, their work, and their history than they ever were before.

At the same time, designers and builders will become better consumers of the services they need—consultants, reprographics, CAD, equipment rentals. Architects and clients will be better informed about contractors, subcontractors, and material suppliers.

The free flow of information about producers and service providers is leading to a "frictionless" economy in which buyers and sellers can find each other much more easily. That inevitably means that long-term relationships anchored mainly in inertia are doomed. As much as anyone in business likes to think that their customers keep coming back because of the great work they do, in truth, an element of client loyalty is based on avoiding what economists call switching costs. For an architectural client, switching costs might consist of the time and effort it takes the client to research, interview, and select a new architect (not a small consideration for most business and institutional clients); the risk associated with trying someone new, including the credit risks of unknown partners; and the learning curve involved in any new professional relationship. When switching costs are high, the customer is loathe to switch suppliers. Clients will resist changing even when they are sure that the new supplier will offer superior service. Convincing a potential client to abandon your competitor and switch to you takes more than just showing them that you are able to do as good a job as your rival. With the networked economy, that equation is changing: switching costs are rapidly declining, because finding new suppliers is so easy.

Professional service firms have long known that many clients simply don't have the tools or sophistication to compare different providers of specialized services except by cost or reputation. If a potential client is shopping for price and doesn't understand why Firm A is better than Firm B, the reduced switching costs afforded by the Internet may make this kind of client harder to keep. Your marketing focus must adjust to this new environment. Effective marketing requires that you skillfully differentiate yourself from the competition and convince clients that your talents uniquely add value to their businesses. Your Web site can go a long way toward helping to educate potential clients about your services.

The Web is a powerful way to talk to clients and build relationships one at a time. The most successful companies in the Internet economy will be the ones who use the Web not as a billboard for advertising, but as an interactive tool. They will use their sites to gather information about existing and potential clients so that they can serve them better. The Web will be a tool to differentiate both themselves and their clients so that services can be tailored to the precise requirements of every project.

Research on the Web

The Internet has revolutionized information access by compressing the distance between information provider and information consumer. Research on virtually any topic is now more available than ever. The research needs of design professionals include market research, product research, and project type research.

Market Research

Every good marketer knows that information gathering is paramount. Web sites abound with information resources for finding and researching potential clients, as well as sites where requests for proposals are posted. AIAonline, for example, offers the Commerce Business Daily, Construction Market Data Early Planning Reports, and ProFile, a directory of architectural firms in the United States. For those doing government work, the CBD is also available on-line from several other sources. State and local governments, counties, school districts, and public university systems have Web sites aimed at procurement of architectural and building services (figs. 7-7 and 7-8). In Canada, national, provincial, and local projects throughout the country are

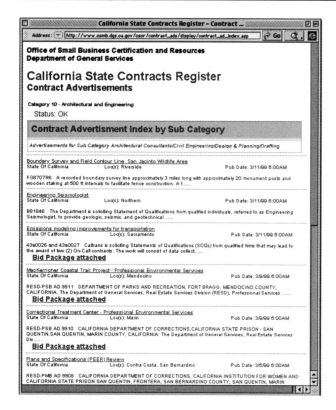

7-7 and 7-8. California uses the Web to provide information about state government contracts and procurement.

being tendered on the MERX Web site. Subscribers can not only submit proposals on-line but can access a historical database of past bids and information on who is bidding for contracts, and users can be notified automatically whenever relevant bids are posted (fig. 7-9).

There has been a proliferation of information resources on the Web that formerly required expensive printed subscriptions or access to a

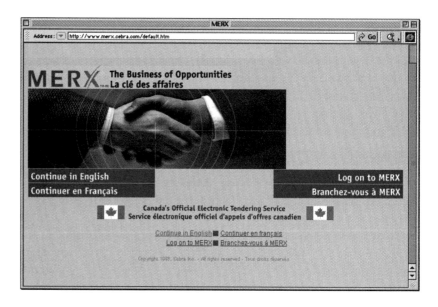

7-9. MERX, Canada's nationwide electronic public tendering system.

high-quality business library. UPI, Reuters, local and national newspapers including *The New York Times, The Wall Street Journal*, and business services such as Dun and Bradstreet and Standard and Poor's can all be found on the Web.

Clients in some areas are beginning to post requests for proposals in the form of Web sites and asking for responses in kind. Web-based statements of qualifications can of course use media that cannot be distributed on paper, such as video, audio, and immersive imaging, and hyperlinked statements of qualifications enable you to present your project team, references, and client list in great detail in a proposal without laboriously copying, assembling, and mailing all this information on paper.

Product Research

One of the principal advantages of the Internet for specifiers will surely be access to up-to-date product information, construction details, and specifications directly from manufacturers' Web sites. They can write specifications with hyperlinks to Web sites that, in theory at least, will always have the latest information. As a critical mass of manufacturers' data becomes available on the Web, it will quickly tip the balance toward this channel of information delivery.

Web-based product information strongly benefits both producer and specifier. Manufacturers of building products realize considerable cost savings by providing information on the Web rather than in printed form. For specifiers, not only is information in this form more convenient, but the power of keyword searches and of hypertext make it faster and easier to use (fig. 7-10). These considerable advantages will not be completely realized until manufacturers' groups (or organizations such as the Construction Specifications Institute) agree on standardized formats for providing product information on-line.

Having a complete, up-to-date, and easy to use informational Web site will become a competitive advantage to manufacturers, but only if they allocate sufficient resources to ensure that their Web sites are self sufficient, not just supplements to paper-based information. Specifiers will trust on-line research only when they know that all the information they need is there. They want to get those catalogs out of the office and not have to juggle between paper and on-line sources. Specifiers will reasonably assume that on-line information is current, so manufacturers must adequately maintain their sites.

Building-product data in paper form has traditionally been provided in printed form by information brokers such as Sweets and Architects First Source. Sweets began a move toward CD-ROM distribution of their materials in the early 1990s, shortly before the Internet boom. Although the CD-ROM format represented a significant costs savings in production and distribution expense and it allowed for somewhat more frequent updates, it was not a big improvement for the information consumer. The CD-ROMs are somewhat easier to use

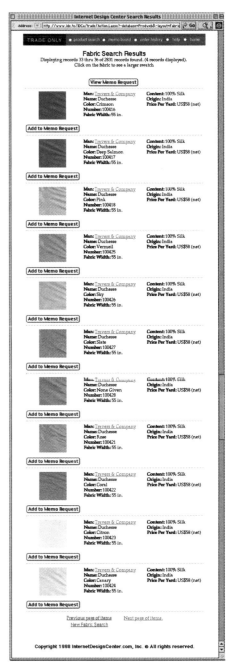

7-10. The ability of browser pages to act as a "front end" to powerful databases makes them an excellent tool for distributing catalogs of all sorts. The Internet Design Center site shows how fabric samples can be previewed on-line and samples can be ordered. (Courtesy InternetDesignCenter.com)

7-11. BuildingTeam.com aims to be a Web portal for AEC professionals. (Courtesy Cahners Communication)

Colin Gilboy, president of Specs-Online (www.specs-online.com), tells manufacturers to design their product Web sites "so that an experienced architect or specifier could complete her design on a Saturday afternoon using just the information available on your Web site."

than the old green catalogs, mainly because they take up less space and are more easily searchable. But in some respects, the CD-ROM is *less* usable than paper versions, because each manufacturer adopted its own style of interface, rather than agreeing on one standard. Users were forced to learn the intricacies of each manufacturer's system, and many became frustrated. Lack of standards is also hindering the Internet as a product information channel.

Sweets hesitated to jump on the Internet, and it now faces direct competition from many new players. It remains to be seen if the old standbys in paper-based product information will also be victorious on the Internet or if new Web-based upstarts will replace them. The business model is quite different. An Internet-based product information broker is, after all, merely providing a collection of links directly to manufacturers' Web sites, deriving income from advertising, whereas Sweets was able to charge both the supplier and the consumer of the information. The Internet has shown it can be brutal to anyone—travel agents, insurance agents, and stock brokers, for example—who is caught in the middle between supplier and consumer.

The emerging model for building product information is that of a gateway or portal site to remote resources (fig. 7-11). If properly implemented, such sites should allow for a high degree of user customization, by remembering preferences and the results of previous searches, for example. Although designers are inundated with unsolicited product information, most appreciate the value of an up-to-date product library, especially when crunch time arrives and products have to be specified quickly; as a result, architects and builders spend considerable resources on maintaining and updating product libraries. Closer, more direct communication between manufacturers and designers should now be possible, with more of the burden of information maintenance shifted to the producer and away from the designer.

In Europe, industry, government, and academic groups are taking an active role in creating gateway sites, viewing them as part of a broader rationalization of the construction industry that is accompanying European economic integration. The British government seeded the Construction Information Gateway (CIG), a portal site to be sponsored by an alliance of construction companies and product vendors (fig. 7-12).

Manufacturers are also looking at *push technology*, in which information is directed to customers, rather than waiting for it to be requested. Architects who want to be informed about new lighting products, for example, will subscribe to a "channel" of information by providing a customer profile describing the kind of information they want and how often they wish to be updated. Instead of their having to search for such information, push technology brings the information to them. Or they can program search criteria into intelligent Web agents that scour the Internet to find the information they want.

In order for intelligent agents to become a reality, manufacturers and service providers must have the ability to describe the attributes of their products in a standardized way. Likewise, the seekers of information need a standardized language to describe the information they need. Searches across the Internet currently are based on information com-

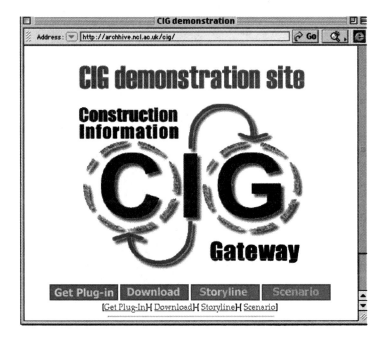

7-12. A prototype of a construction information gateway from the Construction Industry Research and Information Association, London. (Courtesy of the UK Department of the Environment, Transport and the Regions; Construction Industry Research and Information Association, and the University of Newcastle upon Tyne)

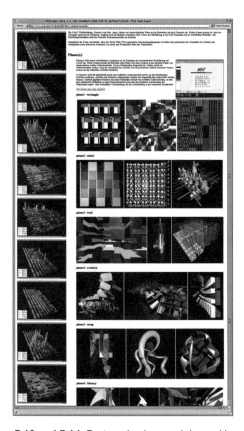

7-13 and 7-14. Design schools around the world are using the Web to showcase their work and connect with practitioners. (Fig. 7-13 Courtesy Professor Maia Engeli, Architektur & CAAD ETH Zurich; Fig. 7-14 courtesy Center for Landscape Research, University of Toronto)

piled by search engines that comb the Web for occurrences of keywords. They completely ignore nontext information and crudely assume that the most relevant documents are the ones with the most frequent occurrence of the keywords. This primitive search capability will be greatly improved with XML, a new hypertext language that uses industry-specific tags, or declarations of data types, to define information with greater precision. With XML, designers will be able to search across the Internet for products with specific attributes: "an ADA-compliant halogen sconce," for example, or "a spray-applied waterproofing finish for exterior wall tile." The designer could send a Web agent to perform the search, check multiple manufacturers' Web sites for data that fit the selected criteria, and then compile it on a Web page for easy comparison. XML is discussed in more detail in chapter 11.

Academic and Project-type Research

Academic institutions were among the earliest adopters and most enthusiastic participants in the Web. Almost every academic department of nearly every university has a Web site, including departments of architecture, landscape, planning, engineering, and related fields (figs. 7-13 and 7-14). Some are using the Web in highly innovative ways.

For the many practitioners who bemoan the lack of relevance in design education, and for the academics who wish to see their research efforts better utilized in the "real world," perhaps the Internet is one way to reconnect theory and practice. Research findings that were previously buried in obscure academic journals are now finding their way onto Web sites, making them truly accessible to practitioners for the

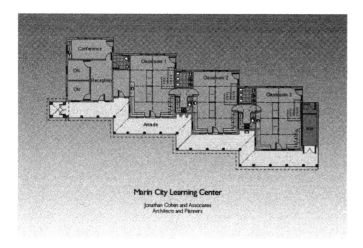

7-15 and 7-16. The design for this preschool by Jonathan Cohen and Associates was informed by advice from experts in early childhood education found on the Internet.

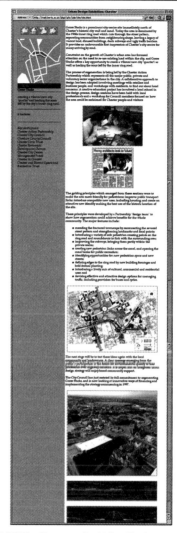

7-17. The Resource for Urban Design Information (RUDI).

first time. For example, my firm, Jonathan Cohen and Associates, was recently commissioned to design two preschools. We were able to use the Web to find up-to-the-minute research on design for early childhood education. We would otherwise never have known this material existed; it was certainly not to be found in the library, even if we had time to look there. Having found the experts in this field, we contacted them directly by e-mail. They were delighted to participate in a practical, real-life design exercise (figs. 7-15 and 7-16). This kind of one-on-one connection between researcher and practitioner would not have been possible without the Internet.

Trading Networks

Electronic procurement processes will soon become commonplace throughout the building industry. Companies such as General Electric have long used electronic trading networks, whereby vendors and cus-

The Resource for Urban Design Information, or RUDI, was begun in January 1996 at the University of Hertfordshire and the library at Oxford Brookes University, with grants from the British government and Sun Microsystems. Its purpose is to provide a substantive, high-quality, interactive collection of materials on urban design for use by researchers and practitioners. Through case studies, articles, resource collections, and discussion areas, it shows the potential of a well-designed Web site to provide rich, highly usable, and constantly updated content on urban design (fig. 7-17). Not only is it an exemplary resource for designers, it is also a wonderful tool for educating community leaders and the public about issues of design for the urban environment.

tomers are linked and information about prices, delivery, inventory, and selection flows directly from one company's database into another's. The GE Trading Process Network has been so successful that GE Information Services has begun selling the system to other industries. Companies are enthusiastic because it lowers their cost of handling routine business transactions. Information is keyed in only once, reducing errors, and customers can handle their own order tracking, technical support, and product customization. Utility companies such as Con Edison and PG&E use it for buying everything from tires to toilet paper.

For many companies, the internal cost of purchasing goods and services often exceeds the value of the product itself. With trading networks, reductions in turnaround time of 50 percent and in internal procurement costs of 30 percent have been reported. When procurement cycles are shortened, inventory levels can be kept lower, resulting in additional savings. For vendors, the cost of doing business is also reduced, but competition is increased, so prices are lower. A universal, browser-based interface to these trading networks makes them far easier to implement than older systems based on proprietary software.

An industry-sponsored organization in the United Kingdom, called Construction Industry Trading Electronically (CITE), was created in 1995 to promote, among other efficiencies, electronic management of the supply chain for contractors. Along with electronic procurement of goods and services for construction, CITE is working on automating materials handling on job sites. Construction, at least in Britain, is beginning to use technology long employed in manufacturing, such bar coding and portable data capture devices.

The Internet now makes such a system possible for much smaller businesses as well, giving them better access to corporate and government purchasing. Constellations of companies are joining forces in virtual confederacies, such as the Automotive Network Exchange, a huge bloc of 1,300 companies supplying the auto industry, trading with each other over private networks and realizing great gains in efficiency.

On-line Plan-checking and Permitting

Clients are increasingly concerned about time lost in lengthy project approvals. In the current business climate, product life cycles are getting shorter: for high-tech companies such as Hewlett Packard, the average is twelve to eighteen months. Time to market is critical for these companies, and anything that delays new product introductions, including time spent waiting for facilities approvals, can have adverse effects on the bottom line. Delays measured in days can mean millions in lost revenue, without even considering sunk costs in land, financing, and fees. Cities that streamline their permitting process have a distinct competitive advantage when companies are looking for locations to build new plants.

Economic pressures like these led to the Smart Permit Initiative in

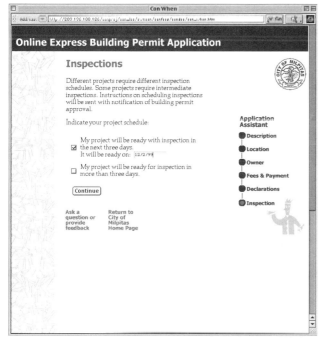

California's Silicon Valley by nonprofit Smart Valley Inc., a public-private collaboration whose mission is to standardize and reform the region's approach to planning applications, building permit submittals, permit tracking, and GIS (figs. 7-18, 7-19, 7-20, and 7-21).

Silicon Valley is a continuous urban area that was once a series of independent farming communities along El Camino Real between San

7-18 through 7-21. The on-line building permit application in Milpitas, California.

Jose and Palo Alto, south of San Francisco. Today the only way to tell if you are in Cupertino or Sunnyvale is by the color of the street signs—until you apply for a permit, that is. Then you encounter the patchwork of twenty-nine local government jurisdictions left over from the valley's agricultural days. Each city has its own planning and building permit agency, rules, and procedures. The high-tech companies that want to build manufacturing, R&D, and office space in the valley care less about which jurisdiction they're in than how long it will take to get a permit. Frightened by the long California recession of the early 1990s, community leaders realized that regulatory streamlining was very much in the long-term economic interest of the area. They adopted these goals:

- Streamline the plan-checking, approvals, and inspections process by applying business systems to permitting.
- Standardize local codes and interpretations.
- Implement on-line permitting, building a bridge to the Internet from internal permitting software.

Linda Joy Weinstein was founding director of the Smart Permit project. In discussions with building officials, architects, and facilities managers, she outlined a vision of paperless plan-checking and an accelerated approvals timeline. The first step was to improve and rationalize the existing paper-based process. Although each of the cities in the valley was using the 1994 Uniform Building Code, they had each encrusted it with amendments. Gathering all the building officials together in one room, she hammered out an agreement to reduce the number of amendments from 420 to 11 that would be applied uniformly throughout the region.

Each city was assigned one piece of the electronic permitting puzzle: standardized forms, accepting payment on-line, digital signatures, and redlining plans. The technology-sharing agreement between the cities means that each will benefit from the work done by others. The city of San Carlos, for example, is developing HTML-based on-line permit application forms that will eventually be used throughout the valley. "We realized right away that this had to be tackled with a regional approach," said Robert Kraiss, Director of Corporate Facilities for Adaptec in Milpitas. He is a director of Smart Valley and a member of the International Facilities Management Association.

Andersen Consulting and the city of Palo Alto developed a prototype Web-based permitting system, incorporating real-time conferencing with shared whiteboard, CAD viewing and markup, permit tracking, security, and electronic transaction processing.

San Carlos brought in a Total Quality Management team to examine the building permit process with a view to finding and eliminating procedural bottlenecks. The team found that plan-check engineers had to follow 180 distinct steps before plans were even examined. There was plenty of room to improve the process even before the next step: applying appropriate communication technology.

Hamid Pouyed was the Sunnyvale Building Official during the implementation of Smart Permit. "The culture of an organization has to change before anything else," he explained. "We tried to instill the department with three themes: customer service, communication, and collaboration." His first step was to redesign the physical space into a comfortable area with sit-down counters. Staff inspectors were trained to convey a spirit of cooperation and respect for the applicant. "Part of responding to the valley's needs is to reduce permitting time," he said. "But another part is making sure that the customer has all the information needed to eliminate costly mistakes that can result in construction delays. We need to take a proactive approach that ensures that the customer has all the information he needs to design a safe building, and that we have the information we need to grant a permit quickly." In other words, smarter permitting is a communication issue.

Randy Tsuda is a city planner and the current director of Smart Permit. He says the original motivation for on-line permitting was fear that Silicon Valley was vulnerable to competition from other locations with more straightforward approvals processes. "Now it's evolved into providing an alternative way of interacting with local government. We're moving toward a virtual city hall concept, where all your dealings with government will be Web-enabled. Unfortunately, we picked the hardest piece first—building permits."

Silicon Valley is not the only place where permit automation is being tried. In Houston contractors use kiosks to access a Web-based building permit automation system while shopping for lumber and tools at Builders Square stores. Houston's system, developed by TeleBuild, allows contractors to maintain credit accounts with the building department from which permit fees are automatically deducted. San Francisco Internet startup NetClerk hopes to become a Web-enabled bridge between contractors and building departments throughout northern California. The NetClerk site will handle forms processing and records storage for contractors needing routine "over-the-counter" permits from multiple jurisdictions. Once a contractor has filled out an on-line form, NetClerk faxes or e-mails it to the appropriate department in a preapproved format.

In Cincinnati a comprehensive reengineering of the permit process began in 1994 as a byproduct of the Cincinnati Area Geographic Information System Consortium (CAGIS). An underlying goal was to integrate data derived from multiple sources and used by several agencies during development review and approval, so that information could be given once and distributed to all parties in need of it. Eliminating redundant tasks, making sequential tasks parallel, and focusing on customer needs rather than departmental turf battles led to months shaved off in both the City of Cincinnati and Hamilton County development permit processes. Instead of forcing clients to wait in line at several city departments, the new permit system takes information submitted on paper, scans it, and distributes it over the city government WAN to every agency with jurisdiction over a project.

The achievement of saving time depends in large part on successfully implementing a networked information management system that integrates many kinds of data: GIS maps, paper-based forms, CAD drawings, tax and utility records, scanned and digital photography, and more. A new category of software company has arisen to meet this need, led by Sierra Computer Systems, whose Permits Plus software was a key to Cincinnati's successful permit automation. Permits Plus is a modular client-server application that works with an industrial-strength relational database. Components include modules for permitting, inspections, conversion of legacy paper-based data, activity tracking, and plan-checking. The system can be customized to agencies' work flows and procedures.

Installing the right software without adequate planning and provision for training and support, however, can be a recipe for municipal disaster, as King County in Washington State discovered. There, an audit ordered by the county council found that the cost savings and efficiency improvements that were expected to flow from implementation of the very same Sierra software used successfully in Cincinnati were not achieved due to significant management problems. It seems that solutions for permit bottlenecks that rely on information technology alone, without accompanying organizational and process reform, are doomed to failure.

7-22 and 7-23. Federal regulations such as ADA and OSHA are available on the Web.

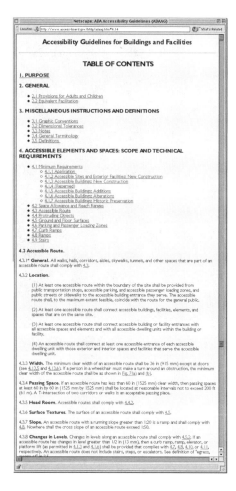

Codes On-line?

Anyone who has worked with building codes knows it is entirely too easy to make mistakes with them. The codes are awkwardly written, confusing, disorganized, and boring. The sheer inconvenience and uncertainty in dealing with code issues is a significant disincentive to innovation.

How much time do designers and builders spend poring over the codes? How uniformly are codes enforced? How much money and time have contractors, owners, and architects lost due to code problems? How many lawsuits could have been avoided had codes been easier to interpret? And finally, how much permitting time is lost due to interpretation issues that are frequently beyond the experience of local building officials?

These questions and more are part of the larger communication puzzle that faces the construction industry. If any form of information lends itself naturally to hypertext, it is the building code (figs. 7-22, 7-23, and 7-24). An HTML version of the code would enable linking to relevant code sections from drawings, specifications, and product literature. It would permit local jurisdictions to publish their amendments quickly and cheaply, with live links back to the master code residing on the code authority's server. Building officials redlining drawings within an electronic permitting process would be able to embed hyperlinks directly to applicable code sections, saving an immense amount of time and reducing the potential for errors. Definitions, tables, and cross references would all be far easier to use.

Then there is the issue of access to public information. When municipalities adopt a model code, it becomes city law. Shouldn't it be available on-line with the other local ordinances, particularly since public safety is at stake?

Tim Kung of the International Conference of Building Officials, author of the Uniform Building Code, says that his organization is considering all options, but that issues of control and compensation have so far prevented building codes from appearing on Web pages. He says that the ICBO wants to be able to control access to what it considers to be its intellectual property. And the business model that ICBO and other model code organizations use is based on selling the books.

One solution might be a system whereby municipalities pay a licensing fee to the code author when they adopt model codes. The fee could be a sliding scale, based on the dollar volume of building permits a city handles, and passed on in the form of building permit fees. Or a subscription-based or per-use fee for accessing the code on-line could be employed. In the end building owners would pay the cost, just as they do now, but making codes more accessible and easier to use would eliminate many downstream costs due to misinterpretation and error.

Beyond just placing codes on-line in hyperlinked, searchable form, Web-based add-ons could easily extend the usefulness of such a system

7-24. Larimer County, Colorado, has placed its zoning regulations on-line, making good use of HTML tables and hyperlinks.

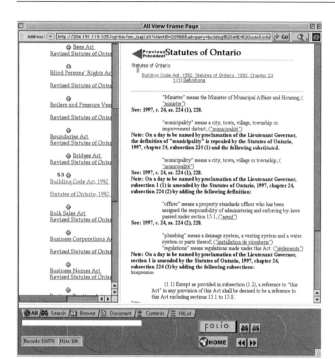
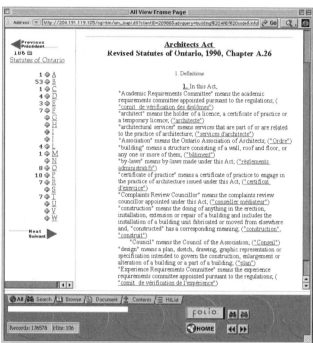

7-25 and 7-26. The on-line, hyperlinked, fully searchable building code for the province of Ontario.

much further. Designers could type in a location and find all the codes relevant to a project; enter a zip code and know immediately what seismic zone or wind zone applies; enter an occupancy type and jump to the exiting requirements; or enter a number of occupants and know the required width of exits or the maximum length of corridors. Information technology applied to the building codes could well be a spur toward more widespread adoption of performance-based standards, which tend to encourage innovation far more than the typically prescriptive approach.

Here is a clear case of an information provider—the code authorities—not responding to the needs of its information consumers—in this case architects, engineers, and builders. As of this writing, the only North American building code available on-line was that of the province of Ontario, Canada (figs. 7-25 and 7-26). Minnesota and Virginia have placed their statewide amendments on the Web, but the underlying model code is not included.

Design Firm Administration

In many fields the cost of services is being significantly reduced by information technology. Stock brokers and insurance companies, for example, have been able to lower fees because of dramatically reduced transaction costs. Can information technology similarly reduce design costs? If not, as other business services become cheaper, will design services seem unreasonably expensive in comparison? The problem, of course, is that design professionals in the building industry generally produce a unique solution that is used only once. Design services cannot be commoditized, and it seems that clients are always demanding more service, not less.

The cost of producing core services may not be falling, but the cost of "back-office" functions certainly should be. We may not yet have achieved the paperless office, but because of information technology investments, administrative staff have declined from 20 to 14 percent, bookkeeping staff from 4 to 0.4 percent of total staff in design firms over the last fifteen years (Laeserin 1999c). The paring of nonbillable staff is most pronounced in younger firms, which set themselves up without receptionists, administrative offices, or even drafting boards.

The Internet promises to further this trend, with opportunities to trim costs and streamline operations. Firms will save on travel, reproduction, and messenger expense, as well as reduced project delivery time. Product libraries and flat files will give way to Web sites and hard drives. Designers and builders will be in more direct contact with clients, partners, and suppliers, with less reliance on intermediaries or support staff.

Human Resources

Increasingly your employees will find you through the Web, which is already the leading channel for recruiting and job hunting in some industries. One of the greatest challenges of managing a design practice is pacing the work to fit the resources available. Matching the flow of work to a fixed number of staff can be very difficult, and an inability to do so is a leading cause of firm failure. Many firms find that they can keep only a small core of permanent staff, relying on imperfectly trained freelancers to fill the gaps when deadlines approach. Virtual teaming may allow you to "borrow" staff electronically from branch offices or even other firms when a short-term need arises. It can allow the sharing of specialized expertise and resources over more projects and multiple offices. A firm with several branch offices may learn how to share professionals with special skills, such as an expert in clean room design or a specifications writer.

MIT business professor Thomas W. Malone has postulated the emergence of an "e-lance economy," in which the fundamental unit of business activity becomes the individual independent contractor whose work is largely self-directed and project-based, performed as part of a temporary network of professionals supported by advanced communication technology (Malone & Laubacher 1998). Indeed, one can imagine that as the effectiveness of networked business-to-business communication grows while the cost declines, more and more organizations will devolve into confederations of Web-linked entrepreneurs.

Intelligent Web agents will make the assembly of project teams more efficient. Just as architectural firms are increasingly global in the markets they serve, so the various skills that must be assembled to produce projects will become less place-bound. Electronic collaboration

---

Web-based As-Builts

For facilities managers, construction documents are organized to build buildings, not to manage them. And they provide an imperfect guide to the way buildings were actually built. As buildings age, the chore of tracking existing conditions becomes harder still. How might an Internet-based project information repository make facilities management easier?

Bill Jepson of the UCLA Urban Simulation Team is developing a hyperlinked "as-built" system for the UCLA hospital complex, which is being rebuilt as a result of the 1994 Northridge earthquake:

> Our plan is to use the system not only to plan and design the new hospital, but to manage it throughout its useful life as well. We have begun a dialogue with various construction contractors which would allow the association of the as-built drawings, which the contractors are required to provide, with each wall or surface in the building. Using this interface, one could walk into any space, click on the wall or ceiling, and pull up the appropriate as-built drawing(s). In addition we would have the contractor photograph each wall before the wall is closed up. These photos (locating the conduits, etc., within the walls) will be indexed to the appropriate wall/ceiling/floor object, so they can be retrieved using the same point-and-click interface described above. This would provide a much more accurate record of the actual placement of the objects (conduit, pipes, etc.) within the wall at a much lower cost than the standard approach used today.

and teaming will enable the assembly of talent regardless of geographic location. Some firms already administer projects from one city and produce documents in a second, for a proposed building in yet a third. The physical propinquity that results when team members are in the same room may not be as valuable as the ability to assemble the best people to do a job, wherever they may be.

In the same way, Internet communications make joint ventures of two or more firms more manageable. You may have more opportunity to obtain work by partnering with firms in new markets. The Internet helps tie together strategic partners, such as the subconsultants with whom you work frequently or a client that represents a significant percentage of work. It may even make design/build easier to implement, allowing the design and build halves to function as separate entities for some projects and as virtual partners on others.

Training and Professional Education

As the design professions become more technology dependent, the demand for training will increase. At the same time, professional societies and licensing boards are increasing their annual requirements for continuing education. Internet-based training is still in its infancy, but the multimedia capability and interactivity of the Web make it potentially an excellent environment for distance learning. The Web makes asynchronous learning possible: teacher and student need not be on-line at the same time, which allows working people to participate when they can. Web-based courses can be a combination of live, interactive events over streaming video, prerecorded lectures with hyperlinks to outside resources, and self-paced exercises.

Internet-enabled Project Management

Building owners are demanding a more efficient project delivery process. They want higher quality, lower cost, and shorter schedules. How can better communication help to bring that about?

Of all the applications of the Internet in the design professions, none has more wide-ranging significance than Web-based project management. It offers the potential to establish a seamless flow of project-based information from player to player, over a project's entire life cycle. Better access to information means learning from mistakes and not repeating them in the next project.

Coordination is the project manager's toughest task—and lack of coordination, the biggest source of problems. A system that shortens and clarifies the connections between pieces of information is certain to reduce mistakes and delays.

The problems of coordination are multiplied under fast-track construction. In the traditional design-bid-build project delivery cycle, there is at least a single moment prior to construction when the entire project is "complete" and theoretically fully coordinated. With fast-

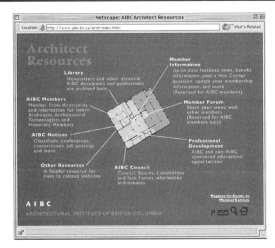

7-27. Professional groups have been among the most enthusiastic early adopters of the Internet. Such organizations as the Architectural Institute of British Columbia are using Web sites to connect with their members on a daily basis. (Courtesy AIBC)

7-28 (right). The home page of the CSI. (Courtesy of the Construction Specifications Institute)

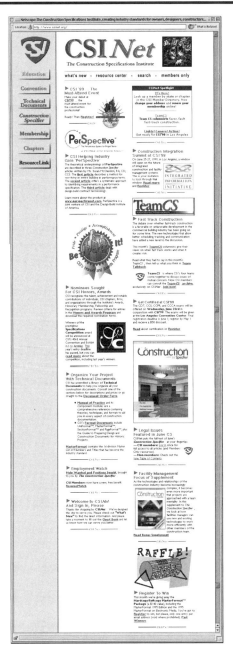

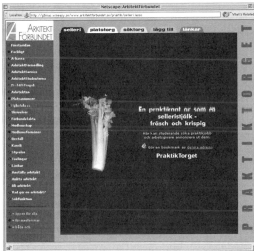

7-29. Arkitekt Forbundet, a Web resource for Swedish architects. (Courtesy Per Lander, editor, Arkitekt Forbundet)

7-30. The International Interior Design Association home page. (Courtesy IIDA)

Professional Organizations on the Web

Virtually all of the professional organizations representing the design professions are on the Web. They are using Web sites to connect more closely with their members than they were able to do with expensive print media. Members are using these sites to find out about project leads, continuing education opportunities, upcoming conferences, and much more. Professional organizations are also using Web sites to introduce their members to potential clients (figs. 7-27, 7-28, 7-29, and 7-30).

track, because design and construction are occurring simultaneously, architects must foresee how a construction change could affect an aspect of the project that has not yet been designed or how a design change could be precluded by something that has already been built. Fast-track construction clearly demands better communication between designer and builder than the traditional sequential process does.

A typical project presents two sets of coordination issues with which managers must contend: *organizational*, across disciplines, and *temporal*, across phases of a project, from programming to design, construction, and facilities management.

One aspect of coordination that presents both organizational and temporal issues is *change notification*. Tracking the history of even minor changes to a design is critical to successful project management. For example, suppose an architect must design doors wide enough to accommodate equipment that will be moved into and out of a room. During the programming phase, detailed information about this equipment is given to the architect, who designs accordingly. Two years later, during construction, someone within the client organization orders new, wider, equipment that does not fit through the doors the architects specified. The new building now has to be remodeled, before it is even completed, because no system of change notification was in place. Keeping track of who changed what, and why, is something that current systems don't do well. With so many players within different organizations working on a project, how can you ensure that when one makes a change, all the others who are affected are notified, and no one else?

In addition to documenting changes, adequate coordination also requires documenting the *intent* behind project decisions. Keeping a record of intentions can facilitate the resolution of disputes and prevent misunderstandings. Moreover, a complete project file that maintains a history of why decisions were made, not just when and by whom, can be extremely useful in the design of future projects. Managers recognize that not all design decisions are made during the design phase of a project; many decisions are in fact made in the field during construction. Systems to capture such on-the-fly or out-of-sequence decision making are needed.

Role tracking is another aspect of coordination that can be supported by better communication. Any large-scale project involves hundreds of people, thousands of decisions, and huge volumes of information. As the project progresses, participants' roles and responsibilities with respect to project information change. Clearly defining roles as they evolve over time in a multiplayer environment is one of the great challenges of project management.

So far, information technology seems only to have increased information overload for project managers. When copying is so easy that everyone on a project team receives every memo and letter, who can possibly read it all? How can you filter out the important messages from the dross? Sometimes many more people than necessary are informed of every change in a project, as the notifier attempts to build a paper trail. The result is that almost everyone is overwhelmed with irrelevant messages, making it easy to miss the few that really count. Michael J. Bocchicchio, who is responsible for managing billions of dollars of construction projects for the University of California, complains that project chatter is more distracting than ever: "The net result is I don't have time for this stuff and throw it all away. Communication is short-circuited."

All of these issues—change notification, documentation of intent, role definition, and information filtering—can be managed more effectively with the Internet. Two broad approaches have been proposed for managing the integration of project data: Electronic Document Management (EDM) and the shared project model, also known as the object model integrated database. Of these, only EDM has advanced to the point of commercial availability.

Electronic Document Management

EDM recognizes that current practice involves a variety of discrete document types: text based (specifications and contracts) and graphical (CAD drawings and models), along with spreadsheets, schedules, and media such as photographs and video. For the near term, these paper-based, discipline-specific formats will continue to be used, but the integration of these documents and access to them can be greatly improved. EDM creates a single gateway to all types of project documentation.

Two models exist for EDM: a centralized registry or a distributed one. With a central registry, all project information is stored on a single server. As documents are created or modified by members of a dispersed design team, the central registry is constantly updated with the latest documents. A central location has the benefit of providing fast access to all project data from a single source. If desired, a system can be put in place to take "snapshots" of constantly reworked documents at set intervals, so that a history is recorded. Networked systems can protect against unauthorized changes to documents, by setting levels of permission and denying access to a file while it is being worked on by another user. But sometimes all this system does is slow the process down, forcing user A to wait while user B modifies a file.

The second model, a distributed system, hands off administrative tasks to an information broker, which provides links to information that may reside elsewhere. For example, the CAD drawings remain on the architect's server but are linked to the information broker, so that anyone with authenticated permission can view, print, or download them without even being aware of where they are located.

In either case, project managers benefit from the following features of EDM:

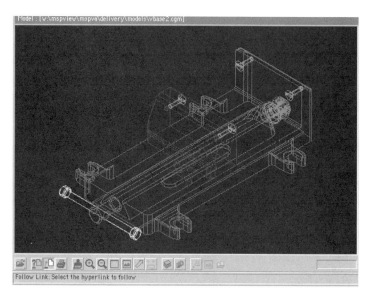

7-31. ModelServer Publisher from Bentley Systems.

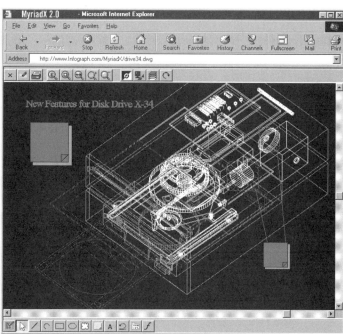

7-32. The MyriadX browser plug-in displaying an AutoCAD file. (Courtesy Informative Graphics)

- Check-in and check-out systems that leave an audit trail of who accessed information and when they did so
- Automatic generation of view-only file formats from original documents, such as Adobe's PDF format and Autodesk's DWF
- Cataloging and indexing of files
- Automatic change notification by e-mail or fax
- Tiered levels of authenticated permissions to access, view, and print documents
- Security and frequent backups of data

A commercial product based on EDM is Bentley Systems' ModelServer Publisher (fig. 7-31). This server program stores CAD information in native format and converts it on demand to a Web-viewable form when requested by any client on the network. In this way, it responds to designers' concerns about publishing drawings in formats that could be altered without the knowledge or consent of the designer. A second advantage is that all subsidiary files needed to print drawings, such as fonts, reference files, and symbol libraries, are resident on the server and need not be transmitted to clients so they can view a file. ModelServer Publisher has been implemented on intranets and extranets and is available on some of the subscription-based project Web site services discussed in chapter 8. ModelServer TeamMate extends this functionality to encompass all types of project files and offers control over access authorization and revision history.

Other such document management products include AutoEDMS from ACS Software, Cyco Software's AutoManager Workflow, and Documentum Enterprise's Document Management System. Such systems support viewing, printing, and markup of multiple document types, including CAD files, word-processing documents, images, HTML pages, spreadsheets, and scheduling documents. EDM systems maintain databases of documents, track authorship and version history, and allow users to compare versions of the same document. Users can view any document in a Web browser and access information within it regardless of the software used to make it (fig. 7-32).

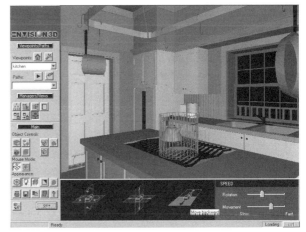

7-33 and 7-34. Envision 3D streams VRML models for faster download. (Envision 3D™)

Three-dimensional EDM

Envision has developed a system for streaming three-dimensional VRML models to support collaboration across intranets and extranets (figs. 7-33 and 7-34). Instead of having to download large files with extraneous information, users can select specific areas of a model and an appropriate level of detail. Users can navigate, measure dimensions, change lighting, select wire-frame or rendered views, and leave attached comments, all within a "thin client" browser application.

The Shared Project Model

The shared project model is the second approach to project data integration. It would replace individual paper or electronic documents with a single knowledge base describing an entire project. Participants would have real-time access to the model throughout the life of the project, in turns contributing their own knowledge and using information contributed by others. Each discipline that a project team comprises, from surveying to finance, would continue to use specialized tools for performing its own aspect of the work, but these tools would have the ability to draw from and contribute to, a common pool of information. For example, a mechanical engineer would continue to work with tools specific to his discipline but within the context of an intelligent information system that does not require reentry or translation of information once it has been created. The key change from present practice is that all specialist tools can transparently exchange information with the shared project model. Elements of a building would be represented as *objects*, containing physical attributes as well as graphical and textual information about the item. This is very different from CAD as it is used today, which automates hand drafting but does not endow what it draws with more than geometric information. So-called object-oriented CAD derives from object-based programming in the software industry, which discovered that complex applications could be quickly and easily assembled from a kit of preexisting parts.

Objects within a building model carry with them dimensional data, as CAD objects do, but also richer information, such as specifications, code and performance data, cost, and information related to construction means, methods, and schedule. For example, an object representing a steel beam would be drawn, first, *architecturally*, with its physical characteristics; second, *structurally*, with its load-bearing properties; third, as a *cost item*; fourth, as a *scheduled process* of fabrication and delivery, and so on. Each participant would draw on the common object to access the information and manipulate it with discipline-specific software. An architect would draw and model, an engineer would calculate, and a construction manager would schedule, all using information from a common project database that is accessible over a network.

Instead of creating standalone CAD drawings and models, architects would contribute the physical design attributes of a building to the larger computer representation of the building as both an object and a process. Now, CAD drawings become just a kind of report, reflecting only one aspect of the total process represented in the model. The shared project model becomes almost a living organism that can be accessed asynchronously by its many contributors. Information is now available in context-specific forms, rather than inflexible paper-based presentation formats. Teams could have multiple "live versions" of a project available simultaneously to support design collaboration.

Several government, academic, and commercial initiatives in Europe and America seek to bridge the gap between the current document-based system and an integrated model-based approach. One European Union

Models and Metaphors

The computer industry likes to use metaphors to describe concepts. Sometimes the metaphorical use becomes so widespread that it supersedes the original term. Many architects have noticed how many terms have been borrowed from "our" vocabulary—*site, user, program,* and of course, the term *architecture* itself. We cringe at such hideous usages as "this software has been completely rearchitected" (from an Autodesk promotional piece).

Sometimes the result is confusion between metaphors and the real-world concepts to which we think they refer. For example, when an architect or builder imagines object-oriented CAD, she probably thinks about real, physical things such as doors or bricks. Actually, "object-oriented" derives from a programming concept in which blocks of code can be assembled into larger components. Java and C++ are examples of object-oriented programming languages.

Model is another term that has come to be used in many contexts. In this book, it is used in at least three different ways. When a discipline-specific model of a design is mentioned, it does not mean a physical model or a computer model, but a model in the sense that a designer creates in his imagination a representation of the final design. In that sense it is a metaphorical model.

A *physical model*, such as those architects make out of wood and cardboard, is easy to understand but limited in its use. It must be physically transported from place to place. But it is a powerful representational tool because it is intuitively grasped and highly interactive. People can move around it and select any view from which to experience it, making it a very seductive form of presentation, as architects have known for centuries. Models can be photographed, of course, but viewing photographs is far less satisfying than physically examining the model because there is no interaction.

A *computer* model is another kind of model. It lacks the toylike charm of a physical model but compensates with versatility, ease of revision, and portability. You can alter the time of day and the season, create walk-throughs and fly-overs, and export views of the model for rendering, video, and immersive imaging techniques such as QuickTime VR.

But a geometric three-dimensional model is only one kind of computer model. It contains only a subset of the qualities of the objects being modeled. Models may include shapes, lines and points, or three-dimensional components such as blocks, cones and spheres.

Other kinds of computer models include parametric, procedural, and generative models. *Parametric models* permit the relationship between elements to be seen. When a variable is changed, its effect is seen on related elements. *Procedural models* add the ability to set parameters for such relationships, ensuring, for example, that incompatible elements cannot be placed adjacent to each other, or that a door is not swinging in an illegal direction. *Generative models* create geometries that fulfill requirements entered by the user, such as: "generate the optimal layout of theater seats for this auditorium" or "create a single-run stair between Floors 1 and 2." Generative models follow rules set by the designer, such as "seat rows shall be 22 inches apart" or "risers shall not exceed 7 inches."

The discussion about shared project models as a new paradigm for describing buildings refers to models that embody three-dimensional geometric information, but also information about the attributes of the object being modeled, such as what it is made of, who makes it, what it costs, how long it lasts, or how many worker hours are needed to install it. The shared project model is not necessarily a literal model at all, but a kind of database. It is sometimes referred to as four- or even five-dimensional CAD, where the three physical dimensions are augmented by time and cost.

---

initiative is called COMBINE (Computer Models for the Building Industry in Europe), which in its first stage focused on project data modeling particularly for design of HVAC systems. In its second phase, COMBINE is studying the larger issue of project data integration within all building design disciplines. COMBINE calls the shared project mode the Integrated Data Model. Work is being done at a theoretical level on the thorniest problem: how to get the various design tools used by architects and engineers to exchange data with the shared project model.

A large-scale initiative now underway by the International Standards Organization is the Standard for the Exchange of Product Model Data (STEP). STEP intends to create an international standard for computer-based description and exchange of the physical and functional characteristics of products throughout their life cycle. The idea is to put this rich information into a form accessible by a wide variety of software applications, including CAD and project management software. Industry-specific implementations of STEP are being developed for the process plant, offshore engineering, shipbuilding, and commercial construction industries.

Working in parallel to STEP is the International Alliance for Interoperability (IAI), a consortium founded in 1994 to develop a mechanism for sharing information during design and construction and through-

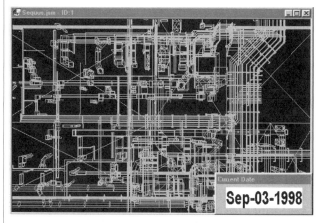

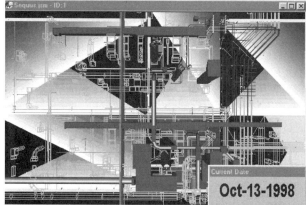

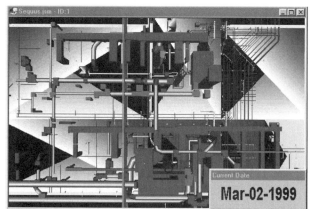

7-35 through 7-38. A four-dimensional (geometry and time) representation of the construction process for a pharmaceuticals plant. (Courtesy Martin Fischer, Stanford University)

The Shared Building Model at Work

Most of the discussion about the shared project model has occurred in academic settings. Practitioners are justifiably skeptical about an idea that has been talked about for twenty-five years with little practical testing in the field. Martin Fischer and Sheryl Staub of Stanford University helped direct a real-world application of the shared building model for the Sequus Pharmaceuticals pilot plant in Menlo Park, California (figs. 7-35, 7-36, 7-37, and 7-38). "We worked with the architect (Flad and Associates), general contractor (Hathaway-Dinwiddie), and principal subs to build a very detailed three-dimensional model for coordinating the mechanical, piping, electrical, and architectural work," said Fischer. "Every cover plate and light switch was in the model. It was a small project (20,000 square feet), but dense ($350/per square foot)." The goal of the experiment was to integrate and manage design, cost, and schedule information using existing tools from Autodesk, Ketiv Data, Timberline, and Primavera, by modeling the relationships between these normally isolated kinds of information.

The project team reported 20 to 30 percent higher design costs (attributed to building the model) but reaped the following benefits during construction:

- 60 percent fewer RFIs than normal
- Only one contractor-initiated change order (normal would have been ten to twenty major change orders per subcontractor)
- Fewer owner-initiated change orders than normal
- A net cost overrun of zero (some contract amounts went up a bit, others went down a bit), which is unheard of for projects of this complexity and nature
- No rework!

out the life cycle of buildings. Its members include architects, engineers, client organizations, product manufacturers, and software companies. IAI is working to define *foundation classes*, a universal code for modeling building elements that enables project information to be shared by the different kinds of software applications in use in the industry. For example, when an architect adds a door, the door *object* will describe not only the physical attributes of the door needed for design by the CAD program, but also the cost, maintenance, supply, and installation properties of the door for use in project costing and scheduling and, later, for facilities management. By examining the design process within each discipline, IAI hopes to reduce to a series of attributes, or *classes*, the information that each particular practitioner requires to do his job. A useful comparison can be made to the bar codes that are now universally used to identify products by scanners at retail check-out stands. If IAI is successful, it will invent a coding system for building parts, a kind of DNA that identifies all known properties of a manufactured building component.

Whether these research efforts will lead to usable tools any time in the foreseeable future remains to be seen. Any new system for project information sharing that requires designers to scrap the substantial investment they have already made in software and training isn't likely to succeed. Significant nontechnical issues must be addressed: data ownership, liability, security, and the big one: who pays? In more organizationally integrated industries, such as aircraft manufacturing and process plant engineering, the shared project model and collaborative, geographically dispersed working groups are already a reality.

The two leading CAD vendors, Autodesk and Bentley Systems, are both making moves toward the shared project model. Bentley proposes a migration path in incremental steps from the standalone CAD of today to the shared project model of tomorrow. Its first commercial product is MicroStation/J. The *J* stands for JMDL, a Java-based language that permits breaking down bits of a building design into easily exchanged pieces of data called components. Components are not the same as drawing objects: they represent pieces of a building process rather than geometric elements of lines, blocks, and layers. The components are then stored on a server accessible to any desktop computer on the network with a Web browser. The database stores the attributes of the component, its revision history, and information about its relationship to the other components.

The common thread that unites these approaches is a reliance on networked computing. If a comprehensive building model is used by all participants in a design project, it must be readily available to them at all times throughout the process.

Internet-based communication is the key to achieving this goal of distributed but integrated project management, whether it is used to establish a central database as a shared project model or simply a file management system that can be accessed from a Web browser. Many firms are setting up intranets and extranets as a first step toward this goal, and that is the subject of the next chapter.

8 Intranets and

As fast as the public Internet has grown, private intranets and extranets have grown even faster. Virtually every kind of organization, but particularly those with multiple locations and those that manage projects involving many participants, has discovered the value of private networks. All the benefits of the Internet—standards-based technology, easy implementation, a browser interface to every kind of information—can also be applied to sharing your private information securely. This chapter explores how AEC firms are using intranets and extranets for internal communication and project management.

Intranets: Your Own Private Internet

A key to successful communication for any design practice is communication within the firm itself. A firm's experience, as embodied by the collective professional knowledge of its principals and employees, is its most important asset. But how is that experience captured, stored, and reused throughout the firm? Is it held in cardboard boxes or in the memory of key employees? Is it available when needed? Or is access to it hidden or difficult? Are people within the firm sufficiently aware of the experience of their colleagues to identify and consult with in-house experts when necessary? How much time are your people devoting to searching for information that is already within the firms' knowledge base but not available when needed? When key employees leave the firm, how much of the firm's knowledge investment leaves with them?

This book has discussed Web sites without always making a distinction between those employed on intranets and those sites on the public Internet; in fact, there is no inherent difference between the two. A site used entirely within an organization will have its own

Extranets

design considerations, however, based on the way it will be used. Most organizations will want to set standards for "look and feel," navigation hierarchies, and graphic design for their intranet sites. A consistent interface will enable employees and partners to save time by not having to relearn each new site. Within a corporation or institution, departments such as human resources can employ the same design elements and navigational structures as accounting. Template sites establish firm-wide design and organizational standards while allowing each department leeway in creating its own site. Departments can then "own" their own sites and be responsible for upkeep.

Don't assume that everyone accessing an intranet is on a high-bandwidth connection. Employees working from home, traveling, or at job sites need information too and may be working with a dial-up modem connection.

Case Study: Ove Arup and Partners

Arup is a far-flung engineering consultancy with five thousand employees in sixty offices and forty countries. Their intranet began as an attempt to "create a road map to the knowledge within the firm," according to Phillip Crompton of Arup's Los Angeles office. The firm was so large that it was difficult to keep track of all the expertise it possessed. Originally Arup had an "overguide," a directory to all the engineers and their experience, and a "skills network." "Whatever engineering problem you were trying to solve, someone in the firm had probably solved it already. The real problem was finding that person," explained Crompton. "We were reinventing the wheel and sometimes even working at cross purposes." Knowledge of the firm's resources was based largely on word of mouth. What Arup needed was a repository of the firm's far-flung expertise, and that need led to the development of an intranet.

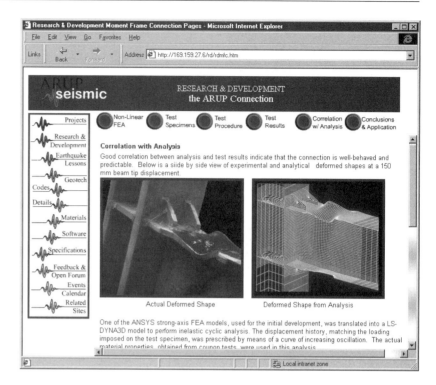

8-1, 8-2, and 8-3. Ove Arup and Partners' intranet. (Courtesy Ove Arup and Partners California Ltd.)

The Relational Database

The spread of Web-based intranets follows the development of the relational database as an overarching technology within large organizations. Relational databases retain small bits of information separately from the larger structures in which they may be used, so that each piece of information can have different relationships over time to other pieces. A simple example would be contact information for a client who has multiple projects with the firm. Instead of repeating that information in a database for each project, it is kept in a separate but linked area of its own. When that information is changed, it is updated wherever it appears.

Relational databases are ideal for allowing a single information pool to serve a large number of people for a variety of purposes, mirroring the client-server paradigm of the Internet itself. An international standard query language, SQL, allows users to access enterprise-wide data from a variety of different sources, freeing the data from proprietary technology, at least theoretically. The system is called Open Database Connectivity, or ODBC. All of the major relational database applications are ODBC compliant.

Until the Web, however, each database vendor (Oracle, Sybase, Informix, and others) had its own implementation of SQL and its own "client" application for accessing the data. The Web changed all that:

Web browsers have replaced proprietary client software because they can display forms and support SQL queries of any ODBC-compliant database, all from within the familiar browser interface.

In large companies, the client-server model of computing has been augmented with a new three-tier system, in which the middle tier is a kind of data broker that collects information from one or more enterprise-wide data sources and repackages it in a user-friendly, browser-accessible form. Such "middleware" (also known as Web application servers) is custom built with programs such as Lasso from Blue World Communications, Microsoft's Active Server Pages, Allaire's ColdFusion, and Apple's WebObjects. Middleware is also the key enabler of electronic commerce, by serving data from catalogs and processing Web-based transactions.

Significantly for design professionals, relational databases can support not only text and numeric information, but also spatial information in the form of points, lines, and polygons, pointing to the possibility of storing such information independently of the proprietary software file types that currently contain them. Such a relational database could be a repository for spatial data, such as CAD and GIS information, which could be made available on an intranet.

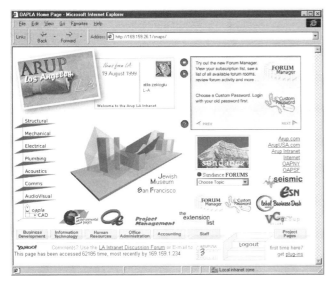
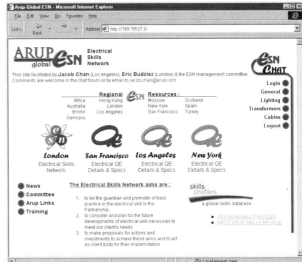

At first, each office developed its own intranet, and the central office did not try to exert much control. This ad hoc approach allowed the firm to experiment widely. After evaluation, firm managers found a common ground where engineering expertise could be indexed by skill sets and by branch office. Now Arup is developing a second-generation intranet that will be more structured, with a recognizable firm-wide interface (figs. 8-1, 8-2, and 8-3).

The Arup intranet includes specifications in Word and PDF formats, details as AutoCAD files (which non AutoCAD users can view with WHIP), and a database that tracks how details have been implemented in firm projects. Engineers can annotate details and specs with notes about how well they worked in one instance or how they failed in another, maintaining a record of their use in real projects. Crompton calls this "invaluable information." The effort that went into development of a detail is preserved, along with the firm's experience with it. The feedback loop between design and implementation is captured, providing a sterling example of the way that communication can be brought to the service of design.

Case Study: An Architect's Intranet

Jill Rothenberg is manager of information technology for ADD Inc., a 150-person architectural firm headquartered in Cambridge, Massachusetts, with offices in San Francisco and Miami. All employees have computers with Internet access. The firm has an intranet and relies on it for in-house communication (figs. 8-4, 8-5, and 8-6). Each day an information page is posted, with events, meetings, and firmwide news. Employees use the intranet to reserve conference rooms, for example, and order food and AV equipment at the same time. New employees are introduced with on-line biographies.

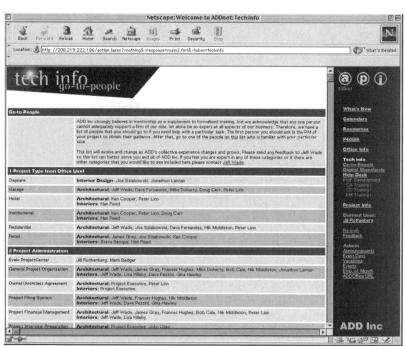

8-4, 8-5, and 8-6. ADDnet, the intranet of ADD Inc. is a valuable resource for the firm's employees. (Courtesy of ADD Inc., Cambridge, Massachusetts)

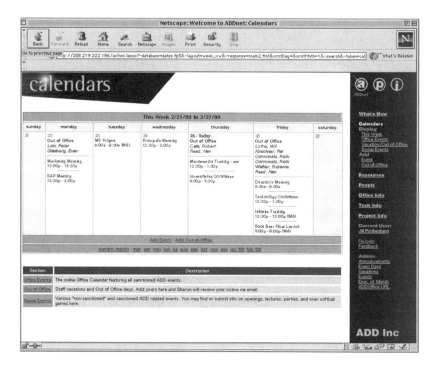

Administrative functions such as vacation scheduling and office policies and design standards are there too. "Our firm was growing so fast that no one knew the person next to him," said Rothenberg. "When problems arose, people didn't know whom to consult, so the intranet has a list of 'go-to' experts within the firm."

Rothenberg feels the firm's sophistication about technology appeals to clients and serves to differentiate ADD Inc. from the competition. "It's made us look very good in interviews," she said.

Extranets: Project-specific Web Sites

Of all the applications of Internet communication in the design and building professions, the project-specific Web site, or extranet, seems to be catching on most rapidly. Here are some of the biggest reasons:

- Contractors can tie together their subs and material suppliers in a way that improves communication and speeds response to bidding requests.
- Building owners, particularly institutional and corporate ones, can use an extranet to create a wide-area facilities network to cover multiple sites and maintenance contractors, manage furnishings and equipment, and take bids from multiple suppliers.
- Designers can use an extranet to connect the project team, improve work flow, and allow clients to participate more actively in the design process.

Many firms are experimenting, but firms that take the plunge and implement project Web sites as part of standard operating procedure will likely see the greatest impact soonest. And the greatest benefits will also accrue to the firms that implement project Web sites beginning with the earliest design stages, rather than waiting until construction starts. The 1996 AIA firm survey reported that 20 percent of architectural firms of fifty or more employees were using project-specific Web sites, and that figure is surely much higher now.

These Web sites are more than just electronic file cabinets. Making project documentation more accessible to all participants and making the flow of information more transparent should reduce administrative costs and shorten project schedules. If information is more complete and accessible, much of the time spent by architects, builders, and owners in simply answering each other's questions is reduced. The extranet can also impose cohesion and order on the massive amounts of data that every project generates. The key is hyperlinking: you can make crucial connections between related bits of information. Hyperlink a window detail to a cut sheet and a specifications section. Hyperlink a structural calculation to a code section. Hyperlink a plot plan to a zoning ordinance. Or hyperlink a three-dimensional model to a building program bubble diagram.

Architects often say they lose money during construction, because it is sometimes impossible to be adequately compensated for the time spent responding to RFIs, change order requests, extra site meetings, and so on. A lot of time is spent mediating disputes between what the architect intended in the design and what the builder or subcontractor assumed in bidding the job. Because historically little or no contact between these parties has occurred during design, the entire burden of communicating the design intent to bidders is placed on the construction documents. Inefficiencies in that communication result in higher costs for both the architect and contractor during construction.

Project extranets can be modeled on your existing project management systems. They will then become an evolution of your current practice, rather than a sweeping change. It goes without saying that no amount of advanced communication technology can overcome poor project management procedures. If your firm has implemented a project management system that works, an Internet-supported version of it

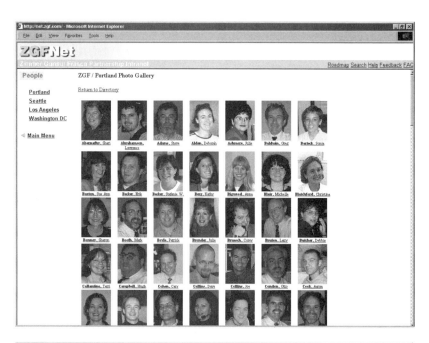

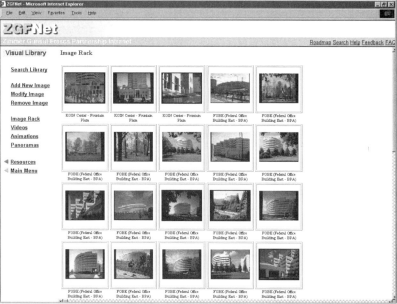

8-7, 8-8, and 8-9. Zimmer Gunsul Frasca's intranet. (Courtesy Zimmer Gunsul Frasca Partnership)

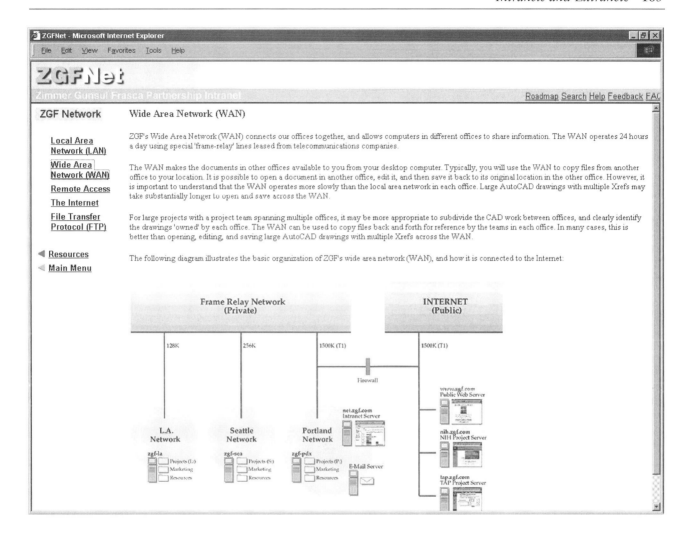

is likely to be even better. But don't expect any computerized system to overcome an underlying lack of organization; technology will simply amplify what doesn't work.

Case Study: Zimmer Gunsul Frasca

Ken Sanders is a partner with Zimmer Gunsul Frasca Partnership, an architecture and interior design firm in Portland, Oregon, with offices in Seattle, Los Angeles, and Washington D.C.: "We began to seriously look at the Internet as a practice tool in 1995," he said. "The browser simplified access to all kinds of information. You didn't have to learn all the tools to view information. For example, a firm partner might not know AutoCAD but needs to view drawings on-line. Most people create just a few flavors of information—but they want to access more. The browser is a unified technology for looking at information."

First, ZGF set up a public Web site. Although pleased with the results, they "realized the really useful application was going to be in

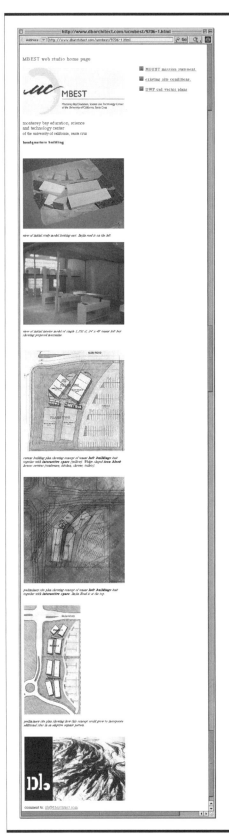

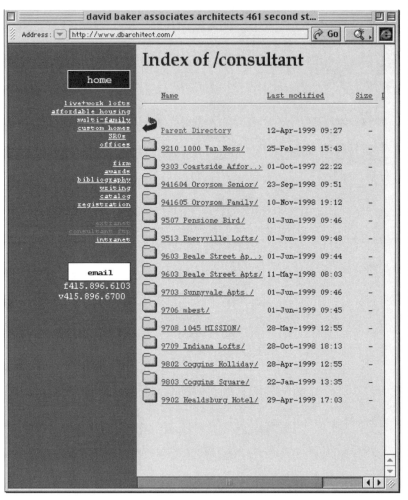

8-10. Even small firms can create their own project-specific Web sites. (Courtesy David Baker Architects)

8-11. David Baker Architects uses this FTP site to exchange files with consultants, clients, and contractors. (Courtesy David Baker Architects)

Extranets for the Rest of Us

ZGF is a large firm with substantial in-house resources and expertise. What can small firms do? David Baker Architects of San Francisco, which pioneered live/work loft housing, creates its own project-specific Web sites. These sites include a gateway to an FTP site for easy file exchange between architect and consultants (figs. 8-10 and 8-11).

managing projects," said Sanders. Late in 1996, they proposed to a client, the Port of Portland, that a Web site be used for tracking and processing RFIs for an airport project. The client agreed, and it worked out well.

Since then ZGF has used extranets for more than a dozen jobs, each different, as well as its own intranet (figs. 8-7, 8-8, and 8-9, pages 184–185). They deploy two kinds of extranets: one for project management during the construction phase, and one early in the design process "just for communication with the client." ZGF likes the ability to customize the Web site to each client. Some are tightly controlled for access, some are very open. Extranets have been created for projects with many stakeholders, including university projects involving facilities managers, administrators, faculty, students, and neighbors.

Sanders is waiting for the commercial extranet services to mature, but he thinks ZGF will continue to use its own home-made Web sites as a "convenient, low-cost" way to improve client communication: "There are always going to be projects that we want to do in a creative way."

Components of an Extranet

As firms adopt this new way of communicating, Web site templates can ease the transition from paper-based to Web based project information systems. Project managers and department heads who are charged with setting up sites can do so more easily with a firm-supplied template. A project-specific extranet might be as simple as an FTP site, or it might include a sophisticated suite of Web-based information management tools, with all the functionality of such groupware products as Lotus Notes.

A project Web site might include some or all of the following features:

- Authentication of users, typically by means of passwords
- Provision for various levels of access for different classes of users:
  - Read-only access to all or portions of the site or to particular types of documents or folders
  - Upload and download permission, to add new files and/or modify and delete existing files
- A messaging and notification system for sending e-mail to project participants, with attachments and annotations
- A calendaring/scheduling mechanism, with a system for managing contact information for project participants
- Relational database access and integration
- Electronic forms design, submission, and management
- Conferencing, which might be synchronous communication—live chat sessions with whiteboarding, as Microsoft NetMeeting offers—or asynchronous, as in threaded discussion groups
- A method of tracking and time-stamping the specific files accessed by a user

8-12. The 24-hour construction Webcam at Texas A&M's Corpus Christi campus. (Courtesy of Texas A&M University—Corpus Christi)

- A method of presenting files for remote viewing and printing that does not require the remote user to have the application that created it, including:
  - CAD and GIS viewers and plug-ins
  - Acrobat or other read-only formats, created on the fly when a document is requested
  - Java-based file viewers

Categories of project documentation available on the site would include:

- Project directories, with contact information for each project participant
- Schedules
- Financial information
- Meeting notes, by phase
- Correspondence, by phase
- Programming documents
- Approvals documents
- Site documentation
- Photos and video
- Surveys
- Aerial photos
- Regulatory information

- Master specifications
- Drawings:
  - Schematics
  - Design development
  - Construction documents
  - Construction sketches
  - Shop drawings
- Presentation and marketing materials
- Models
- Progress reports
- Logs
- Contracts, including:
  - Owner-architect
  - Architect-consultant
  - Owner-contractor
- Time cards and internal management data
- Web-based construction site monitoring (fig. 8-12)

Case Study: An Owner's Perspective

Mark Herman, an architect by training, is real-estate and construction manager of MathWorks, a software company in Natick, Massachusetts.

Herman acted as client for MathWorks' recent corporate headquarters project, a 180,000–square foot, four-story project designed by ADD Inc. and built by John Moriarty and Associates. At Mark's suggestion, the design team used Evolv's ProjectCenter as a ready-made project extranet (figs. 8-13 and 8-14). "It was very useful just for owner-architect communication. It paid for itself quickly with savings in courier expense alone—the architect is forty miles away and package delivery is $25 to $50 a pop," said Herman. But the main benefit was in the design process itself: "I was able to stay much more

8-13 and 8-14. ProjectCenter from Evolv. (Courtesy Evolv)

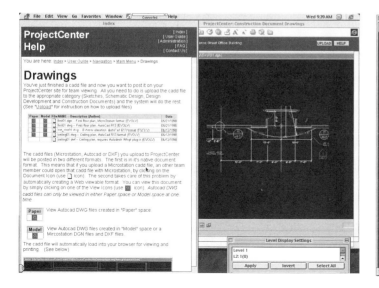

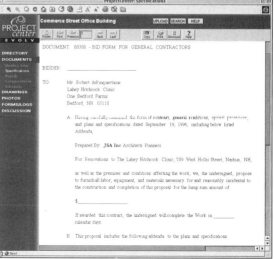

involved in the design without having to spend time in the architect's office. It eliminated what I call the dud meeting—where the architect has worked for a week in the wrong direction."

ADD Inc. posted sketches in the form of PDFs that they exported from MicroStation CAD files. Herman brought them into Photoshop, marked them up, showed them to the corporate stakeholders, and then reposted them on ProjectCenter. "It was much more of an interactive process than we could have had without the extranet," he concluded.

What did he most like about ProjectCenter? "It's almost never down, I get a good sense of security, I'm notified of what's new, and it's intuitive to anyone familiar with the CSI format." He criticizes the interface, however: it lacks polish and it takes too many mouse clicks to get to the information. And he would very much like a nested folder structure, so that he could see several levels into the file hierarchy.

Home-made or Off-the-Shelf?

If you are convinced of the value of project-specific Web sites for managing your projects, you face a choice. Should you create your own system, or use one of the subscription-based services on the market? Companies such as Cephren, Evolv, BidCom, and others offer Web-enabled project management for a monthly fee based on the number of users or the size of the project. Or should you buy an industry-specific solution to install on your own hardware?

In arriving at this decision, your considerations should include:

- Do you have the resources to acquire and support the necessary hardware and software to operate your own server?
- Do you have dedicated access to the Internet—leased lines, T1, or ADSL?
- Do you have, or will you hire, at least a part-time systems administrator to manage a Unix- or Windows NT/2000–based system?
- Are you able to provide physical and electronic security for the system?
- Are you comfortable placing mission-critical data outside of your physical oversight and control?

Part of your decision making will have to do with the image you want to project: just as every project and client is unique, no two project extranets will be identical. The best firms are able to customize services to clients and differentiate themselves by projecting a distinct identity. In this era of customer-focused business strategies, your ability to treat each client differently may be paramount to your success.

Increasingly, the Web is turning what were personal—and expensive—services into commodities. Ten years ago, for example, one could hardly imagine trading thousands of shares of stock for a mere $8, without even having to call a stockbroker. The most successful companies in this environment of declining margins and customer loyalty are likely to be the ones who make their clients feel that services are tailored specifically for them. You can use the Web not just to push services at your clients but to interact with them as well. Your site's interactivity will help you to learn about your clients so that you can serve them better. As more and more business is conducted on the Web, your site will grow into an important means of building relationships and it should reflect your image and identity.

In evaluating your firm and its style of doing business, you may find good reason for spending the resources to develop your own systems in-house. Customization may be as simple as adding or subtracting elements on a template site you created for one project, for use in another project. Firms may see the value of branding their template Web sites with a firm-designed identity, including a consistency in the way sites are organized and navigated. Clients will develop a familiarity and comfort level with your interface. They will always assign a higher value to a service when they perceive it as having been created especially for them. If important business is transacted on a generic, one-size-fits-all Web site, they may find it easier to go elsewhere. In a relationship business, it is another aspect of your service that binds the client to you; your extranet may pay for itself just with the client loyalty it engenders.

Case Study: Reel Grobman Architects

Ken Grobman is principal of Reel Grobman, a thirty-person firm in San Jose, California, specializing in interior architecture. He calls their project Web sites "our mega file drawers." Grobman said, "The largest single thing that's new in the construction world is the Internet. For us, the predominant use is communication with our clients. When you think about what project management consists of—communication, scheduling, and budgeting—the Internet helps us manage all three."

Reel Grobman uses ProjectNet, a subscription-based extranet system from Cephren, for its project-specific Web sites (figs. 8-15 and 8-16). "Lack of communication is the biggest cause of failure in any project," said Grobman. "Change orders and time overruns usually reflect a failure of communication. When all communication is out there for everyone to see, there is less opportunity for misinterpretation."

Grobman believes the extranet saves the time often lost in waiting for client approvals—a day here or a week there can add up. For a $30 million project for Phillips Electronics, he proposed ProjectNet to the client but was asked to justify the expense. "I told them I don't need a 10 percent contingency if we use an Internet-enabled project management system because I know that errors will be reduced due to better communication." He proposed cutting the contingency to 7 percent and eventually reduced it to 3 percent. The client was impressed by his confidence and agreed to the extranet.

Grobman believes using that using the Internet for project communications will soon be commonplace: "All architects will be doing it within a few years." He is not sure there will be a need for

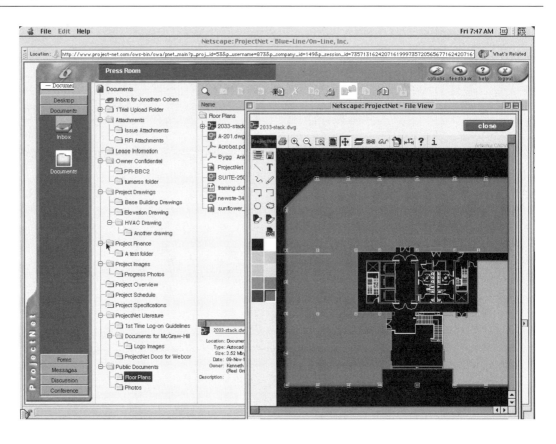

8-15 and 8-16.
ProjectNet from
Cephren. (©2000
Cephren, Inc.)

outside extranet providers to manage it, as Web-authoring tools become easier to use and Internet skills become mainstream in the profession. "I could implement this in-house if I was so inclined," he said.

He considers the extranet a marketing advantage: "It's a differentiator for Reel Grobman—we're perceived as an Internet-savvy firm, and that makes us attractive to high technology clients."

Using Off-the-Shelf Systems

Two kinds of ready-made solutions are available: subscription-based, which require no investment on your part, and systems that you purchase and install on your own network.

The advantages of a subscription-based solution include:

- No investment in hardware or software, although training of personnel is required. Access is via free Web browsers.
- No responsibility for physical security of data or hardware.
- No development expenses for designing a system from scratch. You can test the waters with a trial project without making a major commitment. Commercial solutions offer features, such as audit tracking and reporting, conferencing, and CAD viewing and markup, that would require sophisticated programming to set up in your own system.
- You are free to sample and use more than one system, depending on client preferences. This can become a disadvantage, however, if it means having to juggle several systems.
- Data backup is provided; administrative staff time for site maintenance is unnecessary.

The disadvantages of a subscription-based solution include:

- No off-the-shelf system can reflect your personality and style of doing business. Although these systems can be customized to a degree, the range is limited, and changes are essentially cosmetic.
- Ultimately you are placing mission-critical data in the hands of another organization, and you are asking your clients and partners to do the same. If, for any reason, you cannot connect to your provider's server, you may completely lose contact with your project information. A few of the services allow for local backup of the system on your hardware—a potential life saver if the main server is down or inaccessible.
- You face "lock-in" if you become dependent on proprietary technology. You will not have control over the frequency of upgrades or scheduled downtime. You cannot be sure that the firm with which you are contracting will stay in business through the life of your project.
- Because you are outsourcing all the costs and investment, you have a new monthly expense item. If clients balk at including it as a reim-

bursable expense charged against the project, you will have to pay a monthly fee and expect your consultants to do the same.

■ You may find your firm involved with a different proprietary system for each project or client, multiplying your training time.

Questions to ask a prospective extranet provider include:

■ Is your system based entirely on open Web technology, HTML, and Java? Is it fully accessible from all potential client computers and browsers?

■ Are all the file types used in a typical project accessible for viewing, downloading, and printing from the extranet, including graphic files, photos, correspondence, CAD drawings, and specs? Some systems require that plug-ins be installed on client computers to permit viewing of certain file types; other systems use server-side technology to convert files to viewable formats without plug-ins. If plug-ins are required, make sure they are available for all computer platforms you and your partners use.

■ How is document version tracking handled, if at all?

■ To what degree can the system be customized to our work process?

■ Whom do you consider to be your target market (architects, contractors, engineering firms)? Who are your biggest customers?

■ Whom do you consider to be your main competitors? What differentiates your product from theirs (performance, features, scalability, price)?

■ Can your system readily share data with other such extranet systems? How have you planned for such emerging technologies as object-oriented CAD and XML?

■ What end-of-project deliverables, such as a CD-ROM, does your system include? Is the archived data delivered in a nonproprietary format that can be accessed with available software?

■ How much downtime have your customers experienced over the last twelve months?

■ What kind of support is available—24/7/365? What is the cost per use? Is there a free support period? Do you provide only technical support, or do you help customize the system for particular clients? What about training for employees and partners?

■ Is there a free evaluation period?

■ Are there independent consultants who are familiar with this system and available to help implement and/or customize it?

■ How often are back-ups made, and are they redundant? Where and how are the backup tapes or other media stored?

■ Is the provider also hosting the secure server, or is this subcontracted to another vendor? What is the nature of your relationship? Is there a long-term contract, and do you have a back-up supplier?

■ What insurance can your firm provide against loss of data, loss of confidentiality, or scheduling losses due to downtime?

■ What commitment can you make with respect to frequency of

upgrades? (This is a double-edged sword. You want updates to keep current with the ever-changing technology, such as new document viewers. On the other hand, you do not want frequent and unexpected changes requiring retraining of your personnel or partners.)

■ Who owns the company? (You might find that the largest shareholder is one of your competitors!) What assurances can be given with respect to treating all customers equally and safeguarding confidential information and relationships?

An architect may balk at allowing a contractor to control the administration of systems in which confidential data is kept, and vice versa. As compelling as the idea of linking designer and contractor in a project extranet may be, you may find that managing design and managing construction are different enough to require separate systems. The ready-made solutions currently on the market tend to show a subtle bias toward the designer, builder, or owner, depending on the background of its founders. Evolv's ProjectCenter, for example, was developed by Bill Tucker, an architect. BidCom started as a bidding management system that was targeted to general contractors. Whether any of these systems actually will evolve into something that is universally applicable for every phase of every project is not yet clear. Portal sites may enable builders and architects to filter information from multiple information systems to a customized single desktop. If more than one system is implemented on a single project, care should be taken to ensure that information can flow as freely as possible between the systems.

An Out-of-the-Box Solution
An alternative to building your own extranet from scratch or contracting with a subscription-based extranet service is to install one of several industry-specific products on your own network. Cephren, for example, offers a version of its ProjectNet service called ProjectNet Enterprise for installation on your server and ReviewIt AEC Enterprise from Cubus Corporation can likewise be run on your server or theirs (figs. 8-17 and 8-18).

Framework Technologies' ActiveProject uses a template approach to create project management Web sites without need for programming or knowledge of HTML. ActiveProject sites provide user authentication, a nested file management system, change notification, and viewing of various file types, including CAD files, photos, schedules, and Microsoft Office documents. Thus the system offers the features of the subscription-based services in a package that runs on your server.

ActiveProject consists of two components, Builder and Server. The builder component is used to assemble Web sites graphically that are then hosted by the server component. Once constructed, a site is fully

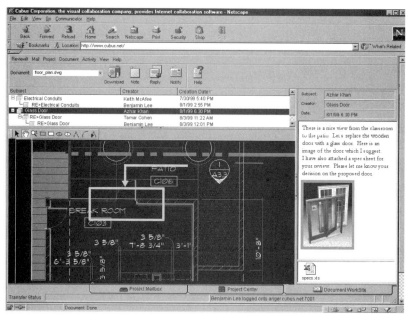

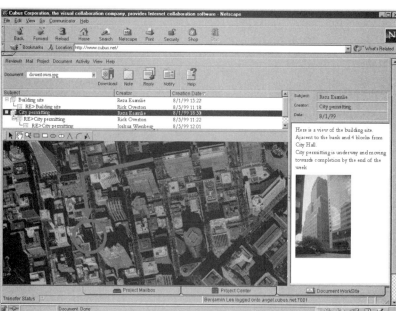

8-17 and 8-18. ReviewIt AEC from Cubus Corporation is a project extranet solution that emphasizes visual communication.

accessible from within a standard Web browser. A "publish and subscribe" feature allows remote collaborators to select the kinds of information that will be "pushed" to them and exclude the enormous amount of irrelevant chaff that attends every large project. ActiveProject is being used to manage Boston's $10 billion Central Artery/Tunnel Project and by Little and Associates Architects to manage a new research complex for Sandia National Laboratories (figs. 8-19, 8-20, and 8-21).

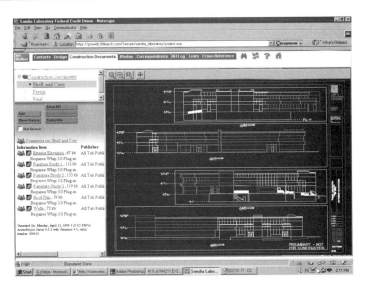

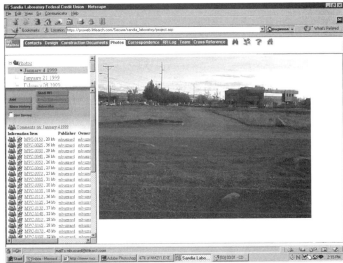

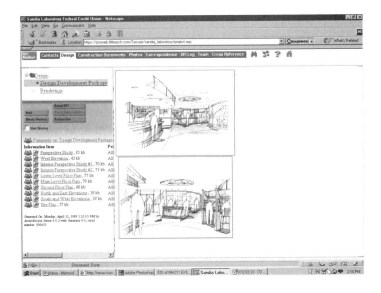

8-19, 8-20, and 8-21. Architects Little and Associates use ActiveProject to manage the Sandia Laboratory project.

8-22 and 8-23. BidCom's project extranet system.

Case Study: Webcor Builders

Andy Ball is Chief Executive Officer of Webcor Builders, a general contractor in San Mateo, California. Webcor was established in 1971 and has about $400 million of work in place.

Andy was an early adopter of Internet project management: "I've had a long-standing desire to really go with a paperless office. It made no sense for me to get truckloads of printed documents, only to throw them out when the next revision came a few days later." He saw an opportunity to facilitate communication with the Internet.

In 1996 he attended a conference of the International Development Research Council, a think tank of large real-estate holders, including many Fortune 500 companies. He saw a presentation on the use of Lotus Notes over a wide-area network to manage large construction projects. Although impressed, he was not enthusiastic about the high cost of implementation and training. But it was a first step.

When he learned about Cephren's ProjectNet system, he knew he had found a more cost-effective alternative. He signed up and used the system in a tenant improvements project.

Today Webcor uses Internet project management for every job over $3

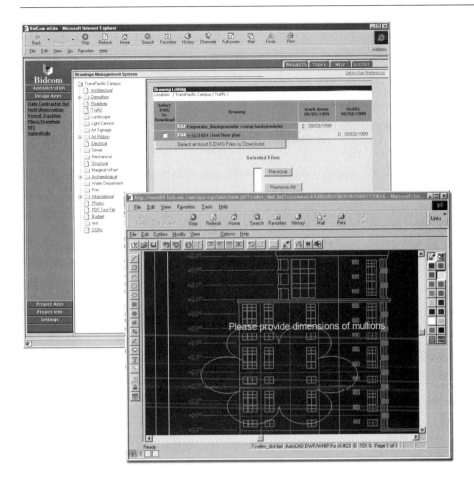

million. They install a T1 line to every job site, then set up a small LAN on the site, which is connected back to the main office in parallel to ProjectNet.

Andy's biggest task is convincing owners and architects. "What we're trying to do is educate people. There is a reluctance to change tried and true methods. It's not yet at critical mass," he said, "but it will soon be something you can't do business without."

He tells owners: "It's wonderful. You don't have to go down to the job site or the architect's office." Most owners are interested, but even if they hesitate, he provides the service at no cost, knowing that it will pay for itself with savings in administrative cost and time: "In our typical project, there might be $200,000 of printing costs and $20,000 in messenger charges." He considers it ideal to have everyone involved in a project on board, but he finds ample value in just his own relationships with subcontractors and suppliers. He tells subs they must make the minimal investment in a computer with Internet access, or they cannot do business with Webcor.

Case Study: Swinerton & Walberg

Charlie Kuffner is a vice president of Swinerton & Walberg, an old-line general contracting company that bills $900 million annually. In September 1997, BidCom came to him with an on-line bidding system.

He had problems with it: Charlie did not want to receive hundreds of e-mails ten minutes before a bid deadline and have to coordinate them all. Last-minute faxes were already driving him crazy. But he also saw potential in connected project management and work flow, especially in tracking RFIs and submittals. And he loved the idea of giving the owner an end-of-job CD-ROM with record drawings and the full history of a project. He gave his suggestions to BidCom, and they listened. In a few months, they were back with a system that Kuffner could use (figs. 8-22 and 8-23, pages 198–199).

The first job was 211 Main Street in San Francisco for Charles Schwab, a $30 million project with 110 subcontractors. He found that 90 percent of them already had Internet access. Surprisingly, the first on-line were small mom-and-pop operations that were running the business from home PCs. Next were big mechanical and electrical subcontractors who were already communicating with their product suppliers on-line. The laggards were the medium-size firms, those with around thirty employees, in low-tech trades such as unit masonry. For the few that cannot receive e-mail, BidCom provides a fax server, so that subs can receive faxes rather than e-mail.

With the system in place, turnaround time for RFIs went from more than a week to two or three days. BidCom offers real-time work flow tracking of RFIs to show exactly where the bottlenecks are. "We saved the owner $300,000 in rent and $50,000 in overtime costs," claimed Kuffner.

Swinerton has used BidCom extranets on projects ranging from the $255 million Soka University in Orange County, California, to $250,000 tenant improvement jobs. Other clients have included Lucent, The Gap, and Stanford University. Swinerton puts connected PCs in every job-site trailer so that subs can log on from the field.

Every project has an initial learning curve, according to Kuffner. Problems have occurred when new subs were coming on board at frequent intervals: each one needed training, and many had slow modems, old computers, and obsolete software. Kuffner is planning to publish minimum and optimum system requirements in its standard bidding documents that will be a prerequisite to subcontracting with Swinerton.

Kuffner concluded: "We've had amazing results. You know how valuable time is in our business—we're saving lots of it, both for us and the owners. We save on staff time, as well as costs; lots of administrative stuff, like the time it takes to fax something. The owner gets to move in sooner, saves on duplicate rent, and starts generating revenue sooner."

Calculating a Return on Investment

The goals of any investment in technology should be stated clearly up front and subjected to as rigorous an analysis of measurable success as possible. Having said that, many firms will adopt intranets and extranets without even attempting to quantify savings, simply to keep pace with competitors. For others the advantages are so obvious that trying to quantify them seems unnecessary. But smart business owners should want to calculate a return on investment (ROI) for an undertaking of this magnitude, even if some of the variables are subjective or hard to measure accurately.

Anticipated gains from implementation of new project communication tools include:

- *Quality improvements* due to better communication among project participants. If an engineer can consider more design possibilities because of computer modeling, that is a quality improvement. If the client feels she was better served by the design team because her objectives were more clearly understood, that is also a quality improvement, even if it cannot be easily measured. General contractors who were formerly focused on production now realize they are service providers, and it is good service that brings repeat customers.
- *Efficiency improvements*, as tasks are accomplished in fewer hours with lower costs. If a structural engineer can download and review structural steel shop drawings, make revisions, and then post the drawings back to a Web site within a few hours, without incurring shipping or administrative expense, that is an efficiency improvement.
- *Time improvements*, as the overall time needed for individual tasks, with or without efficiency improvements, is reduced. If a general contractor can use a project extranet to receive change order approval in three days rather than the ten days it required with paper and fax, that is a time improvement. If improved communications means that tasks that were done sequentially can now be done simultaneously, that is also a time improvement. Time-saving benefits are especially valuable for owners whose revenue streams cannot start until a building is finished.
- *New sources of revenue*, which might include leveraging your expertise with extranets into a billable service you can provide to others, or providing clients with Web-based project manuals for a fee. If you are hosting a server, it seems reasonable to charge your clients and consultants a fee for using the system.
- *Reduced direct costs*. Some kinds of savings are easy to document, such as reprographic costs, photocopying, postage, telecommunications, and travel. Consider that the cost of overnight mail is not just the FedEx charge, but the time your office staff spends writing transmittals, addressing labels, calling when packages don't show up, and so on. A properly implemented Web-based system leaves a perfect paper trail automatically, eliminating the need for paper transmittals and phone logs.

Firms spend quite a bit of time answering requests for information from project participants, ranging from the client to consultants to subcontractors. Many hours will be saved by placing information in an easily accessible central repository. Since time is usually accounted for by project and phase of work, it is sometimes hard to ascertain how many hours a project manager spent addressing transmittal forms, for example, or answering routine questions by phone.

Consider carefully which specific tasks might be improved with an intranet or extranet. How many phone calls will not be made for information that was available in more convenient form on the Web site? How much time would have been spent searching for a paper document that can now be viewed and printed from a Web site? How much reporting that was previously done manually will now be automated? How much of the regained time can be put to use in direct billable time for the firm?

City planners spend a lot of time answering the same kinds of questions over and over again on the phone and at the permit counter. If a significant fraction of these inquiries can be directed to a Web site, then valuable time is saved. Ellen Miller is Manager of the Advance Planning and Research Division of the Baton Rouge, Louisiana, planning department, overseeing the work of fifteen professionals and seven support staff. Their Web site, which offers zoning, demographic information, application forms, and GIS mapping on their 200,000 land parcels, receives about one thousand visitors per month. If you assume that half of those visitors would otherwise call the planners, at ten minutes per call and an average personnel cost of $50 per hour, the Web site saves $6,250 every month.

Much of the value of an intranet or extranet is intangible; such soft earnings are the hardest to measure. What is the value of cementing a client relationship with a custom-designed project communication system? If your client can check the status of his project at any time of the day from anywhere in the world, the goodwill created might well lead to another project or a recommendation to a potential new client. On the other hand, if your system is poorly implemented, causes more frustration than satisfaction, or wipes out your time savings with time lost in maintaining it, then the ROI is turned on its head.

When measuring "soft" savings, such as time saved due to improved productivity, do your calculations after the system has had time to mature. Some people will resist new ways of working even if the new way is faster, better, and easier. It may take as long as six months before everyone in the organization is comfortable with a new system.

You can calculate a return on investment by adding the projected savings to any increased earnings that the project generates and then subtracting the costs. What remains is the net present value. Convert this figure to a percentage of the costs, and you have the ROI. Anything above 20 percent can be considered a good investment.

Be especially careful to assign costs directly. If you are using equipment you already have or were likely to acquire anyway, don't assign its full cost to the ROI calculation. Many firms have already created an intranet or at least a LAN; you should be able to leverage this investment. Most of the hardware and training, and all of the software, is interchangeable between intranets and extranets. Your existing server may be fully usable by the extranet or require only a relatively minor memory or storage

Calculating a Return on Investment for a Web-enabled Project Management System

Costs		Savings	
Equipment		Hard Savings	
	Require a new server?		Reduced postage/shipping expenses
	Upgraded internet connection?		Reduced paper/printing
	Router?		Reduced reproduction expenses
	Wiring?		Savings in voice/fax communications
Software			Travel Savings
Security			More efficient billing
	Need firewall?	Soft Savings	
	Other security products/services:		Productivity gains
Development			Project direct time saved
	In-house resources		Support staff time saved
	Contracted resources		Coordination benefits
Training			Lower exposure to liability claims
	Training for in-house users		
	Training for clients/partners	**Earnings**	
Management		Billable services	
	How often will upgrades be required?		Extranet service billable to client?
	Management resources devoted to extranet		Per-use fee? Per-project fee?
Support			Extranet service billable to consultants?
			Billable to contractors?
Depreciation			Training fees paid to 3rd parties?
			Revenue from outside consulting services
Totals	$	**Totals**	$

upgrade. Software you may have acquired, pages and sites that you have already created, graphics you have already scanned and converted to GIFs and JPEGs—all are reusable on the extranet. One of the principal advantages of digital content is that, once created, it can be cheaply and easily reproduced and used for multiple purposes.

Your training costs may be less than you think. Most of your employees, partners, and clients will already be familiar with using Web browsers. As page creation and site management tools become more sophisticated and easy to use, creating comprehensive Web sites will be easier.

Don't try to do too much all at once. A Web site is *scalable*—you can start small and simple and build from there. Small firms have fewer resources for extranet development than large ones do, but their projects probably have simpler project management requirements as well. They may not need all the advanced features that a sophisticated system offers. It is much easier to begin with a modest system that can be expanded than to contend with something that is inappropriately complicated for modest projects.

Think of all the functionality that you would like your system to possess and then aim for perhaps 80 percent of it—that extra 20 percent may cost another 100 percent to implement. Almost everything will be reusable. It is far better to start small and build slowly than not to start at all. Reevaluate and reassess frequently. Do another ROI calculation after your system has been up and running for a full year—you will have a better handle on the costs and savings. In fact, it may be difficult for many to appreciate in advance all the functionality that your system will bring, and new uses and applications will become apparent as your employees and partners familiarize themselves with it. Be sure to include your partners and clients in the development process: their involvement will help ensure that the system is well used once it is up and running.

9 City Planning

Few fields of human endeavor must evaluate and consider as many variables as city planning. The communication needs of planners parallel in many respects those of designers and builders, but they also encompass the public realm of politics and economics as well. Having the enhanced ability to collect, organize, and disseminate information in numerous data types is extremely useful to planners. The ability to make linkages between all the disparate pieces of information that bear on urban issues makes decision support for city planning far more comprehensive.

Computer-based planning tools such as Geographic Information

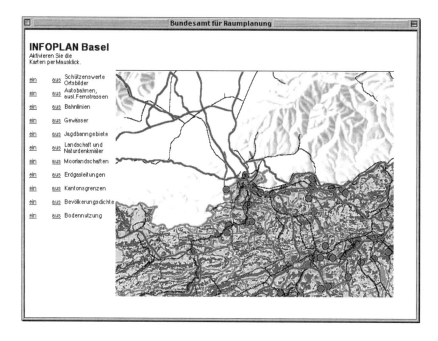

on the Internet

Systems (GIS) and visualization and simulation techniques, when coupled with the Internet, become powerful agents for analysis and persuasion. Greater access to information, including census and economic data, traffic flows, and property valuation data, makes it easier for planners to make informed choices. The vast amounts of information that cities collect about themselves is being made available for use by professionals and citizens alike. At the same time, the emergence of a powerful and accessible new medium of communication offers opportunities for enhanced public awareness of urban issues and of proactive, community-based planning and design (figs. 9-1, 9-2, and 9-3).

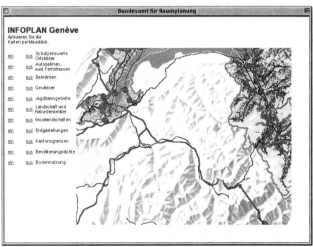

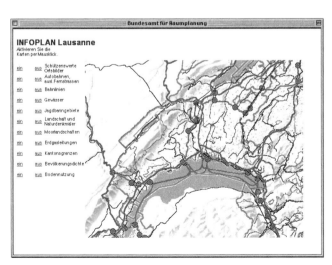

9-1, 9-2, and 9-3. The Swiss Federal Office for Spatial Planning offers GIS mapping for each canton. Layers of information can be clicked on or off.

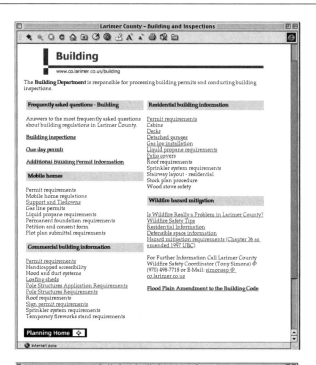

9-4. Larimer County in Colorado has placed its building and inspections regulations on-line, making use of hypertext to link related information.

9-5. Boulder County, Colorado, uses HTML tables and hypertext to make its zoning regulations easy to navigate.

Since most planning takes place within public agencies, let's look at ways that planning agencies are starting to harness the communications power of the Internet to serve their clientele.

Public Outreach

The first step for most planning departments is to set up an informational Web site with some or all of the following categories of planning information:

- Public hearing notices and agendas
- Notices of planning applications received and their status
- FAQs about procedures: how to apply for permits, fees, time lines, standard conditions of approval, and the like (fig. 9-4)
- Zoning ordinances, with tables, diagrams, and definitions; hyperlinking makes this information more usable than paper versions (fig. 9-5)
- Zoning maps, overlay districts, historic and other special districts (fig. 9-6)
- Downloadable planning publications, such as specific area plans, downtown plans, comprehensive plans, and environmental impact statements

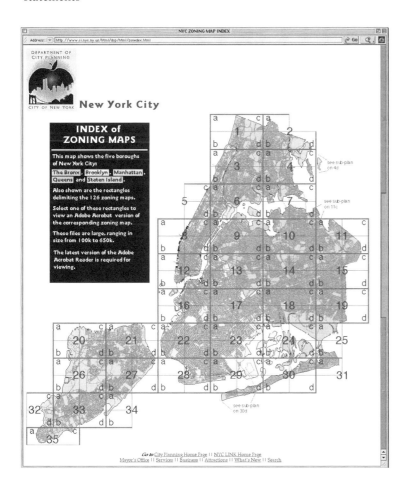

9-6. The on-line index to the zoning maps of New York City.

■ GIS information—street maps, assessors' information, seismic and flood zones, Sanborn maps, census information, neighborhood association boundaries, school district boundaries, utility information (fig. 9-7)
■ Application forms, either as HTML forms or in downloadable PDF format (fig. 9-8)
■ Hyperlinks to e-mail addresses of planning staff, planning commissioners, department heads, city council members

A second-stage planning Web site integrates navigable, searchable GIS information: advanced mapping functions, assessors' information, floodplain and seismic zones, and address finders (figs. 9-9, 9-10, and 9-11).

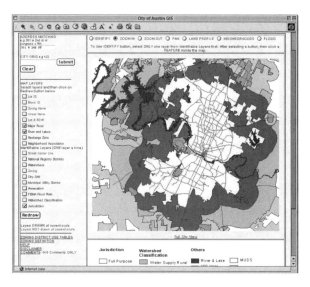

9-7. GIS mapping for Austin, Texas, is easily accessible on the Web. Layers of information can be clicked on or off.

9-8. Santa Rosa, California, puts zoning application forms in PDF format for download and printing.

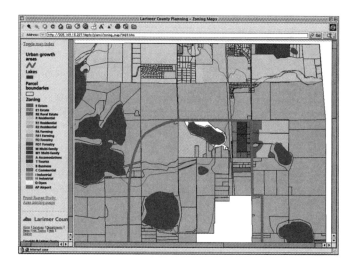

9-9. Colorado's Larimer County uses its GIS system to display land use and parcel information.

9-10. On-line GIS in Mecklenburg, North Carolina, provides detailed information about properties.

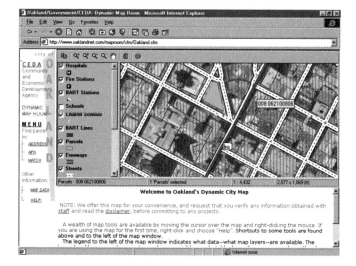

9-11. The Dynamic City Map of Oakland, California. Parcel information is layered over high-resolution aerial photographs.

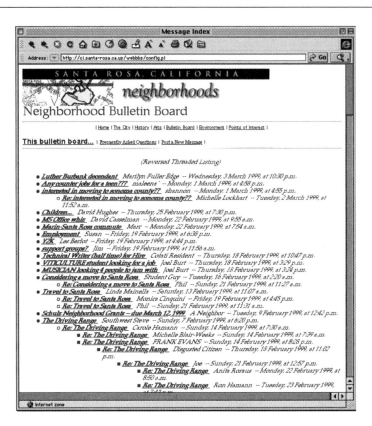

9-12. A discussion forum can be a useful tool for citizen participation in city planning.

Tips from the Field

Julie Crisp runs the planning department Web site in Portland, Oregon. She said, "The comments I receive most often are about how happy people are to find zoning information on the Web. Our purpose was to provide users with this visual aid in order to get their questions straight before calling or visiting the permit center."

Her suggestions to planning department Webmasters include:

- Once you decide to put information on-line, make sure you are committed to the resources necessary to keep the information up to date.
- Create a mission statement and a goal. Have a clear policy for what will be on the site, who will be linked to it, and how it will be maintained.
- Do not try too incorporate too much information into the site at first. Start off with a manageable chunk, and increase gradually.
- Follow the plan, and after a year or so revisit the goals and evaluate. Restructure if necessary. Keep the site fresh and straightforward, and design it for the users, not the techie who manages it.

A third-stage site introduces interactive features, which might include:

- A system for on-line filing and tracking of applications
- A forum or discussion area for citizen comment about current planning issues and zoning applications, discussion of general plans, specific area plans, proposed special districts and redevelopment proposals (fig. 9-12)
- Customizable mapping of zoning districts, overlay zones, parcel maps, and the like, allowing users to select layers of data

Case Study: Wake County, North Carolina

Tim Clark is Senior Planner and unofficial Webmaster of his eleven-person department. Wake County's planning department went on-line in September 1997 with a Web site that sought to be informational and easy to use (fig. 9-13). Clark had this to say about the experience:

The 1990s have seen a major change in people's expectations of local governments, as well as local governments' response to those expectations. People want excellent customer service at a low cost. People also expect to be better informed about, and involved in, local government policy decisions. As examples, people want immediate access to information or services and many would prefer to look for it themselves, rather than try to find the person who has that information. People also want information to be timely and accurate, e.g., zoning and subdivision regulations which have been updated to reflect recent amendments.

At the same time, planning departments, especially in fast-growing areas, are faced with the challenge of doing significantly more work with less personnel. Simple information dissemination tasks such as answering general inquiries, copying and sending out ordinance updates, and disseminating information on pending development requests to the general public all take valuable time which could otherwise be spent on the work program. The need to provide public information in a computerized form has been particularly acute in the Wake County planning department, where there is no clerical support, staff size has decreased, and the work program continues to expand.

The significance of this innovation is that planning departments can significantly improve their ability to provide timely, accurate, and robust information, to get public input, and generally to increase public satisfaction with the planning function while allowing for a more efficient use of staff.

We believe we have taken a visionary approach and embraced Internet technology as a whole new way to conduct our business, incorporating it into our everyday practices. This ranges from simple tasks

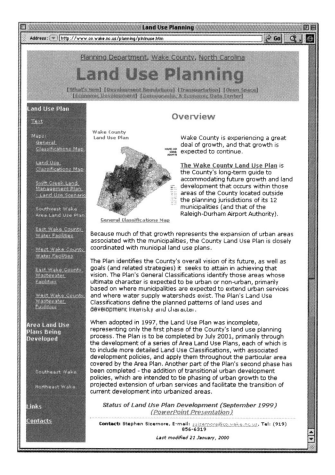

9-13. The Wake County Planning Department Web site.

such as directing people who want an updated copy of our ordinances to the Web, to giving the general public timely access to agendas, including the back-up memoranda, for the boards and task forces we support, to soliciting public input into planning decisions. We are able, because of the Lotus Notes Domino technology, to immediately attach written material to the Web, thus giving access to our data warehouse.

Our use of the Internet for publications has made significant improvements in public familiarity with our plans. One reason that plans often collect dust on the shelf is that very few people obtain them, and if they do, the plan is usually out of date. By keeping the plans up to date on the Internet, our experience has already shown that people read them, and they know that what they read is current. Similarly, the ordinances on the Internet are current, including an ordinance supplement, which allows the viewer to determine what changes have occurred recently. Placing our publications on the Internet has not only made those products more accessible to the public but has also cut down significantly on our copying and mailing costs.

Our implementation of this program has been very effective. We have significantly improved public participation and customer satisfaction with us through our Web page. We constantly receive compliments on our Web page, directly from the feedback feature and from public officials and peers. We believe the Web page and the information contained in it show excellence in thought, graphics, and presentation and enhance our ability to provide full, clear, and accurate information on planning issues to citizens and decision makers.

When the Internet users do call us, they are better informed about the issues, so the conversation is generally more focused and effective. For those who cannot, or choose not to, use the Internet, we are more available because we are not spending as much time with Internet users. We believe this technology has great transferability for any planning department that will establish its Web page as a priority and devote resources to implementing and updating it.

Case Study: Pasadena, California

Chris Ryder is a management analyst and Webmaster of Pasadena's planning site, which has grown to over a thousand pages and has won awards from the Los Angeles and California chapters of the American Planning Association (fig. 9-14). He reported on his department's experience with its Web site:

> We saw how using the Web could help increase service to the public. So far, we're getting excellent reviews from our customers. Certain permit ordinances and applications, such as grading standards and commercial development guidelines, are getting a lot of hits. Customers receive immediate guidance to the process they need to go through and what submittals they need to make without having to make the trek down to city hall.

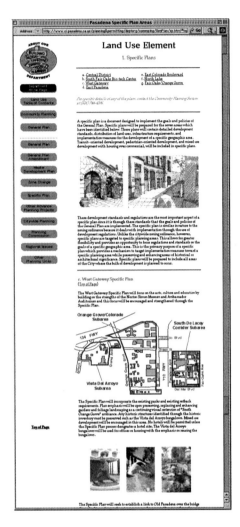

9-14. Pasadena's Planning Department uses its well-designed site to make planning information more accessible to customers.

We are also starting to get more hits on the meeting pages so people can find out what the agendas are coming up in the next week. We provide pages for each of Pasadena's nine neighborhoods so residents can see what is happening near their homes.

We are in the process of developing six specific area plans and plan to use a Web site for each one to involve residents in the discussion. These sites will be interactive, with comment blocks and links to related information.

As more customers learn about the Web site, they are starting to look there for information and applications instead of coming into our permit center, which is exactly what we had hoped: getting more information to customers and giving us more time to work on other projects.

Most people in urban areas don't know much about the history of the place they are living in. The Internet can provide much easier access to all the information cities have about their physical characteristics and history.

Chris Ryder offers these tips for planners building Web sites:

1. Have a plan. Figure out what information your customers would be interested in, what would be helpful to them, and what they can access from home instead of coming to your building. We found that most people don't know the difference between advanced planning, current planning, or building, so we made sure that we developed effective ways for people to find our information. We have our departments listed, but we tried to stress the services people wanted and what questions our customers would ask, rather than which department they needed.
2. Know who your customers are. Try gearing different pages to those who will use them. For example, our Permit Center pages are a bit more bland because developers and architects aren't concerned about friendly and fun, they just want information. Our neighborhood pages are a bit more friendly, so we can appeal more to residents and neighborhood groups.
3. Speed up your site. On all our pages we took into consideration that people want information as quickly as possible, so watch how many pictures are involved and make sure somebody on your Web team knows how to make the pictures load as quickly as possible.
4. Keep your pages current. Don't have meeting or neighborhood pages unless you are committed to updating them.
5. Make sure that you involve your planners and staff in the process, and be clear what they will get out of the final product. If you have a great Web site but nobody uses it, then it is waste of time, so use your whole staff to evangelize it. Give staff guidelines about what they can access, how to instuct customers, and so on.

Case Study: Philadelphia
Gary Jastrzab is a planner with the Philadelphia City Planning Commission. His department has a staff of sixty, including around

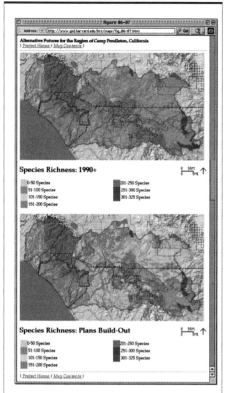

Address: http://www.gsd.harvard.edu/brc/maps/fg_86-87.html

Alternative Futures for the Region of Camp Pendleton, California
| Project Home | Map Contents |

Species Richness: 1990+

0-50 Species
51-100 Species
101-150 Species
151-200 Species

201-250 Species
251-300 Species
301-325 Species

Species Richness: Plans Build-Out

0-50 Species
51-100 Species
101-150 Species
151-200 Species

201-250 Species
251-300 Species
301-325 Species

| Project Home | Map Contents |

9-15. Biodiversity and landscape planning: Alternative futures for the region of Camp Pendleton, California. (Courtesy of Harvard University)

What Is a GIS?

A geographic Information System (GIS) is a set of mapping tools for collecting, storing, manipulating, and displaying data with a spatial component. GIS has many uses, from analyzing census information to mapping cancer clusters to finding the best location for a new McDonalds (fig. 9-15). Geographic Information Systems have three components: hardware, software, and properly trained personnel to use them. In recent years, increasingly powerful personal computers have put GIS at the disposal of smaller agencies and firms.

As with CAD, GIS maps employ layers—sometimes called "data themes"—that enable users to filter information visually and to make connections between related data sets.

GIS is a classic example of the "garbage-in, garbage-out" maxim. The most important and time-consuming aspect of any GIS is collecting and storing the base information. If it is not accurate and complete, then nothing that follows from it will be useful.

forty professional planners. He initiated the departmental Web site and does most of the upkeep on his own time.

For us, it's another channel for making information available. The pages viewed most frequently are those related to statistical data about the City of Philadelphia. The PCPC "Guide to Data Sources" received the most hits during this period, averaging about two hundred "views" per month. This document lists public and private sources of frequently requested planning and marketing data for the Greater Philadelphia Region and includes the names of data providers, postal addresses, telephone numbers, and Internet URL and e-mail addresses.

The second most-viewed document is our "CityStats" publication (in PDF format), which contains a series of tables with demographic and economic data for the City of Philadelphia and the region, followed closely by the agendas posted for our semimonthly City Planning Commission meetings. We also receive a fair number of e-mail inquiries for specific planning, development, and marketing information about the City of Philadelphia via our Web site. In our role as information clearinghouse, the use of the Internet has given our agency another medium in which to provide this information.

The Web provides a great opportunity to make the information resources of a planning department available to a wider public, both in terms of educating the public about important planning issues and providing more immediate access to the data needed to make informed decisions about public policy and physical development options.

Spatial Data Analysis and Planning Visualization

As noted in chapter 5, the Web will dramatically increase the demand for GIS, as it provides the ideal vehicle for delivering GIS maps directly to businesses and the public. An astonishing amount of public-domain information is already available from government agencies such as the U.S. Geological Survey and the Census Bureau. Until now, most of that information, although technically in the public domain, was not very accessible. Many local governments have invested heavily in GIS, only to see the information used by only a handful of people. The Internet will change that by opening a much wider distribution channel for these maps.

Some localities are moving to integrate their GIS systems on a regional basis. The Smart Permit Initiative in Silicon Valley, discussed in chapter 7, is seeking to create a region-wide GIS to counter the unfortunate habit of individual local jurisdictions to develop systems that are incompatible with their neighbors'. This region-wide GIS will be fully integrated with the Internet and accessible to planners, architects, developers, and citizens via the Web. A standardized list of data themes will help the valley make intelligent decisions on issues of region-wide impact, including land use, transportation, open space, and jobs/housing balance.

Planners are turning to visual and interactive media to engage the public in important decisions regarding land use, transportation, and redevelopment. Michael Shiffer of MIT has developed a Collaborative Planning System (CPS) for group decision support in city planning. For Shiffer, an effective computer-mediated planning system must, at a minimum, be able to:

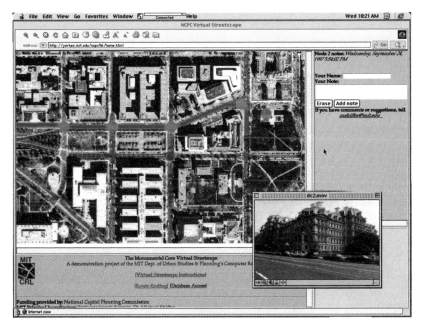

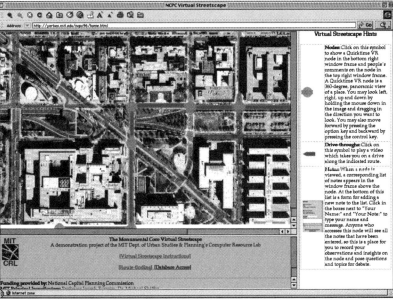

9-16 and 9-17. A Web-based multimedia urban design visualization system, developed for the National Capitol Planning Commission by Michael J. Shiffer of the Massachusetts Institute of Technology. (Image courtesy of Michael J. Shiffer and the MIT Urban Studies Computer Resource Lab)

- Use *multimedia* to convey otherwise abstract information to nonspecialists, with an unthreatening interface geared to the nontechnical user. Appropriate media might include scanned maps, photos, video, QuickTime VR, and sound. Shiffer believes the potential for multimedia in urban simulation is unlimited. He wants systems that accurately simulate traffic noise and model the effect of sound-screening devices or that simulate aircraft sound from various locations, accounting for wind and other variables. Shiffer is developing the means to model the impact of traffic congestion on neighborhoods, not just with the dry data that traffic engineers usually generate—trips per hour, levels of service, and so on—but in ways people can actually experience, by allowing users to call up video images showing level of service *D*, for example, with accompanying sound clips of prerecorded traffic, so that they can understand what the planning jargon really means.

- Employ virtual *navigation systems* to allow stakeholders to familiarize themselves with the areas being discussed.

- Provide a method of *evaluation*, enabling users to rank attributes and preferences from among presented alternatives.

- Provide for *annotation* by users, and therefore act as a spatially oriented collective memory. It must allow for brainstorming by groups, allowing participants to make connections from among the various pieces of information. Such systems must be able to "mature"—that is, their usefulness will improve over time as more users interact with them and build layers of information.

9-18 and 9-19. The Metro Planning Department in Portland, Oregon, uses the Web to enable citizens to envision housing density.

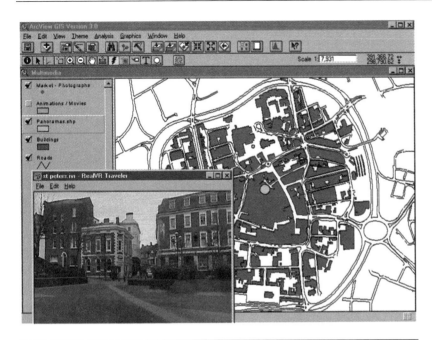

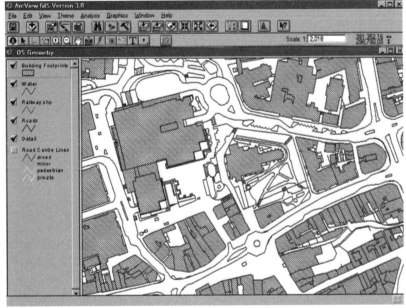

9-20 and 9-21. VENUE: Virtual Environments for Urban Environments, from University College, London.

A recent Web-based CPS system was developed by Shiffer for Washington's National Capital Planning Commission (figs. 9-16 and 9-17, page 215).

Density is a hot button in many planning controversies. Opponents and supporters each make conflicting claims about how a proposal will or will not increase density, and what that will mean to the community. But even experienced planners find it almost impossible to visualize density impacts accurately with the tools that are commonly used. Such issues lend themselves to multimedia or at least visual explication (figs. 9-18 and 9-19).

An interesting convergence is taking place between GIS and multimedia that holds great promise for planning and urban design visualization on the Web. Planners are beginning to harness GIS to map not only existing conditions but "what if" scenarios under alternative development options, including different densities of development. GIS-generated worlds can be realistic representations of cities or imagined terrain maps showing invisible geography.

A group of urban designers and geographers formed Virtual Environments for Urban Environments (VENUE) at University College, London (figs. 9-20 and 9-21, page 217). Their premise is that GIS can be brought down to the fine scale used in urban design and, coupled with multimedia, become a tool for design and visualization. Particularly valuable will be the ability to study and model the sequences experienced as one moves through urban space. Working with GIS vendor ESRI, they are developing tools for sketch planning with integration of multimedia and immersive imaging techniques.

Case Study: ESLARP and EGRETS

The East Saint Louis Action Research Project (ESLARP) began in 1987 as a community assistance program sponsored by the departments of Architecture, Urban Planning, and Landscape Architecture at the University of Illinois at Urbana-Champaign. The city of East Saint Louis, Illinois, had seen its population decline by nearly one-half between 1960 and 1990, due to industrial abandonment and the consequent migration of blue-collar jobs to other areas. It was considered a prime example of urban blight in America. By 1990, over half the population was living below the poverty level. Unemployment was nearly 30 percent.

The community turned to the university for help but extended this challenge: don't draw beautiful plans that will rot on the shelf; show us how to use your planning and design tools so that we can rebuild this city ourselves. The project began with a pilot neighborhood planning workshop in the fall semester of 1990 and grew into a comprehensive interdisciplinary program with an on-site, staffed neighborhood technical assistance center.

A component of the project is called EGRETS (East Saint Louis Geographic Information Retrieval System), an innovative program for providing this underserved community with some of the most sophisticated tools of the planning profession. Brian Orland is a professor of landscape architecture and director of the Imaging Systems Lab (IMLab) at UIUC. In 1994 he had a problem that had nothing to do with East Saint Louis: in the strategic land-planning studios he was leading, his students could not afford to plot their color maps. One day, as he walked across the campus to where Mosaic, the first Web browser, was under development at the National Center for

9-22 through 9-26 (pages 219-220).
EGRETS is an innovative program that provides GIS services to the impoverished community of East Saint Louis.

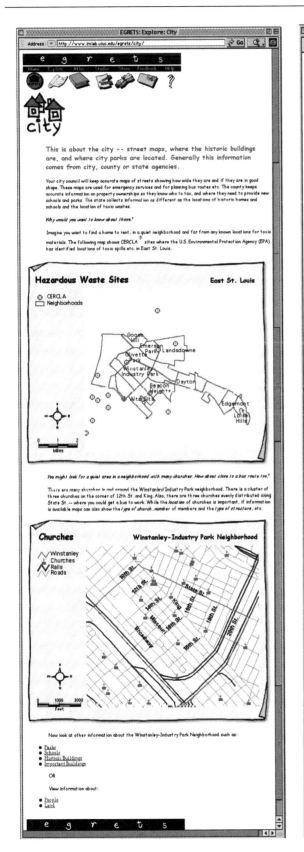

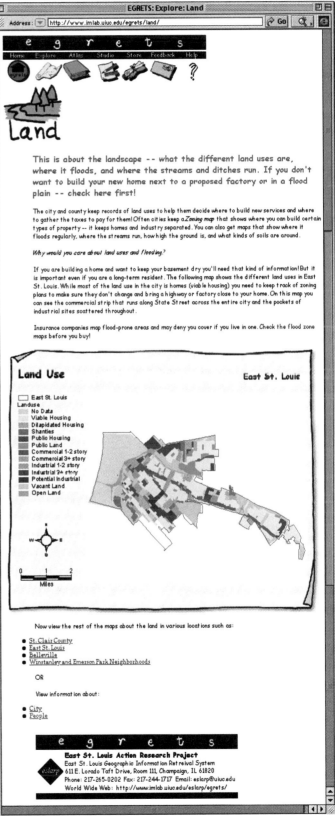

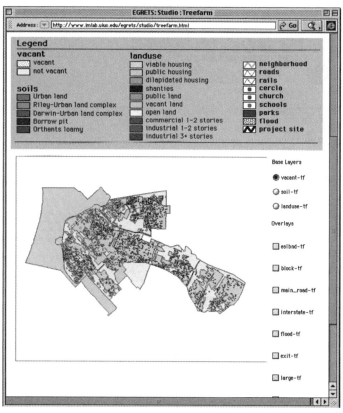

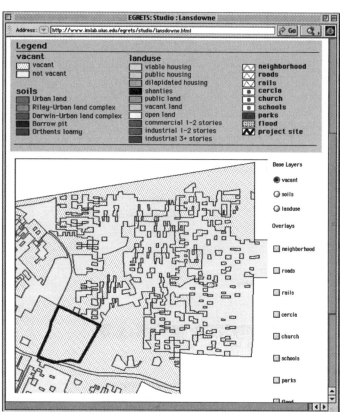

Supercomputing Applications, he realized that the Web was going to become the ideal platform for publishing GIS information. Soon an intranet was in place to allow sharing of map data between students and faculty, obviating the need for hard-copy prints.

Orland saw an application for this idea in East Saint Louis: "Most people do not know the wealth of information that is available about their community and how it could be useful to them." He and his colleagues set out to create a Web-enabled educational resource to make mapping data available for this community along with training in how to use it (figs. 9-22, 9-23, 9-24, 9-25, and 9-26). He designed a Web site that sought to accomplish three things:

1. Educate people about information and maps and how they can make use of them. For example, knowing the location of toxic waste sites or flood zones would clearly be valuable information for anyone buying a house or locating a business. This became the Tour section of the site.
2. Create an archive of searchable maps that already existed. This became the Atlas section of the site. His team used the Excite search engine to permit natural language searching using metadata. For example, if someone implements a search using the keyword "people," the search engine associates that with maps containing information about population.
3. Let visitors create their own maps by selecting "themes"—data layers—using a Java-based GIS viewer. This became the Studio section of the site.

A practical use for the GIS data came into play when the local transit agency was considering extending an existing light-rail line. The Emerson Park neighborhood wanted the line to come through it. They enlisted the EGRETS group and, using detailed maps, showed how the transit line would spur economic development and access to jobs. The transit agency was convinced and rerouted the line through Emerson Park.

Now the EGRETS team is conducting surveys of neighborhood conditions. Based on drive-by assessments of visible trash in neighborhoods, they use GIS to generate maps showing the condition of properties throughout the city in a highly visual way. It provides an effective early warning system about neglected properties. The program is an adaptation of Smart Forest, the IMLab's forest management visualization tools, to the urban environment.

10 Participatory

Today important land-use planning and community design decisions must be made with the participation of community residents. Yet such decisions are frequently made in the context of emotional confrontation between the sponsors of development proposals and their opponents, with public officials caught haplessly in the middle. Worse, such confrontations are often fueled by misinformation and misunderstanding on both sides. Public participation is hampered by inadequate access to information about proposed projects. And uncertainty about public reaction to development proposals creates a major element of risk for their sponsors, who must invest time and money without knowing if their proposals will be approved. It is clearly in a project sponsor's interest to hear from everyone who might have an interest in a project and to know early on what issues might influence the approvals process.

Until now, the barrier to citizen participation in planning decisions has been high, and consequently the rate of participation has been low. If being physically present at a public hearing, a neighborhood association meeting, or a planning workshop is a requirement for citizens to participate in planning decisions, then participation will be limited to those with spare time, a small and diminishing segment of society. As a result, planning decisions tend to be skewed toward the demands of a vocal minority, and important voices in the community are not heard.

The ways in which city planning decisions are made, and the way in which the public can interact with these planning processes, are beginning to change because of the Internet. One of the outcomes of this change will be much wider participation by the public than has previously been possible. This public participation will be supported by access to high-quality, media-rich information about development proposals and the issues surrounding land-use planning decisions.

Design and Planning

Interactive multimedia offer powerful new tools for representing physical issues such as land-use, traffic analysis, and density. GIS, together with computer-generated urban visualization techniques, provides opportunities to inform and involve the public as never before. The Internet can enable fuller, more informed participation in planning decisions by citizens and public officials alike (fig. 10-1).

One result of the environmental and preservation movements has been the growth of a class of citizens well educated in the language and possibilities of design who feel that architecture and city planning are appropriate topics for public discussion. For design professionals, this trend has been a mixed blessing. On the one hand, early consultation with users and neighbors can help identify issues and options the designer might not otherwise have considered. On the other hand, who needs yet more opinions in a design process that already seems overcrowded with kibbitzers? One thing is certain: there has never been a greater need for designers and planners to communicate effectively with diverse groups of people.

The Internet promises to be a participatory medium as well as an informational one. It can be a powerful tool for enabling community-based design. Planners and designers are beginning to use the multimedia capabilities of the Web to make complex visual and spatial concepts accessible to a broad public. And they are using the Web's interactive features to create a place for focused discussion and information exchange about specific developments.

Case Study: The Oxpens Quarter Initiative

Most public debate of proposed projects pits the project sponsors on one side against the neighborhood activists on the other. The process is reactive rather than proactive, and sometimes it is downright destructive. The problem for planners has been to involve the public in

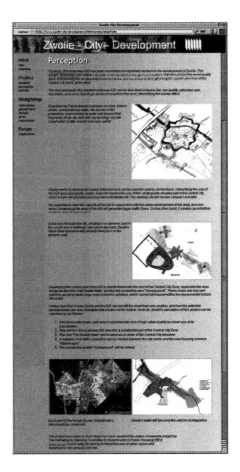

10-1. A Web-based design competition for Zwolle, the Netherlands.

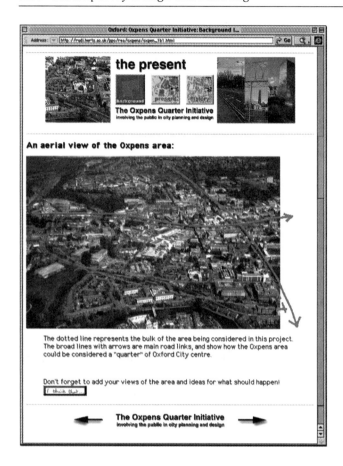

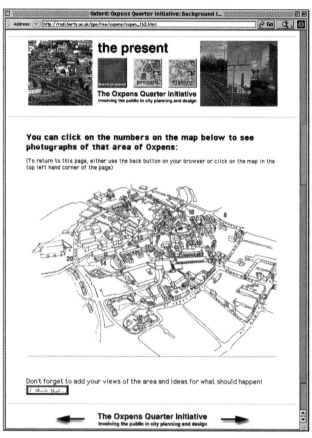

10-2 through 10-5. The Oxpens Quarter Initiative, a pioneering project in Web-based community planning. (Courtesy of Roger Evans Associates and RUDI)

creating shared visions, rather than *reacting* to someone else's. In Oxford, England, an innovative process was undertaken to involve the public in creating just such a vision. Oxpens, in the southwestern corner of the city, had been victimized by heavy-handed redevelopment in the late 1960s. Since then it had been developed haphazardly and was characterized by low-density, automobile-related sprawl. Oxpens had no cohesive identity, and it provided a notoriously bleak environment for pedestrians. Everyone felt that something was missing in this part of town, but when specific remedies were proposed, the ensuing debate tended to become confrontational, leaving developers and residents equally frustrated.

Instead of waiting for developers to come forward with new building schemes, the Oxford city council launched the Oxpens Quarter Initiative. Roger Evans Associates, an urban design consultant, was asked to engage city residents in a freewheeling discussion of possible futures for the Oxpens area. To reach the broadest cross section of the population, they offered several venues for participation:

- an awareness-raising event at a shopping center
- a treasure hunt through the study area
- a telephone hotline

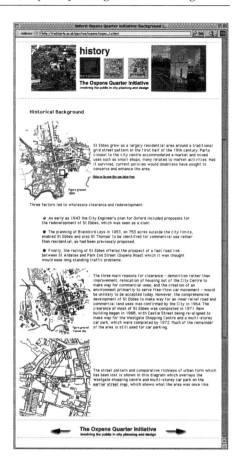

- a public workshop and exhibition
- a multimedia Web site

The Web site includes on-line discussions of various topics and specific locations within the study area, allowing residents to learn more about the area's history, provide comment to the project sponsors, and talk to each other about the issues (figs. 10-2, 10-3, 10-4, and 10-5). Hosted by the Resource for Urban Design Information (RUDI), it has become a worldwide model for how to implement an Internet-enabled community participation process.

Case Study: The South of Market Foundation's Living Neighborhood Map

The South of Market area in San Francisco (SoMa) is a former industrial-maritime zone that has re-emerged as a unique economic incubator for the city and the San Francisco Bay area. It is home to over nine thousand small businesses, including traditional light manufacturing, as well as a burgeoning multimedia industry. Design firms and software companies have long been attracted to SoMa's airy industrial loft spaces and relatively low rents.

The South of Market Foundation (SOMF) developed a dynamic

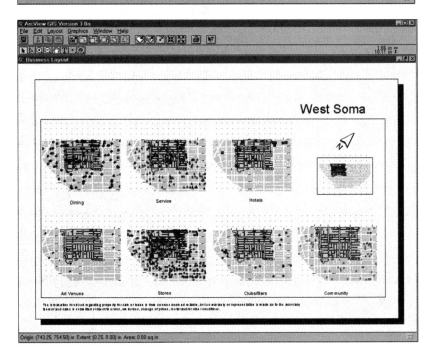

10-6, 10-7, and 10-8. The South of Market GIS project. (Courtesy of South of Market Foundation and GIS Planning, Inc.)

GIS-based "living neighborhood map," which catalogs the community's ever-changing matrix of people, businesses, and buildings and continuously archives its growth. It played a prominent role recently in clarifying the impacts of change in the neighborhood and giving support to planning decisions.

SOMF initially used its living neighborhood map to document the importance of the proximity of light industry and the multimedia

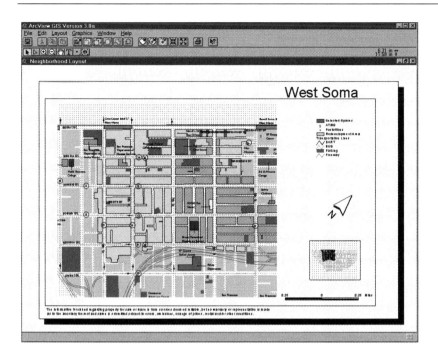

industry to downtown. Mapping was combined with interviews to probe the importance of various location factors to small businesses. The locations of demolition, renovation, and new building permits were overlaid on a business map that included employment and sales information. Change among commercial rent prices was also mapped, as were important economic linkages between business types.

The map's unit of analysis was the individual building parcel. Address-level information about businesses, residents, buildings, and land values was linked to a parcel map using GIS. A user could study any number of blocks, portions of blocks, or individual parcels and buildings. Data could also be analyzed and mapped by attribute, such as business type, household income, and number of employees (figs. 10-6, 10-7, and 10-8).

Cheryl Parker, who directed the SOMF project, said, "Such freedom of information revolutionizes the ability to track change in a community. Unlike traditional data sources like census data, time and boundary limits pose no constraints. Living neighborhood maps have several powerful applications in local community development. These include analytical uses, political applications, and as interactive tools which promote economic development. Community-wide access to up-to-date location-based information is giving neighborhood people a voice in their local economy, while mapping and field checking can mediate among stakeholder groups disputing land uses."

During the 1990s, an unusual type of gentrification was taking place in SoMa. Residents feared that small businesses were being driven out by pressure for new loft housing close to downtown. The San Francisco Planning Department publicly stated that not one business had been displaced by new residential construction and urged rezoning to support even more intensive residential construction in the area. Using ten-year-old census data, planners did not have an accurate view of recent trends in the area. The living neighborhood map became a planning tool that helped people understand the intricacies of the local economy and the importance of adjacency to various types of businesses. "Everyone began to see the situation for what it really was," said Parker. "Rather than reacting through emotion, people could present intelligent and well-informed fact-based economic arguments. Such an articulate and well-organized community, in turn, forced the planning department to engage in its own very rigorous study, employing the same GIS methodology used by the foundation."

Its own GIS studies convinced the planning department to revise its policy completely. It concluded that industrial lands were well utilized and development pressure was indeed causing certain industries to be displaced. The department committed itself to finding land elsewhere within city limits to develop high-density residential districts and to attempt to preserve the light industrial character of SoMa. To document its case, the planning department mapped and field-checked all uses on a parcel-by-parcel basis and came to the same conclusions as the SOMF.

Parker views the whole episode as reflecting very well on technology as an enabler of intelligent community participation in planning: "By both improving the quality of information and providing a means for working together, people stopped reacting through emotion, hearsay, and opinions and were thus much more credible and powerful in arguing in the public arena for their rights as a community. GIS played a role akin to a neutral moderator throughout the story. It assisted people who were very much at odds with each other in finding a common ground for communicating."

Venues for Web-based Community Planning

Debates about planning and development tend to become adversarial very easily. Community-based planning is most likely to succeed when it is sponsored by a neutral moderator in a trusted venue. This is as true on the Internet as it is with traditional forms of participatory planning. What kinds of neutral platforms are appropriate for encouraging discussion of planning and design issues on-line? Aside from local planning agencies, three such platforms are community networks, non-profit planning organizations, and regional planning boards.

Community Networks

A number of communities have created public networks expressly for fostering electronic democracy. The first of these was Santa Monica's Public Electronic Network (PEN), which began in 1989 with two components: a system for allowing residents to send e-mail to public officials, and an electronic bulletin board for public discussion of civic issues. It was hailed at the time as reflective of the city's belief in "human-scale community, participatory democracy, and one-class society," aided by technology. The city councillor David Finkel, who cast the only vote against PEN, quickly became a convert. "What democracy is all about is engagement," he said. "What urban life as we know it in the 1990s is all about is disengagement." He appreciated the ease with which residents could communicate with elected representatives and agency heads, without the usual bureaucratic gatekeepers blocking the way. Everyone from the police chief to the local congressman was soon hearing directly from citizens.

Everyone who lived or worked in Santa Monica was given a free account with e-mail and access to the on-line conferences, which quickly became a huge hit with city residents. Conferences were organized into issue areas, including one devoted to land-use planning, growth, and zoning issues (fig. 10-9).

PEN began before the Web, so it has always been a text-based, nongraphical system. Although that limits its ability to host much discussion about visual issues, it has led to a kind of intimacy among participants that is remarkable. One early on-line conference bemoaned the

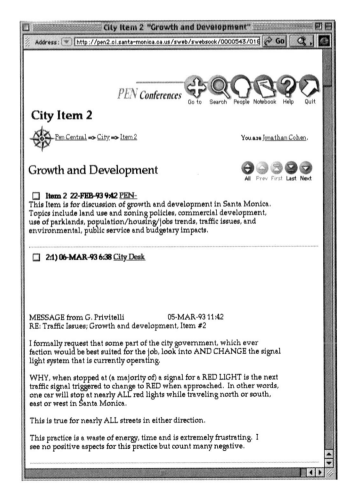

10-9. Santa Monica's PEN was a pioneering on-line community.

growing population of homeless people on Santa Monica's streets. After several months of heated discussion, it was revealed that one of the most articulate participants in the conference was Don Paschal, himself a homeless man who was logging on at the public library. He told the conference that he could not work because he had no place to shower or store his things during the day. That shocked people who had never knowingly spoken to a homeless person before, and it led to the founding of an on-line committee to sponsor the construction of a public shower and locker facility. The committee met and worked on-line for six months before their first "live" encounter. The facility was built and is operated by the Salvation Army.

Keith Kurtz is the current director of Santa Monica's Information Systems Department and in charge of PEN. He said the city uses PEN to stimulate discussion of planning issues, but in an informal and unstructured way. An example he cites is public discussion now underway of how to reuse a historical beach house built by William Randolph Hearst. The city acquired it after decades of neglect, and PEN is being used to build a consensus about its future.

The National Telecommunications and Information Administration, part of the Department of Commerce, has been a spur to development of community networks throughout the United States. Approximately $16 to $20 million is granted annually to community groups and local government agencies, so that nonprofit organizations can have access to the same communication tools that the private sector enjoys.

One such recipient is the Blacksburg Electronic Village, a joint venture of Blacksburg, Virginia, Bell Atlantic, and Virginia Tech. In 1993 the university's existing data network was extended to include the surrounding town—its government, institutions, businesses, and residents. By 1997 69 percent of Blacksburg's 36,000 residents were using BEV to access the Internet, compared to only 16 percent in surrounding Montgomery County. Office and apartment buildings and new home subdivisions were wired with high-speed connections. Access is free for residents, and Web hosting is offered to community groups. There are bulletin boards, e-mail lists, and on-line chat programs (fig. 10-10). Local businesses, two-thirds of which have Web sites linked to BEV, have used it as a springboard to international exposure and sales. Schools, libraries, and senior centers are all wired. A training center offers classes in Web design. The program has been so successful that the BEV now offers a turnkey electronic village solution to other communities seeking to build civic networks. Like any business engaged in e-commerce, BEV carefully tracks the usage trends and demographic characteristics of the people using the system.

Carol Bousquet, head of the Blacksburg Planning and Engineering Department, had this to say about the Blacksburg Electronic Village:

> We have been actively seeking opportunities to tap this resource to reach the citizens we serve and to improve our processes and products.

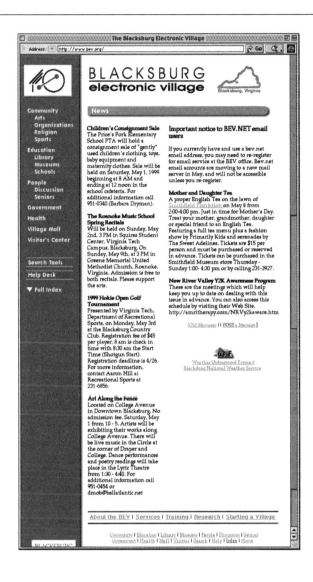

10-10. The home page of the Blacksburg Electronic Village.

Blacksburg is in the midst of updating its comprehensive plan. As we began this process, we distributed a survey throughout the community about preferences for the future. In addition to hard copies, the survey was made available, and responses were received back, through BEV. Once a draft "Portrait of Blacksburg in 2046" was developed based on the survey responses and community meetings, we made it available under the Comprehensive Plan section of the Blacksburg home page. Under this category, we have also posted completed drafts for greenways, bikeway-walkways, solid waste management, sanitary sewer, water, transportation, and others. Each of these listings notes an e-mail address to send comments. Citizens can also provide comments easily to any town office by clicking on a form which will then be e-mailed to the department of their choice. Members of the community can receive applications for building permits, certificates of occupancy, and work order permits. Soon all permits for the town will be available through BEV.

The Internet has provided opportunities to expand dialogue between organizations regarding planning. In addition, we have sent statements of the town's position to state and national politicians. To do this electronically enhances our ability to respond to proposed legislation in a timely manner. We continue to seek new opportunities to reach the public and to use the Internet to enhance our planning efforts.

Nonprofit Civic Organizations

Nonprofit civic organizations provide another opportunity for Web-enabled public participation. The San Francisco Planning and Urban Research Association (SPUR), a nonprofit public policy think tank, proposes to use a Web site to encourage public participation in the redevelopment of Mission Bay in San Francisco (fig. 10-11). Mixed-use housing, commercial development, and a new campus for the University of California are now planned for the area, a former industrial/maritime zone. Plans call for the creation of fifteen thousand housing units and thirty thousand new jobs.

The goals of this Web site are to increase effective public participation in the design of a major redevelopment proposal and to enhance access of the public to information about the context, the proposed solutions, and the process that will be used to make deci-

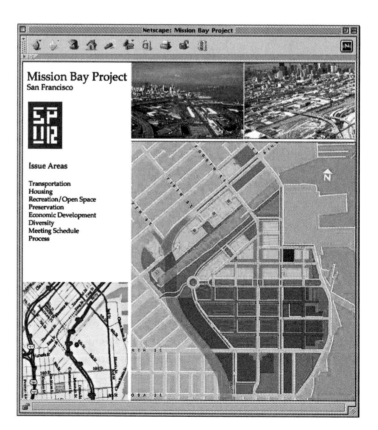

10-11. A Web site for community education about and participation in the Mission Bay project in San Francisco, developed by Jonathan Cohen and Associates in conjunction with SPUR.

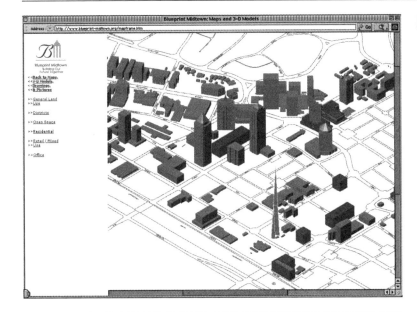

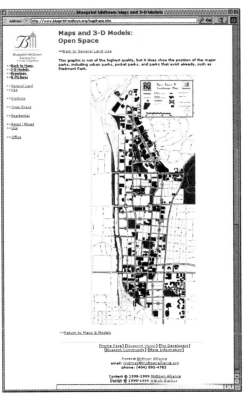

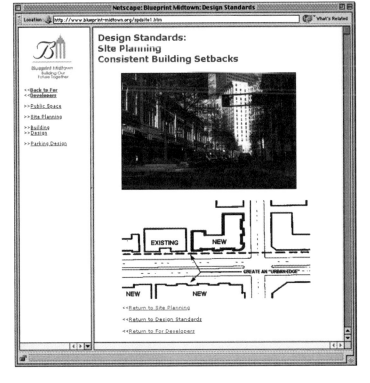

10-12, 10-13, and 10-14. The Midtown Alliance of Atlanta uses its site to promulgate development goals and guidelines. (Courtesy of The Midtown Alliance and A Nelessen Associates)

sions. A secondary goal is to prove the effectiveness of the Web at broadening the reach of public participation in community design and to encourage its use in other communities. Information about the site and surroundings, the physical and historical context, and the rationale for development will be explained with maps, aerial photos, GIS information, QuickTime VR panoramas, historical drawings, and photos. Issues that the proposed development raises for the community will be presented evenhandedly, including transportation impacts, provision of affordable housing and open space, implications for the tax base, and economic impacts. Specific development proposals will be modeled on the site using photomontage, VRML, and other techniques of architectural representation, to allow citizens to understand and experience the development options as accurately as possible.

Rather than waiting for developers to propose projects, some communities are beginning to plan proactively, and they are using Web sites to promote their planning goals. The Midtown Alliance in Atlanta, for example, began a community visioning process in 1995 that focused on improving public safety, encouraging appropriate land use, promoting arts development, creating pedestrian-friendly streets, improving public transportation, and spurring economic development.

Through a community-based consultation process facilitated by planner Anton Nelessen, a diverse sampling of midtown stakeholders was asked to evaluate the existing conditions and arrive at a consensus regarding a future direction for the area's transportation, zoning, and urban development. Using a variety of media, the Blueprint Midtown Web site presents this vision in detail, together with recommendations for site and building design, streetscapes, and land use that will enable developers to implement it (figs. 10-12, 10-13, and 10-14, page 233).

Regional Planning Boards

Regional planning boards, such as the Association of Bay Area Governments, the Puget Sound Regional Council, and the Regional Plan Association in the New York area, are excellent venues for Web-enabled public participation in planning. Such regional planning issues as transportation, jobs/housing balance, and affordable housing are particularly difficult to engage with the public using traditional techniques, because of the physical difficulties and expense of reaching people over a wide area.

Transportation and Infrastructure Planning

Civil engineering projects are a major part of the built environment and just like city planners, transportation and infrastructure planners are faced with the challenge of educating and involving the public in decision making. The Web is beginning to play an important role here as well, as the following examples demonstrate:

■ The Institute for Civil Infrastructure Systems (ICIS) was established within New York University's Robert F. Wagner Graduate School of Public Service in January 1998. Its purpose is to foster means for civil infrastructure agencies to listen and respond to community goals, values, and expectations in planning transportation and other large infrastructure projects. ICIS views the Internet as an important tool for involving and informing the public about such projects and having an effect on the decisions that lead to their construction. Its Web site is a clearinghouse of participatory case studies for communities to use to broaden public consultation in infrastructure projects.

■ In the course of preparing a draft environmental impact statement (DEIS) for the rerouting of U.S. Highway 93 in Arizona, the Federal Highway Administration and the consulting firm CH2M Hill prepared an interactive Web site for presenting alternatives and receiving comments. The present highway crosses the Colorado River on the top of Hoover Dam, presenting a number of safety and congestion issues. The Web site allows visitors to view simulations of the proposed alternative routes, taken from eye level and aerial viewpoints (fig. 10-15). After viewing the simulations, visitors are invited to make comments on the DEIS, which are entered into a searchable database.

■ The Pennsylvania Department of Transportation has created a Web site to involve Harrisburg area citizens in the Intelligent Transportation System Early Deployment Study. The Web site describes proposed transportation technologies, which are aimed at enhancing mobility, improving safety, and reducing environmental impact. The public is invited to complete a stakeholder survey that will identify the transportation needs and problems in the Harrisburg metropolitan area. The site provides point-and-click contact information for the project managers, as well as information and links to other agencies and organizations that are project participants.

In Europe and America, three-dimensional visualization techniques have been used to aid public understanding of transportation projects before they are built:

■ The Austrian digital arts group Ars Electronica created a VR "cave" to show citizens the effect of a new road proposed for their neighborhood. Everyone who lived in the area was invited to the cave, where neighbors could place themselves on the balcony of their homes, view the existing and then the proposed road, and listen to simulated road noise. This simulation was invaluable in improving understanding and developing the consensus needed to get the road built.

■ To enable public visualization of a proposed cable-stayed bridge in Rotterdam, a VRML model was constructed and placed on the Internet. Visitors to the Web site could experience the bridge from any of four vantage points: an aerial view, a view from the bridge, a moving view from a tram car crossing the bridge, and a view from the water (figs. 10-19, 10-20, and 10-21, page 237).

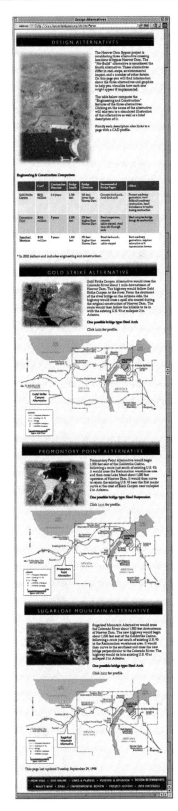

10-15. The range of options for the Hoover Dam bypass is modeled on this Web site.

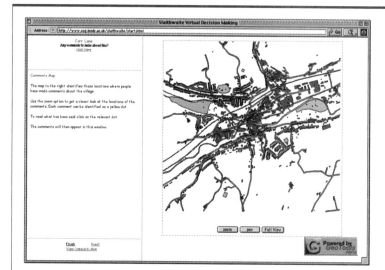

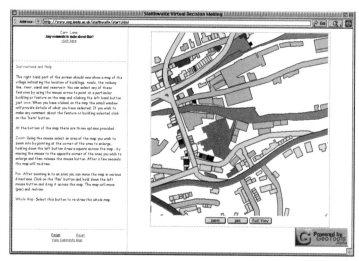

10-16 and 10-17. The people of the West Yorkshire village of Slaithwaite in Great Britain are being given a greater say in local planning decisions via this Web-based experiment in community participation. (Courtesy School of Geography, University of Leeds)

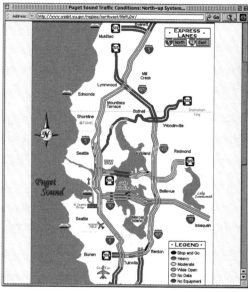

10-18. Real-time traffic information for the Seattle region.

Tools for Participation

Some of the tools and techniques available to Web site designers to foster participation in design and planning include:

- Meeting schedules hyperlinked to agendas and other supporting material. Citizens can review the same material prepared for planning commissioners, for example, before they enter the meeting room.
- On-line forms are used to enable Web site visitors to enter data, leave comments, request more information, ask to be contacted, and so on. Planning staff should compile such responses and post results back onto the Web site to complete a feedback circle.
- "Click-throughs," a technique already widely used in e-commerce, shows site administrators which pages were visited, for how long and in what order. Such information provides clues to visitors' interests and concerns.

- Threaded discussions allow visitors to join the debate on a particular topic or start a new one. The full exchange on a topic can be reviewed at any time. Participants visit when convenient—they never need to be on-line at the same time, yet a very lively discussion is possible.
- Java applications permit visitors to view maps and models interactively, zooming and panning from within a browser window (figs. 10-16, and 10-17).
- Some sites provide real-time traffic information, weather conditions, and live Webcams (fig. 10-18).
- E-mail links are provided to enable direct communication with public officials, project sponsors, consultants, planning staff, and neighborhood associations.

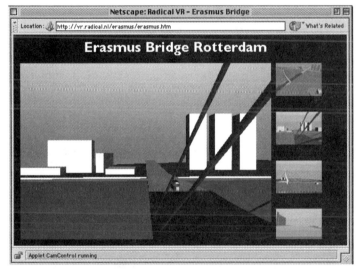

10-19, 10-20, and 10-21. A Web-based VRML model of a proposed bridge for Rotterdam. Viewers can select from several saved viewpoints, including the view from a streetcar as it traverses the bridge. (Courtesy of Lex van der Sluijs, Radical Holding, BV; designed and produced by Lex van der Sluijs MSc. ©1997, Radical Holding BV)

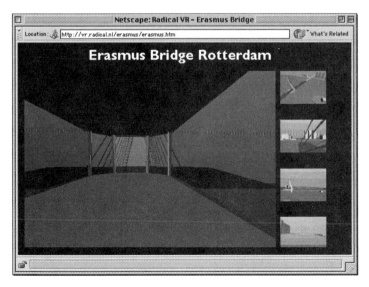

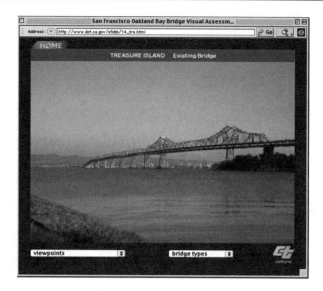

10-22, 10-23, and 10-24. Alternatives for rebuilding the San Francisco–Oakland Bay Bridge are presented on a Web site by the California Department of Transportation.

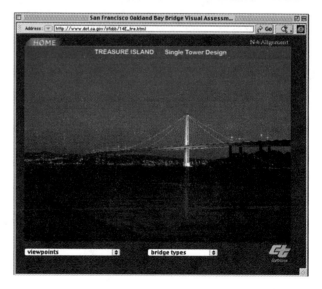

■ The California Department of Transportation created a Web site for citizen review of design alternatives for the rebuilding of a portion of the San Francisco–Oakland Bay Bridge (figs. 10-22, 10-23, and 10-24).

The Centre for Landscape Research (CLR) at the University of Toronto envisions a radical transformation of practice in the environmental design disciplines through the use of networked communication. CLR defines its objective as finding "a spatial language supported in a computational media accessible to everyone if society is to make more intelligent environmental decisions." The Crossings is an experiment in developing an interactive hypermodel of a landscape that can be used collaboratively via the Internet. To construct such a model, a group of landscape architects and artists borrowed the simulator used by the port of Rotterdam for training the pilots of huge tankers. The simulator uses a 360-degree array of twelve powerful Silicon Graphics workstations (fig. 10-25).

10-25. The Centre for Landscape Research (CLR) at the University of Toronto envisions a radical transformation of practice in the environmental design disciplines through the use of networked communication.

Information and Equity

Some people feel that Internet access is not widespread enough to offer a truly democratic means of participation, that the Internet has in fact created a wider chasm between information haves and have-nots. It's an important point, and wider public access to the Internet should certainly be a public policy goal. But many people are effectively excluded from planning debates already, not because they don't have a computer, but because they do not have the time, inclination, or education required to participate. With the traditional methods of fostering participation, such as planning workshops and neighborhood association meetings, the percentage of the affected population that participates is very low, in all kinds of neighborhoods, rich and poor. If the Internet can raise that rate several-fold, as conservative projections indicate, should planners hold back because a group of people that is already excluded might continue to be excluded?

Instead, planners should design participation programs to include a significant outreach component to underserved communities. Schools and libraries, even in the poorest areas, are now or will soon be equipped with computers and Internet access. Public access computers should be supplemented with planning-related education programs directed specifically to disadvantaged portions of the population.

The Internet offers planners the opportunity to provide access to information to those who have been historically excluded from it. One such effort, called Neighborhood Knowledge Los Angeles (NKLA), has been undertaken by UCLA's School of Public Policy and Social Research. Recognizing that data about such known precursors of urban blight as unpaid tax and utility bills and unremedied building code violations was gathering dust in city halls, a group of researchers and students sought to create a single Web-based gateway to public information about Los Angeles' housing stock. With grants from the National Telecommunications and Information Infrastructure Assistance Program and the Los Angeles Housing Department, the UCLA team collects data from a variety of sources—the Department of Water and Power, the Housing Department, the Building and Safety Department, and the tax collector—and maps it to individual parcels throughout the city, using GIS technology from ESRI (fig. 10-26).

Neal Richman, associate director of UCLA's Advanced Policy Institute, said, "I'm excited about using these technologies to share information and therefore share power. We've been able to break down all these little fiefdoms of isolated information." The Community Development Technology Center in Los Angeles trains community development corporations, neighborhood groups, and private citizens in the computer skills needed to use NKLA to assist in neighborhood preservation and development efforts. "These are people who don't typically have access to computers," said Denise Fairchild, president of the center. "NKLA provides powerful access to

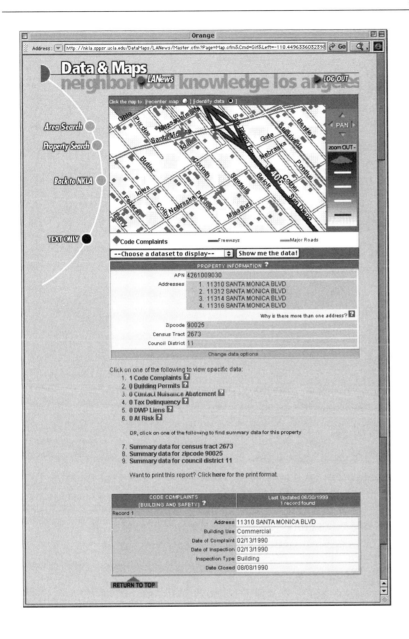

10-26. Neighborhood Knowledge Los Angeles.

information they wouldn't get otherwise. They can see trends in their neighborhood, see sore spots, and see how they can intervene or look into it further." And nonprofit housing developers such as Civitas Housing use NKLA to scout potential sites for rehab projects.

By shining light on information that was previously inaccessible, NKLA has even had an impact on city policies and enforcement procedures. Now every multifamily housing structure in Los Angeles will be inspected regularly, even if no complaint has been received, and inspectors will carry pen-based computers with a two-way link to the city database, so that code violations can be tracked as easily as Hertz cars and FedEx packages.

11 Islands of

New construction and renovation account for roughly one-tenth of the U.S. gross national product and directly employ nearly 6 million people. Worldwide spending on construction exceeds $4.5 trillion dollars annually, around $500 billion in the United States alone. AEC is a huge industry, yet it is in many ways the opposite of an industrial process. Its products are unique prototypes built in place one at a time. The economies of scale that apply to mass production generally cannot be realized in design and construction. It simply is not economical to spend the same kind of resources designing and constructing a single building as are spent designing a product that may be manufactured thousands or millions of times.

Compared to manufacturing, the AEC industry is very fragmented. Each project is a one-time collaboration of many organizations—owner, designer, builder, subcontractor, material supplier. The industry is characterized by small companies and by significant levels of outsourcing in both design and construction firms. The cost of entry into the business is low, and the failure rate is high. The work is more labor intensive than manufacturing, and productivity is comparatively low. Construction is also highly cyclical relative to the overall economy, increasing the risk. Construction firms tend to be undercapitalized and operate with low overheads relative to the size of projects undertaken. Relatively small firms have traditionally served local, rather than national, markets. The largest construction companies have tiny market shares compared to their counterparts in manufacturing industries. Turner Corporation, the largest general contractor in the United States, ranks a lowly 375 in the Fortune 500, and most AEC firms are far smaller than that.

Industry-wide standardization of means and methods is almost non-existent, and the organizations that purport to speak for the industry are themselves fragmented and weak. Most of the innovations that do

Automation

occur are focused on construction materials and techniques, not the product delivery process. Innovations tend to be closely held by companies and not widely disseminated throughout the industry. Because design and construction functions are highly compartmentalized, the innovations that might flow from interdisciplinary synergy are suppressed as well. Not only has fragmentation resulted in inefficiency, but the productivity gains forced by competition in other industries have not occurred either. Competition in construction is often reduced to price alone, rather than value, in part because the very fragmentation of the industry makes value difficult to measure. Even as construction has boomed in the last decade, profit margins remain low.

Fragmentation also exists because building is regulated locally. For many building types, several layers of government must be approached for permits. Even if codes were standardized, regional variations in market conditions, climate, and labor practices tend to make building a relatively small-scale, local affair. Because of its local nature, the AEC industry has been protected from the pressures of globalization that have had a profound impact on manufacturing, beginning with the auto industry in the 1970s. But these pressures, as painful as they have been for manufacturers, have been a major stimulus to reform and efficiency.

In the building industry, remarkably little is spent on research and development, less than 0.5 percent of annual revenue, compared to 3.7 percent in manufacturing, according to the U.S. Census Bureau. There is also a low rate of spending on education and training, particularly for the rank-and-file workforce and lower levels of management. The industry has historically been characterized by an unusual amount of upward mobility from craft worker to manager or owner, with little formal education required. Front-line workers in construction receive an average of twenty-four hours of training per year, compared to thir-

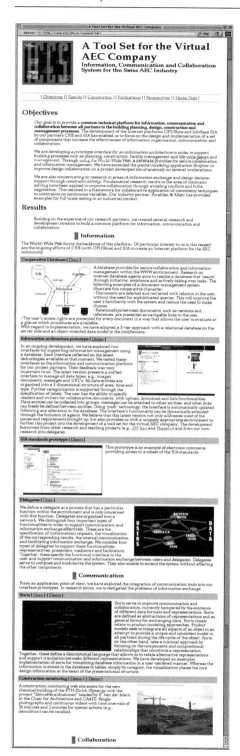

11-1. A Toolset for the Virtual AEC Company. (Courtesy of David Kurmann, ETH Zurich)

ty-four in all other industries. Construction labor is hired on a per-project basis, with most companies keeping only a small cadre of permanent employees. Formal training in the building trades has traditionally been offered by joint union/employer-sponsored apprenticeship programs. Because employment is project-based, the worker's relationship with the craft union is usually far stronger than his attachment to an employer, but as union influence has waned, so has the level of worker training. In North America, as compared to Europe, there is little publicly supported training in construction trades to replace it.

Increasingly, building is about managing information as much as managing products and services. Just like the agriculture and mining industries, the construction industry will inevitably change from a low-skill, high-labor industry to a knowledge-added endeavor requiring a higher level of investment in training, technology, and business process engineering. Without investments in training and R&D, firms cannot innovate. Without innovation, firms cannot differentiate themselves in the marketplace.

In manufacturing CAD/CAM integration has resulted in productivity gains that the building industry can only dream about. Product design and manufacturing have been fully integrated—one informs the other. General Motors, for example, routinely involves suppliers in parts design. Boeing is able to preassemble whole aircraft designs digitally, then share pieces of the model with component subcontractors.

In modern manufacturing the entire relationship between design and production has been turned around. Results have included a shorter product cycles, more choice for customers, and real competition based on product value. Designers do not simply create products that are functional and attractive; their designs must consider efficient fabrication and maintenance as well. Manufacturers want designs to be produced with minimal factory retooling, for example, and expect designers to consider such factors along with traditional ones. Increasingly manufacturers are able to respond to the smallest change in market demand and customer preferences. The key to the feedback loop between design and production has been information technology, the ability of manufacturers to gather information from the production line and from customers and suppliers and then incorporate it into the design process.

In contrast, it is sadly the case that builders and designers rarely evaluate even their own products through post-occupancy data collection. The feedback loop between design and production that is so valuable to manufacturers does not exist in the building industry. Post-occupancy evaluation, if it is done at all, is too often carried out in litigation. That's a shame, because lessons learned in completed buildings could be applied to the next design. Scholars have long talked about "buildings that learn": structures that evaluate themselves and feed back information to inform the design process, but little has been done to bring this practice about. For now, this kind of vital information is lost.

Evaluation can become an integral part of the design process, but only when significant changes have been made in the way that information is collected, shared, and reused throughout the industry. Better project monitoring and information flow require closing the loop of design–construct–inhabit/operate–evaluate–design, making it a circular process rather than the traditional linear one. The industry must shift to a process that incorporates life-cycle-based decisions all the way from initial programming and site selection through to the eventual retirement of the building. This can only occur when the flow of information throughout the building process has been integrated (fig. 11-1).

The industry's fragmentation derives in part from the historical separation of design and construction that evolved over the course of the last 150 years. Ironically, it was a separation heavily influenced by early manufacturing. Design became a linear process, modeled on the assembly line: raw materials come in at one end, and finished goods go out the other. Programming would lead to design, and as components of knowledge or skill were added along the way, the result would be a set of documents that prescribed for the builders precisely what they were to do. Eventually this assembly-line paradigm became institutionalized in the architectural profession, spelled out in the project phases described in the AIA documents. Each phase—schematic design, design development, construction documents—resulted in a product that became the raw material of the subsequent phase. Not until one phase was completed could the next begin. All design work became the domain of professionals, and those further downstream in the process—the contractor and product manufacturer—were largely excluded. In this model, production has little opportunity to inform design early enough in the process for it to be effective.

Yet if you ask architects to describe how they work, most will describe it as an iterative, cyclical process. They begin by tackling the largest issues of a design problem first and then, through a process of trial and error, proceed in ever-tighter circles of refinement until an ideal solution is achieved. They listen, propose solutions, present them, revise them—synthesis, analysis, and evaluation, again and again. That is quite a different reality than the onrushing freight train envisioned by the AIA documents.

The strict division between design and construction functions began to break down as building systems became increasingly complex. After World War II, the percentage of the total work devoted to electrical and mechanical systems began to increase sharply. All the performance specifications, design/build subcontracting, shop drawings and material samples, mock-ups, and laboratory tests that a typical project generates testify to a design and construction process that is far more interwoven than the AIA documents would lead one to believe. The lines drawn between design and production have blurred so much that the distinction may already be obsolete.

Whole-Life Costing

Why is the ability to track life-cycle costs of building products so important? A rule of thumb is that for every dollar spent on the construction of a building, ten dollars will be spent on maintenance, repair, and renovation. Unplanned and unexpected maintenance and renovation costs may amount to half of all money spent each year on existing buildings. Whole-life costing is a means of comparing options and their associated cost and income streams over a period of time. Costs to be taken into account include initial procurement costs, opportunity costs, and future costs. Initial costs include design, construction, and installation, purchase or leasing, and fees and charges. Future costs include operating expenses, such as energy use, cleaning, inspection, maintenance, security, and management over the life of structure. Loss of revenue must also be taken into account; the business losses of a retailer who cannot sell goods during maintenance work, for example, might exceed the original cost of construction. And opportunity costs represent the loss of revenue that might have flowed had the capital been invested elsewhere.

Islands of Automation

The amount of information generated in construction projects is huge—yet communication among the participants is disjointed. It has been estimated that a staggering 30 percent of the cost of buildings is lost because of poor communication within the industry.

Paul Teicholz, founder of Stanford University's Center for Integrated Facilities Engineering, has spoken of islands of automation, in which most design work is done in the isolation of a single discipline. Before joining Stanford as a Research Professor of Civil Engineering, he was the manager of information technology for Guy F. Atkinson Construction Company. Teicholz saw inefficiencies in the construction process; computers were being used only to automate specific tasks, rather than in an integrative way to advance the project. He attributed many preventable errors and countless overruns of time and cost to communication inefficiencies. He believed that owners were given little insight into how the design they commissioned actually worked. "During construction, we spent most of our time firefighting—that's what we called management."

How to integrate the multiple disciplines of design, particularly at the early, conceptual level, where changes can still be made without significant cost or redesign, is the challenge. And beyond the design team, the challenge of integrating design information with the broader business goals of the client and project is even greater (figs. 11-2, 11-3, 11-4).

The first applications of information technology to the design and construction process made the completion of individual tasks easier: drawing a set of construction documents, preparing a specification, creating a CPM chart. They did nothing to integrate the overall process or to make it easier for the various participants to coordinate their activities; they did not do a good job of interoperating. Integration was now even more difficult, because incompatible systems used by individual disciplines created artificial barriers that hadn't existed before.

In a typical design process, each discipline constructs its own "model" of the building and represents its understanding of that model using symbols and language that is unique to that discipline. These symbols are laboriously translated into formats that other disciplines can use. Often they are imperfectly understood by other members of the design team, including those responsible for overall coordination, typically the architect. For the most part, design information remains within "knowledge domains," behind walls of jargon and incompatible means of representation.

Throughout the AEC industry, automation has proceeded in a piecemeal fashion, with each discipline developing its own largely incompatible symbols and methods. Tools have been developed primarily for the benefit of the individual firm and the tasks it performs, rather than for the benefit of overall project goals. Architects use CAD to automate document production; contractors use project manage-

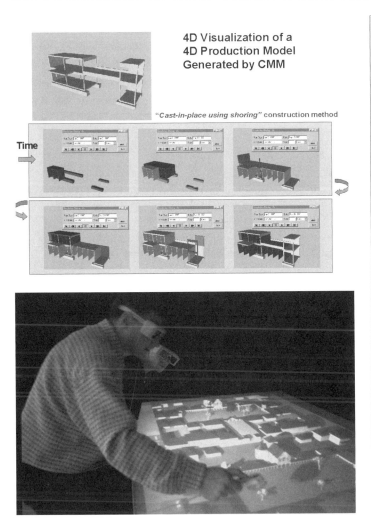

4D Visualization of a
4D Production Model
Generated by CMM

"Cast-in-place using shoring" construction method

Time

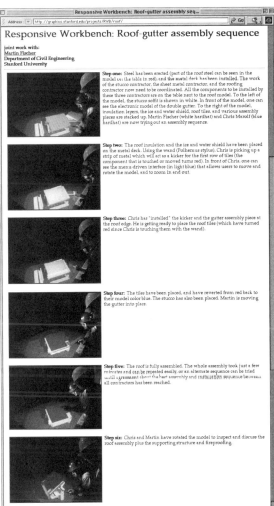

ment software to generate schedules and spreadsheets, estimates, and contracts; suppliers use their systems to track prices and deliveries. For architects the computer replaced the drafting board but did not alter the basic paradigm of producing drawings as standalone, paper-based documents. The difference now is that the paper documents are merely reports of information stored in computer files, rather than drawings that once both reported and stored information. Hence the widespread confusion over what constitutes a digital "original."

Most document formats are still based on historical paper equivalents, using standard drawing sets and paper sizes. When information is handed off from one participant to another, it is usually in the form of an exchange of paper documents, even though the information was created on a computer. So the printed page remains the only common interface between all the discipline-specific computer applications. Software companies have contributed mightily to this problem by locking in their customers to proprietary, mutually exclusive file formats that compound the difficulty of collaboration.

11-2. At Stanford University, researchers under the direction of Martin Fischer are experimenting with four-dimensional CAD, which integrates the geometric and temporal aspects of the building process. The erection of a building is visualized as if in time-lapse animation. (Courtesy Martin Fischer, Stanford University)

11-3 and 11-4. Stanford University's Civil Engineering department is experimenting with advanced three-dimensional visualization for construction. (Courtesy Martin Fischer, Stanford University)

Now that the powerful communications capabilities of the Internet are so widely available, the problems of communication within the AEC community have become that much more painfully clear. Just when we have the capability of communicating more effectively, such communication is frustrated by the incompatibility of our languages. It's as if we've all just been connected to a telephone system only to discover that we haven't a common language.

The second wave of information technology in AEC is signaled by the arrival of a networked model of computing. Networked computing presents the opportunity to reform the entire building enterprise. It can do this by integrating information from many sources and then redistributing it to the many points of execution where it is needed. This second wave could revolutionize the industry.

In 1996 the National Science and Technology Council established seven national construction goals, which included a 50 percent reduction in delivery time, a 50 percent reduction in operations, maintenance, and energy costs, and a 30 percent increase in productivity (output per work hour). At a workshop on how to achieve these goals held in 1996 by the National Institute of Building Sciences (NIBS), forty-one organizations representing builders, designers, and property owners concluded that the major obstacles were "in the process—a process that starts with the need for a timely decision to begin and continues through site selection, community involvement, zoning approval, regulatory clearance, design, plan reviews, permits, construction, commissioning, operation, maintenance, renovation, and ultimately, demolition" (NIBS 1996).

In the United Kingdom, authorities are getting involved in reforming an industry they view as lagging in innovation and productivity. Small wonder—government accounts for 40 percent of British construction industry business. A 1994 report by Sir Michael Latham entitled *Constructing the Team* was scathing in its criticism of an industry riddled with conflict, cost overruns, quality lapses, and process inefficiency. The report led to a thorough government review of its own practices as a client and the issuance of a set of government procurement guidelines that sought to standardize contracting procedures in the public sector. One outcome of Latham's report was the formation of a joint government-industry Construction Industry Board, to represent the industry and promote change. The CIB's early work has focused on developing a set of "best practices" for construction companies, including an emphasis on research for innovation and improved project communications among client, designer, and builder.

One early result has been the development of a Generic Design and Construction Process Protocol by a joint industry-academic group led by the University of Salford. Its premise is that no amount of information technology applied to a fragmented process will untangle it. Any centralized system of distributing project information will stand a greater chance of succeeding if preceded by reform of the underlying process. The Integrated Information Initiative of the Construction Specifications Institute agrees; it is developing an Integrated Information Model for the construction industry that will be scalable across many types of projects.

The integration of information throughout the building process requires breaking out of traditional boxes. Individual professional groups such as the American Institute of Architects have striven to standardize the process of service delivery within their own domains, but none has tried to create a standard process of conceiving, designing, erecting, and managing a building. Robert Johnson, Director of the CRS Center for Leadership and Management in the Design and Construction Industry at Texas A&M, believes "the push for data integration has to come from the building owners. They have the most to gain and the biggest leverage over the process."

Rationalization of the industry is likely to mean major organizational and contractual changes for both designers and builders. A full team approach is needed, with budget, project scope, and scheduling considered in earliest design. Allowing project information to flow from designer to estimator to builder to owner and back again should be the goal. It will mean moving the involvement of builders forward in the process to capture their expertise in costing and constructibility, and it will mean giving designers a meaningful role later in the process, so that they can apply lessons learned in building and operating facilities to the next project. The key to this integration will be the effective deployment of information technology to capture, store, and reuse vital project information.

The existing contractual structure of the industry (and the boundaries of responsibility drawn by the professional liability insurers) conspire against such organizational changes. There are also cultural, educational, and social class differences between professionals, businesspeople, and tradespeople. There are issues of proprietary expertise, intellectual property, and copyright. Importantly, there is as yet no industry mechanism for allocating risk and reward for innovation. If an architect proposes a successful design innovation, for example, the benefits are likely to flow only to the owner. If the innovation turns out to be failure, however, the architect may find herself defending a lawsuit.

Design and construction are fraught with liability risks. Although they claim to put the client first, architects, engineers, and contractors are well aware that any given project might be a profitable success for one party and a purgatory of financial ruin for another. Even when the process is relatively smooth, it is a rare project that perfectly aligns the financial goals of architect, owner, consultant, and contractor. The low level of trust and divergence of goals among project participants is a major source of project delays, errors, and lawsuits, and it serves to stifle innovation as well.

The practice of open bidding legally required in most public sector construction reinforces this divergence of goals. Not only do low-bid awards completely preclude the possibility of information sharing between designer and builder, they expose public agencies to the practice of lowballing. Rather than delivering the highest value to the owner, low-bid contracting works against the very idea of life-cycle costing.

New Modes of Project Delivery

The industry has responded to customer demands for better integration with new modes of project delivery, notably *partnering* and *design/build* (sole-source delivery). Both offer the possibility of compressing the project delivery schedule and informing the design process early on with construction phase information. Partnering, a term borrowed from manufacturing, refers to a management structure that facilitates collaboration across contractual boundaries between designers and builders. Partnering may be project specific or a strategic, long-term relationship between companies. The idea is to align the objectives of each organization to the overall goals of the project. In a relationship between an architect and a contractor, for example, partnering does not alter the contractual obligations between the two parties, or between each of them and the client. A variant of partnering called Construction Management at Risk involves selecting a contractor during the design phase for cost and quality input, who then builds the project for a "cost plus" fee. The advantages of such an approach include better coordination between design and construction and support for fast-track scheduling and earlier ordering of long-lead-time items.

Design/build, on the other hand, puts design and construction functions under a single contract and changes the historical relationship of parties. As with partnering, design/build contracts may be undertaken by two companies in a permanent or temporary relationship, but in every case there is one entity with overall responsibility. In the vast majority of design/build arrangements, the designer is a subcontractor or employee of the builder.

Many architects feel threatened by a loss of independence in design/build, as well as a perceived deemphasis on aesthetics and design values. Many also feel that owners do not appreciate the inherent conflict of interest in having the architect employed by or in partnership with the contractor. Some architects are leading a movement toward designer-led, rather than builder-led, sole-source delivery, but without much success. In 1998, for example, only one out of twenty-seven design/build contracts awarded by the Veterans Administration was designer-led. The reason for this is pretty clear: over the last several decades, architects and their insurers tried to insulate themselves from construction safety issues. Language was added to design contracts disavowing the "means, methods, and sequences of construction." As a result contractors, not designers, developed the bonding capacity and financial capitalization required by lenders.

Some home builders have long integrated development, design, and construction functions within their organizations. Architects are quick to point out that such hybrid organizations rarely produce outstanding design, which they believe can only come from an independent design firm. Nevertheless, a comparative study sponsored by the Construction Industry Institute of 351 building projects ranging in size from 5,000 square feet to over 2 million square feet indicated that, when all other variables were constant, design/build project unit costs were 6.1 percent lower than design/bid/build, and overall project schedules were 33.5 percent shorter (Konchar 1998).

As a result, design/build is gathering steam. The Department of Commerce predicts that by 2001, sole-source design/build firms will be responsible for over 50 percent of U.S. construction projects, up from only 10 percent ten years ago. This trend is spreading into public-sector contracting as well. In many states, laws that forbade sole-source public contracting are being repealed, and some federal agencies are embracing design/build as well. New York's Tishman Construction, for example, recently sole-sourced a 1 million–square foot federal office building in lower Manhattan. The U.S. Navy recently undertook a large-scale redevelopment of the Washington Navy Yard, employing an innovative two-stage process known as "bridging." In the first phase, an architect was hired to develop preliminaries based on a programming phase. Then a design/build contract was awarded to a general contractor (figs. 11-5, 11-6, 11-7, and 11-8). The Naval Facilities Engineering Command expects to award design/build contracts in this manner for at least 60 percent of its projects in fiscal year 2001. A new $70 million Internal Revenue Service complex in Chamblee, Georgia, completed in 1999, was commissioned by the General Services Administration using a similar two-phase process.

The perceived advantages of design/build for the owner go beyond a compressed project schedule and single source of responsibility. The design/build entity is held to strict liability for defects in construction; there is no "standard of care" provision protecting the designer, and therefore the warranty is arguably stronger. Some design/build contracts contain performance warranties, even covering consequential damages such as lost profit. Such contracts make projects easier to finance by ensuring that the owner will have an uninterrupted revenue stream with which to pay back a loan.

Design/build has long been the norm in some countries. In France, for example, the same company commonly designs and builds, then occupies the building for as long as ten years before transferring it to the ultimate customer. This arrangement, known as design/build/operate, is starting to catch on in North America as well, especially among companies looking to outsource as much as possible of their facilities support functions. In Japan some integrated design/build firms have been in business for three hundred years. A university degree in *Kenchiku* (meaning both architecture and construction) prepares students for careers in any aspect of the building industry. And in the United Kingdom, in part as a result of the Latham report, a

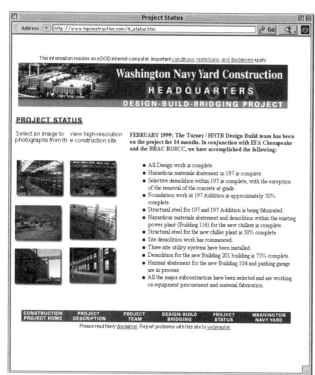

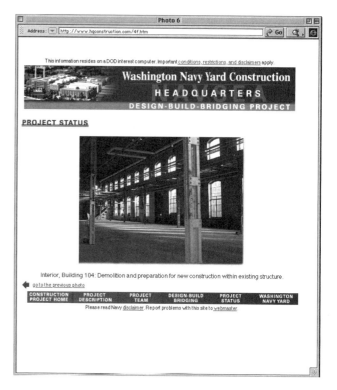

11-5 through 11-8. The Washington Navy Yard is being restored and redeveloped using a design/build bridging project.

private finance initiative will permit design/build contracting of significant public-sector projects, including thirty new hospitals.

Networked Organizations and the Project Information Manager

Design/build is in some respects a regression to a vertically integrated, industrial style of organization—exactly what manufacturers worldwide are moving away from. Companies such as Nike have demonstrated how large enterprises can successfully outsource all production while concentrating on design, marketing, and coordination. Is there an alternative to design/build that would improve efficiency in the building industry without changing its traditional reliance on small firms?

By making external communication cheap and secure, the Internet is changing the equation, offering the possibility of connecting the various players in a building project with a networked organization. A network of small, independent, but tightly integrated firms each contributing to a cooperative process and supported by enhanced communication, may be a better fit to the AEC industry than either the rigidly compartmentalized system that is in place now or the outmoded industrial model suggested by design/build. Such a flexible alliance of specialized firms, which come together for projects, disband, and then re-form, can be highly innovative and effective, if supported by an ability to capture, store, use, and reuse crucial project information. Quality and innovation are enhanced because each member of the networked organization contributes its specialized expertise, which adds to an ever-expanding knowledge base to the benefit of all.

A new process is needed for sharing information, not only during a project but from project to project. Well-documented project histories can be the foundation for programming and budgeting the next project. Stakeholder participation can begin much earlier and take a more important role in the design process. Collective memory can supplant individual experience. But none of this is part of traditional architectural or construction management services. Who will be in charge of this more rational design process? Clearly, the one who controls the project information will be the most powerful member of the building team. Will it be the architect, the construction manager, or someone new?

The project information manager (PIM) may combine characteristics now associated with architect, quantity surveyor, and construction manager. The duties of a PIM encompass a comprehensive overview of a project, not just in one moment in time but throughout a process that extends from site selection and programming through facilities management. It is a natural extension of the architect's traditional persona as the generalist, the professional who can maintain an overarching vision of a project while drawing from specialists the many kinds of expertise needed to create it.

What services might the project information manager provide?

- Building process designer
- Interface designer
- Information intermediary—the one who selects, filters, classifies, and maintains information
- Maintainer of standards and quality assurance
- Coordinator of specialists
- Keeper of the knowledge base, including every factor a building project must contend with: the building program, the financial and political issues, climatological and anthropometric data, along with the products, systems, and techniques of building

The project information manager would be at the center of a flexible, networked organization, a temporary grouping of physically dispersed, independent companies (fig. 11-9). Such a virtual organization would be founded on trust—a willingness of participants to share goals, risks, and information. The culture of networked organizations is based on information sharing rather than hierarchical command-and-control. Entrepreneurial small business units are free to innovate, and these innovations are diffused throughout the enterprise. In this environment, standards—accepted ways of doing things—become ever more important, enabling specialists who have never worked together to become productive quickly, in the same way that makeshift surgical teams of doctors and nurses are able to work effectively in emergencies, using well-defined protocols and procedures.

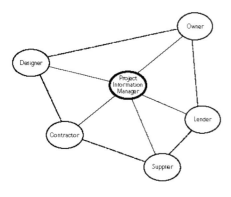

11-9. A networked organization is based on information sharing and trusted relationships.

Successful models of such networked organizations already exist. The Hollywood film industry, for example, is in many ways an interesting analog to AEC. Until shortly after World War II, movies were made under a studio system in which a few vertically integrated large companies controlled every aspect of production, distribution, and exhibition of films. When this system collapsed under antitrust pressure in the 1950s, movie production shifted to teams assembled on a project basis. The transformation from industrial-style to networked organization took place in just a few years. Powerful talent agencies became the equivalent of project information managers, brokering deals by assembling specialist teams—actors, directors, writers, and technicians—and packaging them for investors and financiers.

Another example of a networked organization can be found in the textile mills of Prato in northern Italy. Beginning in the early 1970s, several large (and failing) textile firms were broken up into small, autonomous units specializing in one or two steps of the production process. By 1990 Prato was home to thousands of small manufacturing shops, averaging fewer than five employees each. The firms pooled their research and development efforts, made large investments in CAD/CAM technology, and flourished as quality and innovation soared. Prato became the most important cluster of fabric design and manufacturing in Europe, with annual revenues of $4.5 billion. In the same way that Hollywood talent agencies assumed the role of broker and deal maker, a new kind of "infomediary" appeared in Prato—the *impannatore*. These independent agents provide the crucial coordination services for design and production of fabrics, putting together temporary teams of small firms to fulfill the particular requirements of each customer.

Perhaps the finest example of a networked organization is the Internet itself, which, after the first seeds were planted by the government, grew rapidly as a self-governing, cooperative organization without central control. By allowing specialist companies to concentrate on core competencies, networked organizations make better use of management resources and allow innovation and close customer relationships to flourish. When information can be shared instantly and inexpensively across dispersed project teams, the need for centralized bureaucracies and large fixed overheads is greatly reduced.

Object-oriented CAD and XML: The Future of the Web?

Two emerging technologies—object-oriented CAD and XML—promise to be the enablers of a more integrated design and construction process within networked organizations. Object-oriented CAD is an entirely new paradigm for modeling physical objects. At present, CAD files carry little more information than the pencil drawings they replaced. A CAD program can draw a window, for example, with an exquisite degree of geometric precision, but it cannot write a specification for the window or add the window to the manufacturer's order book or schedule the window's delivery and installation or supply its U-value or the expected life of its painted finish. The idea behind object-oriented CAD is that rich information about building components could be modeled in a form accessible by a wide variety of software applications and used throughout a building's life cycle without conversion or translation into other formats. Properties including shape, behavior, performance data, and transport requirements, along with embedded links to relevant code requirements and test results, could all be included in an electronic "object." When an architect adds a door, the door *object* will describe not only the physical attributes of the door needed for design by the CAD program, but also the cost, maintenance, supply and installation properties of the door for use in project costing and scheduling, and later for facilities management.

The second key enabler for networked AEC is a new Web language for describing information—Extensible Markup Language (XML).

As the Web grew far beyond its origins as a simple means for scientists at CERN to share information, the Web browser became the all-purpose application for interacting with every kind of information source, including large databases distributed across multinational enterprises. But the limitations of HTML to describe information have prevented the Web from reaching its full potential. XML is seen by many as the solution for overcoming these limitations. *Extensible* means that authors can add their own self-defining tags (or "declarations") to Web documents that identify information semantically and thus go beyond the relatively primitive formatting, linking, and display options offered by HTML.

While HTML describes how data should be presented, XML describes the data itself. For example, the tag <PHONENUM> might indicate that the information that followed was a phone number. Or <INSULVAL> might tell the browser that the next bracketed chunk of text describes the insulating properties of a material. HTML and XML have a common ancestor, SGML, which has been used in highly sophisticated data-sharing applications since the 1960s. In 1998 the World Wide Web Consortium announced a standard for XML, a new public-domain hypertext language intended to combine the descriptive properties of SGML with the simplicity of HTML.

A number of industries and scientific disciplines—medical records and newspaper publishing among them—are already using XML to exchange information across platforms and applications (fig. 11-10). XML can be tailored to describe virtually any kind of information in a form that the recipient of the information can use in a variety of ways. It is specifically designed to support information exchange between systems that use fundamentally different forms of data representation, as for example between CAD and scheduling applications.

The success of XML to enable the kind of open information sharing that is needed to integrate the building process hinges on finding a

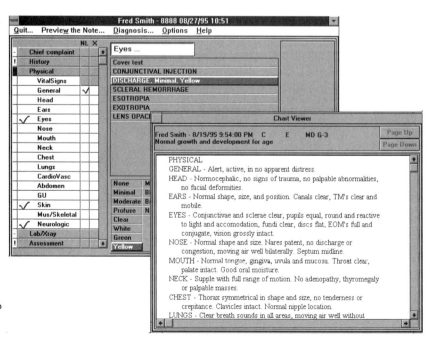

11-10. XML in use to tag medical information so that customized charts can be generated on the fly. (Courtesy ChartWare Inc.)

way to standardize AEC terminology. For any language to function, there must be agreement on the precise meaning of terms. Semantic integrity means that words used should mean the same to the sender as they do to the receiver. Traditional means of achieving this aim with human languages have included dictionaries and glossaries. If computers are to exchange information with each other without active human intervention, however, a much higher degree of precision is needed.

At present, different players within the AEC industry use the same term in somewhat different ways. For example, a *door* can be, depending on context: (1) an opening in a wall; (2) an assembly consisting of a frame, a leaf, and hardware; (3) a scheduling item; (4) a cost item; (5) a product to be manufactured and delivered; or (6) a building asset to be tracked and managed. An industry-specific implementation of XML will need to be precise enough to clarify these different usages and be flexible enough to grow over time.

If XML is widely adopted, it will enable data sharing and electronic commerce in the building industry on a scale not previously imagined. When XML is used to write project specifications, for example, a contractor will be able to extract both quantitative and qualitative data and match it with information from manufacturers' and subcontractors' Web sites. A manufacturer will be able to scan a set of contract documents and match specified items with items in its own catalog, take an order, and move it into production and delivery. Once that product arrives at a job site, carrying the same XML code written by the original specifier, a construction worker using a scanner and handheld computer will enter it into the master schedule for the project.

XML tags can identify every attribute of products and building components, from bending strength to reflectivity. In fact, XML could be used to describe virtually all the objects, documents, services, and organizations needed to complete a project. Because data about these attributes is divorced from the program used to create it, information is no longer imprisoned by file types and software incompatibility. Because much richer information can be described in XML than with HTML, Internet searches will be far more focused and robust than they are at present.

Linked or embedded style sheets enable the data within XML documents to be displayed on the fly in a variety of different ways, depending on the requirements of the end user. Because XML separates data from presentation, XML documents could contain information that would be visible to some users and invisible to others. Instead of making many small requests from the server, XML-enabled browsers can download data in larger chunks and manipulate it offline, relieving network traffic bottlenecks. Users can filter the information themselves, extracting only the specific data needed, or create collapsing and expanding views of the data on demand. The implications for Web-based operation manuals, equipment schedules, and the like are enormous—a maintenance engineer, for example, could easily

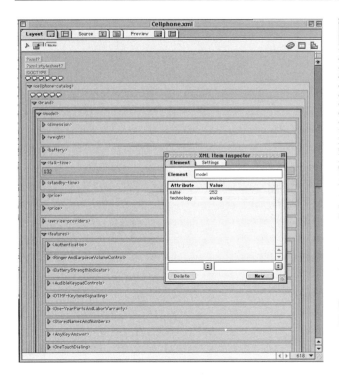

11-11 and 11-12. Some Web-authoring applications can already create XML documents. Here are two versions of a page describing cell phones, shown in Adobe GoLive.

extract only the specific information needed to service a building component from a mass of data that would otherwise be overwhelmingly complex (figs. 11-11 and 11-12).

One application of XML will allow users to access different aspects of a single database and display them in a customized way. For example, in a shared project database, an architect's Web browser might be configured to display only geometric data, that is, the physical form of a design. The contractor's Web browser might display only information about schedules and costs, using exactly the same set of data stored on the same remote server. The architect and contractor would be able to work with the information using Java applets downloaded as needed by their browsers. The architect would not need to have CAD software on her laptop while accessing the database from her hotel room, because all of the functionality needed to work with the model would be supplied by the applet itself.

With XML and object-oriented CAD, entire sets of construction documents could be prepared in the form of live Web sites rather than a collection of static documents. The project file is now completely divorced from any paper representation of it; an unlimited variety of context-based views of the same information is now possible. The very notion of discrete types of standalone documents—plans, specifications, correspondence, schedules—would become obsolete.

Preliminary steps have already begun. In August 1999, Bentley Systems proposed that *aecXML* become the hosts for developing an XML **schema** customized for the building industry. An aecXML Working

Group, led by interim executive director Jerry Laiserin, intends to work in tandem with the ongoing integration efforts of the International Alliance for Interoperability (discussed in chapter 7). In order to limit the scope of its task and to avoid duplication with IAI, accXML will initially not deal with geometric properties, although XML is fully capable of handling them. Eventually, however, it is anticipated that XML and object-oriented CAD will coexist and reinforce each other.

In September 1999, the first meeting of the aecXML Working Group was held in Dallas, Texas, and by teleconference in Reading, England. Over 130 companies and organizations, a cross section of the AEC industry, attended. Five subcommittees were formed, charged with laying the groundwork for XML implementation in the following areas:

- Design, schedule and cost
- Catalogs
- Procurement—matching buyers and sellers of goods and services
- Project management, defined as everything needed to turn documents into buildings
- Facilities management

A parallel effort called E-Construct aims to develop and implement an XML vocabulary that will be the basis of a trading network for construction-related goods and services throughout the European Community. There, the difficulty of integrating AEC across disciplines is compounded by the different national languages and building material classification systems used in each country, as well as regulatory and licensing differences and variations in the historical roles of designers and builders. The aim is that a Italian engineer will be able to design a structure in France that is built by a German contractor using materials and services from anywhere in Europe.

The promise of Internet-delivered product data goes far beyond replacing brochures with Web sites. Products could be classified with far richer detail than they are at present. Properties including shape, behavior, performance data, and transport requirements, along with embedded links to relevant code requirements and test results, could all be included in an electronic specification. Java applets could allow a Web site visitor to extract data about products in a variety of useful ways: comparing the price and performance of various models, checking available options and finishes, or studying the energy consumption of a product when used in a particular sun exposure.

From there, it isn't hard to imagine product models also carrying information about life-cycle performance. Instead of serving as a static single-use document, a product specification could actually "learn," not only during the design and construction process but over the life cycle of all buildings known to contain the product. Performance issues, maintenance, and replacement data could all be integrated into such a "living" specification.

12 Copyright and

Among the most frequently voiced concerns I hear in my seminars concerns unauthorized copying. If the Internet makes it so easy to download material and make high-quality copies, aren't designers just "giving it away" when they place their work on Web sites? What will prevent competitors from stealing or misrepresenting your work as their own? Couldn't developers and builders copy your designs and use them elsewhere without your knowledge or consent? Doesn't that present a potential liability issue for the designer?

The economic concept of *information goods* is a useful way of considering any form of professional expertise for hire. Information goods have the following characteristics:

- Information is costly to produce and cheap to reproduce.
- Once the first copy is produced, most costs are "sunk" and can't be recovered.
- Multiple copies can be made at roughly constant cost regardless of volume.

Virtually all creative content can be digitized even if it was not initially created on a computer, and the Internet has become the primary distribution channel for every kind of digital material, including architectural design. It seems that creative content has become far more liquid and dematerialized. The Internet has dramatically reduced the cost and increased the ease of distribution of electronic information of all kinds. It allows perfect copies of digital material, legal or illegal, to be made at virtually no expense.

You cannot stop illegal copying, and such copying is now easier than ever. But if you have ever had your work shown in the press (and designers love to see their work published), you have already exposed it to illegal copying. For that matter, the very act of building brings the risk of

Intellectual Property Concerns

unauthorized copying and of false claims of authorship. Increased exposure to illegal copying is simply one of the costs of the digital age. But while you may have exposed your work to the risk of copying, you have brought it to a vastly larger audience than you ever had before.

The Internet is not the first instance in which technology has made copying easier and reduced the cost of distributing information. When photocopiers were first introduced, the publishing industry was highly alarmed at the ease with which bootleg copies of books and magazines could be made. Before videotaping became a household technology, the movie industry fought it tooth and nail. The truth is that photocopying actually *increased* the demand for books, and videotapes became a huge new revenue source for Hollywood.

Why? Because creative material must be experienced to be appreciated. By exposing more people to your product, you are actually increasing your potential customer base, even if you are giving away a sample of it. The software industry routinely gives away demos and stripped-down versions of its products. By allowing people to experience the software, they increase the demand for it. When inexpensive videotapes became widely available, many more people started watching movies. Far from being the threat to the motion picture industry that Hollywood feared in the 1970s, the rise of home videos actually saved the movie industry by enlarging its market. Are videos copied illegally? Of course they are, but that has not prevented studios from making a fortune from the legal copies.

Similarly, software piracy actually drives part of the demand for legal copies. Placing your software on people's hard drives is the surest way to create a demand for it. Most users would rather try out software before buying it. If they don't end up using it, it really cost the software author nothing. And most people will gladly pay for the software they actually use. Certainly, when the user needs technical support or a copy of the manual or an update to the latest version, he is likely to buy it.

Copyright law in the United States is built around the notion that ideas themselves are not protected, only the physical expression of them. A conversation, a recited story, or an improvisation cannot be copyrighted because it lacks physical form. A musical performance cannot be copyrighted until it is recorded. The law protects the particular expression of an idea and, until recently, that entailed making some sort of container for it, in the form of a book, movie, painting, or architectural drawing. The physical container locked the contents into a fixed, inalterable, and difficult–to-copy format. Architectural ideas are protected by copyright only when they are assembled into a design and presented in a physical medium such as a drawing or model.

The invention of the printing press dramatically increased the rate of literacy, because the availability of books gave people a reason to learn to read. So the ease of copying brought on by this technological change greatly increased the demand for authors. Observers have likened the Internet to Gutenberg's invention and predict a golden age for creators of all kinds, with more opportunities for creativity, individual expression, and varied forms of distribution.

Instead of worrying too much about protecting your services from copiers, think about how you can deliver the most value to clients by improving services or by offering new ones. Let the Internet be an opportunity rather than a threat. Suppose, for example, you can increase the value of your services by making them more accessible to the client or easier to use. If you begin offering a project extranet as part of basic services, for example, your clients should be willing to pay more for the greater access to their information you have provided them.

What Is an Original in the Digital Age?

In architecture, we have the long-cherished notion of an original. So strong is the hold of paper that building officials routinely ask for an original drawing that has been stamped and wet-signed by the architect. This notion is not easily transferrable to the digital age; there may be no real difference between an original and copy. Thankfully, the concept of "record drawings" lives on the form of CD-ROMs. These can be snapshots of a project taken at a given point in time, and they cannot be altered. Meanwhile, the digital rubber stamp waits to be invented.

Versioning

In the 1970s, the Grateful Dead allowed fans to tape live concerts freely. The result was a worldwide fan base driven by the so-called private tapes. Hearing a tape persuaded music fans to attend concerts, and attending concerts made the fans want to buy albums. The Dead were practicing what has come to be known as *versioning*: giving away a limited form of a product in order to increase demand for the higher-quality version that must be purchased. The Grateful Dead became one of the world's most successful rock bands by in effect giving away a low-quality version of their product. It cost them nothing, and it stimulated sales of recordings and concert tickets.

Many companies have discovered that versioning is often the best way to create demand for a product, now that the Internet has reduced the marginal cost of reproducing information to practically nothing. For example, *The New York Times* offers free access to most of the newspaper on its Web site. What does it get in return? Visitors must register, giving the *Times* and its advertisers valuable information about customers. Moreover, although the basic content is free, visitors who want premium services must pay for them. For example, although searching the *Times* archives is free, there is a charge for downloading articles. The basic version increases the demand for the premium version by making people aware of it. *Doom*, the gory shoot-em-up computer game, began in 1993 by giving away the first few levels of the game. Fifteen million people downloaded it for free, became hooked, and were glad to pay for higher levels when they reached the market.

Some architects who are clever with their Web sites use a form of versioning. Instead of trying to impress visitors with pictures of beautiful award-winning work, they place articles and case studies on-line, in effect giving away some of their expertise in the hopes of hooking a potential client who needs more. Firms with specialized practices can create a demand for what they do by giving potential clients enough information to discover that they need the firm's services. By widely circulating a sample of your work, you may actually fuel demand for the higher-quality version of it, for which you can charge a fee. An architect who offers house plans on-line might make some basic plans available as a free download (it costs nothing) but charge a hefty fee for customizing the plans to a particular site. Or a higher-value version of the same house plans might come with the rights of repeated use.

The value your clients derive from your work has to do with their relationship with you and the information and services you provide. For service firms, the Internet is both an opportunity and a threat. It's a threat because it effectively globalizes virtually every type of business. With so much information available with easy access, clients will find it much easier to form new supplier relationships. You may find yourself competing not with just the firm around the block but with companies throughout the region and world. It's an opportunity because it affords the potential to learn from your clients and end users, to interact closely with them, and to customize your services to suit each particular client and project.

For every creator of intellectual property, whether music, literature, films, software, or architectural design, the Internet has changed the way people assign value to what they do. No longer does the work product itself have much intrinsic value—an MP3 file downloaded from the Internet sounds every bit as good as a CD you bought at a store. The Web version of *Newsweek* has just as much information as the printed version on the newsstand.

For architects, who have been trained to esteem the beautiful object, whether a drawing, a model, or a piece of furniture, it's hard to let go. But soon, if our work product has any physical manifestation at all, it will be temporary and valueless. Our ideas will become part of the great river of digital content that flows on the Internet.

In his article, "The Economy of Ideas," John Perry Barlow, one of the founders of Electronic Frontier Foundation, said:

> Whether you think of yourself as a service provider or a performer, the future protection of your intellectual property will depend on your abil-

ity to control your relationship to the market—a relationship which will most likely live and grow over a period of time. The value of that relationship will reside in the quality of performance, the uniqueness of your point of view, the validity of your expertise, its relevance to your market, and, underlying everything, the ability of that market to access your creative services swiftly, conveniently, and interactively.

Appendix

Questions for a Potential Internet Service Provider:

- How much space (in MB) on your server will you allocate for my Web site? (This will range from 2 to 50 MB). What do you charge for each extra increment of 10 MB? How much space is allowed for FTP? For e-mail? What do you charge if I exceed my limit, and how do you calculate it?
- Is there a usage limit? (There may be limit on the amount of "traffic," that is, the total volume of files served from your Web site per month.)
- Do you permit FTP upload and download directly to the directory where my Web site will be located? Some large ISPs, such as Pacific Bell Internet, limit users to uploading or deleting one file at a time, which makes managing an active Web site extremely tedious.
- Do you allow custom scripts (CGI) to be uploaded to your Web server? Do you provide a directory of common scripts that can be shared by all sites on your server?
- Do you support Microsoft FrontPage server extensions?
- Do you support password protection of my Web site?
- Are there limits on the size of e-mail attachments? (This issue is crucial if you plan to transfer large files such as CAD drawings. Some ISPs will actually cut off a message in mid-transmission when it exceeds their maximum size.)
- Do you provide technical support to all computer platforms? (Macintosh users especially may be concerned here.)
- How is the data that is stored on your servers backed up? How frequently? Are back-up media stored off-site?
- What is your record of down time?
- Do you have an uninterruptible power supply (UPS)?
- Do you have redundant connections to the Internet backbone?
- What are your fees?
  - Is there a set-up fee?
  - Is there a usage fee beyond x hours?
  - Do you charge extra during peak hours?
  - Are accounts flat rate or metered?

  With this information, you can estimate your monthly fees based on projected usage.
- Are local dial-up numbers provided for all the areas you need? (Consider

branch offices, job sites, client offices, and so on. Check for both modem access and ISDN numbers. Are there alternate numbers in your local area? Make sure these are local calls from your location, and remember that not all calls in your area code are local. Try dialing the call-in number during peak periods—generally late afternoon on weekdays—and see if you get a busy signal.)

- Is there a toll-free number for calls from out of town? What is the charge for using it? (You might find that its cheaper to make a long-distance call to your local dial-up number)
- What is the ratio of dial-in customers to modems? Do you add more lines as the customer base increases?
- Do you support 56K on all phone lines?
- How many e-mailboxes are given with the basic account? How much for each additional?
- Do you require the use of proprietary software to access the account or use any of its services?
- Will you sell my information to mailing lists or other companies?
- Support issues:
    - Is customer service available at all hours, every day?
    - Is support a local or free call?
    - Can support be obtained by e-mail?
    - How large is the support staff relative to customer base? Is the staff trained in all computer platforms? Try visiting an ISP's on-line help pages. Are they clearly arranged with ready access to good information? And try calling the support line a few times. If you are kept on hold for an unacceptably long time, look elsewhere for Internet service.

Glossary

alias A shortcut pointing to a file or document. A **domain name** such as www.greatbuildings.com is an alias to an **IP address**.

analog Technology that conveys data as electronic signals of varying frequency and amplitude. Radio/television broadcast and telephone technology is analog. A **modem** converts digital signals to analog and back again. Compare to **digital**.

anti-aliasing A method for smoothing "jaggies"—the stairstep effect caused by pixellation in a bitmapped image.

application A shortened form of *application program*; a piece of software that is used for performing specific tasks, such as word processing, drawing, or managing a **database**. Applications are frequently referred to in this book and elsewhere as *tools*.

ASCII American Standard Code for Information Interchange, pronounced *askey*. The most common format for representing text characters in computers and on the Internet. ASCII uses seven **bits** of data to specify each character in the alphabet as a pattern of 1s and 0s.

asynchronous See synchronous/asynchronous communication.

authentication A process for determining if someone is or is not who he declares himself to be.

backup A copy of the data stored on a computer made on such media as tape drives, Zip or Jaz disks, or other hard drives, in case the computer's hard drive fails.

bandwidth If you compare the Internet to a great river of information with many tributaries, bandwidth can be thought of as the water-carrying capacity of any point in the system. Sometimes discussed as if it were a plumbing system, as in "How big is your pipe?" High-bandwidth connections to the Internet are provided by T1 lines and DSL, while dial-up **modem** connections are low bandwidth.

beta-testing In the software development process, distributing the product to a test group of potential end users, to identify problems and elicit feedback. Beta-testing is the second stage of testing candidate software, after alpha-testing.

binary The base two number system that computers use to express numbers digitally. Thus 1=1, 2=10, 5=101, 10=1010, and so on.

bit The smallest unit of digital data. A bit has a value of either 1 or 0. Abbreviated with a lowercase *b*, as in "56 Kbps modem." Compare to **byte**.

bookmark A saved **hyperlink**. The Netscape **browser** uses the term bookmarks; Internet Explorer, favorites.

boot, boot up To start up a computer. The operating system is loaded into **RAM,** and the computer is then ready to run applications.

bps Bits per second, a measure of the speed at which data is transferred. 1 Kbps=one thousand bits per second, 1 Mbps=one million bits per second.

browser A client program that uses the Hypertext Transfer Protocol (**HTTP**) to make requests for, and then display, Web pages on behalf of a computer user. The first browser was Mosaic, released in 1992.

byte A chunk of digital information that is eight **bits** long. Abbreviated with a capital *B*, as in "64 MB of RAM." A **kilobyte** (KB or Kbyte) is approximately a thousand bytes (2 to the 10th power, or 1,024 bytes). A **megabyte** (MB) is 2 to the 20th power, or 1,048,576 bytes. A **gigabyte** (GB or"gig") is two to the 30th power, or 1,073,741,824 bytes. And a **terabyte** is 2 to the 40th power or approximately a thousand billion bytes (a thousand gigabytes). Compare to **bit.**

cache A place for temporarily holding information. Web browsers create a cache folder on the hard drive to store visited pages. When you revisit a page, it is pulled out of the cache instead of being **download**ed again from the Internet and thus will display more quickly.

CGI Common Gateway Interface. A standard way for a Web **server** to process information submitted by a Web **client,** such as form entries. The term also refers to the scripts that trigger such a process.

CLI Command-Line Interface. A user interface that requires typing arcane commands to instruct the computer. DOS and UNIX are examples of operating systems using a command-line interface.

client Can refer either to hardware, that is, the computer on the **network** that is requesting information from the **server;** or to the software used to interpret and display the information received. A **browser** is a type of client software.

client-server A **network**ed computer system in which information is stored on a **server,** a computer that warehouses information and makes it available on demand to **client** computers on the network. The **Internet** combines aspects of a client-server system with a **peer-to-peer** system. An individual **node** on the Internet is in a peer-to-peer relationship with the other nodes and in a client-server relationship with individual users and subnetworks.

compression The reduction of file size to save storage space or transmission time. Some graphic file formats, such as GIF and JPEG, have compression built in. Programs such as WinZip and Stuffit perform compression on files and folders so that they move more quickly through the Internet.

cookie A small file that helps an interactive **Web site** "remember" information about visitors. Cookies enable user preferences to be retained from visit to visit. A newer system, called *cupcakes,* allows users to create and edit a personal profile that can be accessed by Web sites.

database A collection of information that is sorted and stored so that it can be easily accessed and updated. A relational database retains information in small pieces that can be accessed and recombined in different ways. SQL is a standard language for making queries from a database.

dedicated connection An Internet connection that is constant: always "on."

dialog box Part of a GUI; prompts the user to enter information needed by an application to perform a task.

dial-up connection An Internet connection initiated by a **modem** dialing an **ISP** over an ordinary telephone line. The connection is intermittent.

digital Technology that conveys messages by reducing the components to one of two states: on or off. On is expressed as the number 1; off, as 0. Data transmitted or stored with digital technology is expressed as a string of 1s and 0s. Each of these state digits is referred to as a **bit,** and a string of eight of them is a **byte.** Compare to **analog.** See also **binary.**

domain name A unique name for a **Web site,** followed by a period ("dot"), and a broader classification of the site's sponsor: .gov (federal agency), .edu (educational institution), .org (nonprofit organization), .mil (military), and .com (commercial); or by a two-letter country domain such as .uk, .fr, and .ca. (United Kingdom, France, and Canada respectively). Compare to **IP address.**

download/upload The process of sending or retrieving an electronic file from a server. When you retrieve your e-mail, you download your messages from the mail server at your **ISP.** FTP is used to upload and download files to a Web site.

dpi Dots per inch. Usually used to describe the resolution of a printed document.

DSL Digital Subscriber Line. A technology for sending a high-bandwidth signal on ordinary copper phone lines that cohabit with regular voice and fax signals. The connection goes directly from the subscriber to the telephone central office and then to an **ISP.**

e-mail Electronic mail, one of the **Internet services,** used for sending text messages to individuals and groups. E-mail *enclosures* are files attached to an e-mail message that may require some other kind of software at the receiving end to use. Such enclosures may involve **encoding** and/or **compression.**

encoding On the Internet, the process of converting an e-mail attachment to a text file consisting of **ASCII** characters.

encryption A system for converting data into a form, called a *cipher,* that cannot be understood without a "key." Decryption is the process of reconverting the data into a readable form.

Ethernet The most widely installed technology for creating **LANs.**

extranet A private **network** that uses Internet protocols and the public telecommunication system to share an organization's information with its suppliers, vendors, customers, and other selected groups. In design and construction, extranets are used to support project management by connecting the participants and providing a repository for shared files.

FAQ Frequently asked question.

file system The system for naming and organizing files within a storage device. Most **operating system**s use a hierarchical, inverted-tree-like file system. The root directory or folder contains all other files and folders.

firewall A system to protect a private **network** from unauthorized outsiders. The term can refer to both hardware and software, as well as monitoring and management tools.

flaming Verbally abusing someone publicly on a newsgroup or mail list.

font A set of text characters in a specific style and size, for example, Times New Roman, 18 point. *Font* and *typeface* are often used interchangeably. Fonts must be installed on a computer in order for them to display and print, although some types of electronic documents, such as PDF files created by Adobe Acrobat, have fonts embedded in them.

FTP File Transfer Protocol. An **Internet service.** Used to **upload** and **download** files to a directory on a **server.**

GIF Graphics Interchange Format. An Internet file type for compressed **raster images.**

groupware Software designed to support group collaboration over a **network.** The most popular groupware is Lotus Notes. Lotus (a division of IBM) has acknowledged the triumph of the **browser** by recasting Notes as Domino, a client-server system for creating browser-based intranets.

GUI Graphical User Interface, pronounced *gooey*. In contrast to a command-line interface, a GUI allows the user to control the computer more intuitively, using icons, windows, pull-down menus, scroll bars, and the like. The first widely available implementation of a GUI was created for the Apple Macintosh in 1984, using ideas developed at Xerox's Palo Alto Research Center. A GUI uses visual metaphors to relate computer functions to everyday life: desktop, trash can, etc. **Compare to CLI.**

helper applications Software that enables a **browser** to display a particular type of file. **E-mail** programs also use helper applications to open received attachments.

home page The entry point of a **Web site**; the HTML document that visitors see first and that links them to the interior of the site.

host On the Internet, a **server** with full two-way access to other servers. A **host** resides at a **node.**

HTML Hypertext Markup Language. A simple computer language that tells the **browser** how to display elements on a **Web page**, such as text and graphics, and where to look for linked items. It does so with markup tags between beginning and ending brackets that provide instructions for display.

HTTP Hypertext Transfer Protocol. The set of rules for exchanging text and media files on the **World Wide Web.** HTTPS is the secure version used for electronic commerce.

hypertext, hyperlink A means of organizing pieces of information with associative connections (links) between them. The **World Wide Web** makes use of hypertext by allowing text and media to be linked to other resources on the Internet.

intelligent agent A program (sometimes called a *bot*) that gathers information on the Internet without the active participation of the user.

Internet backbone The high-speed data conduit that moves data in large volumes between regional subnetworks around the world. A better analogy than backbone would be a river, which collects water from many tributaries.

Internet service provider (ISP) A company that provides Internet access and service to customers at the retail level. ISPs may serve a national or regional market.

Internet services The various types of communication supported by the Internet. These include e-mail, the **World Wide Web, FTP,** and others. Each Internet service is governed by a **protocol**, such as **HTTP.**

interoperability The ability of computer systems and software to work with other systems without special effort on the part of the user. As **network** computing has been widely adopted, interoperability has become crucial. The Internet standards of **TCP/IP, HTTP,** and the like are good examples of successful interoperability.

intranet A private **network** that uses Internet protocols for internal communication within an organization. Some or all of the **Internet services** may be supported: e-mail, newsgroups, FTP, and the Web.

IP address Every **node** on a **TCP/IP network** has a unique address in the form of a numeral, such as 140.174.162.14. A **domain name** is an **alias** to an IP address.

JPEG Joint Photographic Experts Group. An Internet file type for compressed **raster images.**

kludge In hacker language, an awkward and inelegant solution that works but does not earn respect.

LAN Local Area Network. A **network** of personal computers within a limited geographical area, typically a single building. LANs can be **client-server** or **peer-to-peer.**

memory In computing, a holding place for instructions and data. One kind of memory is RAM, where the computer's central processing unit stores the operating system and application software in current use. Information kept in memory is more quickly available to the computer than that stored on a hard drive. When the computer is turned off, this kind of memory is emptied.

meta In information technology, a more comprehensive or underlying definition. The new Internet language XML is said to be a meta language because it is a language for defining languages. Some search engines can read meta tags that Web authors insert in pages to categorize broadly the information contained in the page.

modem A contraction of modulator/demodulator. A device that converts digital signals to audible sounds for transmission over a telephone line. A modem at the receiving end is required to reconvert the signal to a digital stream.

multitasking The ability of a computer to perform several operations at the same time, for example reading **e-mail** while **downloading** a file.

Netiquette Internet manners. Sending **spam** is a violation of netiquette.

network An arrangement of points or **nodes** interconnected by communication paths. Networks can be described by their schematic structure, such as a star or ring, or by their spatial distribution, as in **LAN** and **WAN**. Networks can be further characterized by the type of physical link employed (e.g., copper wire, fiber optic), by the communication protocol used (**TCP/IP**, Appletalk), and by the type of signal carried (voice, data).

newbie A new Internet user.

newsreader An **application** for reading, subscribing to, and participating in network newsgroups.

node On a **network**, a single connection point, which may be a redistribution point to other nodes (called a *gateway*) or an end point (called a **host**).

operating system The software that controls basic computer functions. Operating systems in widespread use include Windows 95/98/NT, Mac OS, and the various types of UNIX: Solaris, Linux, A/UX, etc.

packet switching A telecommunications scheme in which messages are disassembled into pieces ("packets"), sent over the **network**, and reassembled by the receiver.

peer-to-peer **Networks** that allow any computer to initiate transactions with any other. The Internet is a peer-to-peer system with respect to its nodes. Each node may be in a **client-server** relationship with individual users and subnetworks. Compare to **client-server**.

pixel A contraction of picture element. The smallest indivisible piece of a computer display or **raster image**. The physical area of computer displays and the size of individual image files are both described by their pixel dimensions.

pixellation The effect caused by enlarging a **raster image** to the point that the individual pixels become visible, often causing a stairstep effect.

platform The underlying computer system on which **application** programs can run. Wintel and Macintosh are examples of personal computer platforms.

plug-ins Add-on programs that permit **browser** software to display additional file types. Popular plug-ins include Apple's QuickTime and Adobe's Acrobat Reader.

PPP Point-to-Point Protocol. When a **modem** initiates a session with an **Internet service provider**, it must first establish a connection, using PPP, before **TCP/IP** services can be served.

point of presence An access point to the Internet. Each **ISP** has a unique point of presence.

protocol A means of establishing the ground rules and common language that two or more computer systems will use to converse with each other. Protocols can be built on top of each other and are sometimes referred to as *high-level* or *low-level* protocols. **TCP/IP** is the "low-level" protocol that forms the basis of the Internet. Built on top of TCP/IP are higher-level protocols such as **HTTP, FTP,** and **SMTP.**

push-pull *Push* is the delivery of information at the initiation of the sender; *pull* is an exchange initiated by the requester.

RAM Random Access Memory. Can be thought of as a computer's short-term **memory,** which makes computer instructions quickly available to the computer's microprocessor. Data in current use by an **application** is stored in RAM rather than on a hard drive to make operations faster.

raster image A digital image consisting of **pixels** with values of brightness and color.

resolution The number of **pixels** within a digital image, or the number of pixels that can be displayed on a monitor, expressed as an *X* by *Y* value. A monitor that can display 1,024 by 768 pixels is said to have higher resolution than a monitor with 800 by 600 pixels. In the context of printers and scanners, resolution refers to the number of dots per inch (**dpi**).

ROM Read Only Memory. A built-in, "hard-wired" section of memory that contains basic instructions for allowing the computer to **boot.** ROM is not erased when the computer is shut down, as **RAM** is.

root folder The folder (or directory) that contains all other files and folders in a **Web site.**

router On the Internet, at the fork in the road at the junction of two or more network paths, a device that decides which route an incoming packet should follow to get to its destination.

scanner A device for digitizing printed pages such as photographs, typed text, magazine pages, and the like.

schema The formal organization or structure of a set of data. In data modeling, you identify the data objects you wish to classify and how they relate to each other. The structure that defines how these classifications are made is a schema.

script A sequence of instructions written in computer languages such as Perl and JavaScript. Different from a program, because a script does not stand alone; it triggers an action to be carried out by another **application.** A common use for scripts on the Internet is to instruct a **server** about what to do with information that Web site visitors supply in on-line forms.

search engine A **Web site** that finds Internet resources matching criteria selected by a computer user.

server Can refer either to hardware, the computer that answers requests from **clients,** or to the software required to perform these operations. Each kind of **Internet service** requires a particular kind of server software: Web server, mail server, etc.

shareware Software that is distributed on the Internet using an honor system that asks users to pay for them after an evaluation period.

SMTP An Internet **protocol** used for sending and receiving **e-mail.**

snail mail A disparaging term for the U.S. Postal Service.

spam Unsolicited commercial ("junk") **e-mail.**

storage device A container for computer files. Hard drives, CD-ROM drives, and tape drives are examples. Storage devices "read" and "write" the information to such media as magnetic disks.

streaming Technology that permits sound and video files to begin playing back before they are completely **download**ed. The download continues as the first part is playing on the viewer's screen. As in broadcasting, media are presented as they come "over the wire" and need not be stored in the viewer's memory. Viewers can jump forward to any part of the full video without having to wait. Streaming media employ **compression** to reduce download time.

synchronous/asynchronous communication Communication between two or more parties, which can occur at the same time, such as a telephone conversation (*synchronous*), or at different times such as an **e-mail** exchange (*asynchronous*).

TCP/IP Transmission Control Protocol/Internet Protocol. *TCP* is the method used to break data messages into pieces (packets) for transmission on the Internet and to reassemble them at their destination. *IP* is the system of addressing and routing the messages. TCP/IP is the foundation of the public Internet and private **intranets** and **extranets**.

terabyte. See **byte**.

threaded discussion On a **newsgroup**, electronic bulletin board, or **e-mail** discussion list, a sequence of comments about a specific topic. It includes the original message and subsequent follow-up messages from other contributors.

TIFF Tag Image File Format. Used for exchanging raster images between programs, including those used for scanning images. A TIFF file is often given a ".tiff" or ".tif" file name suffix to ensure compatibility with UNIX and Windows systems. TIFF files are commonly used in desktop publishing and image-editing applications.

upload See **download/upload**.

URL Uniform Resource Locator. Sometimes called a Web address, but a URL can also point to an **FTP** site or a local folder. An example of a URL is HTTP://www.greatbuildings.com/index.html, which translates in English to: "Please go to a **server** called www.greatbuildings.com (which is itself an **alias** for an **IP address**), where, using **HTTP**, fetch for me a **hypertext** document called 'index.html.'" The **browser** first has to look up the **domain name** "greatbuildings.com" by visiting the domain name server maintained by your **Internet Service Provider**. This server resolves the domain name into an IP address.

usenet A gigantic collection of discussion lists built around interests and affinities. These can be publicly accessible on the Internet or privately hosted on **intranets** and **extranets**.

user interface The boundary between computers and humans; the system for giving instructions to the computer.

utility A small program that enhances the capabilities of the **operating system**. Utilities are used for tasks such as disk repair, file **compression**, or searching.

vector graphic A digital image created using mathematical statements. Drawing elements such as lines and circles have properties such as length, thickness, and angle, and images defined by them can be scaled and viewed from different angles.

VRAM Video RAM. Special memory chips used to display information on monitors. The amount of VRAM in a personal computer will affect the size and color capacity of the monitors it can support.

videoconferencing A system that supports geographically distributed group discussion with video and sound. Videoconferencing on the Internet requires a high-**bandwidth** connection between participants.

virtual reality The simulation of real or imagined environments that can be explored interactively on a computer using the mouse or keyboard.

VRML Virtual Reality Modeling Language. A language for describing three-dimensional, interactive space.

WAN Wide Area Network. A geographically dispersed network. Typically connects the various locations of a single organization. Compare to **LAN**.

Web page A single **HTML** document, usually part of a larger **Web site**.

Web site A collection of **Web page**s, or **HTML** documents, together with their associated graphics and other media, and a system that links these elements together. A Web site resides on a **server**, from which a **browser** can make requests for pages.

Wintel Personal computers with microprocessors manufactured by Intel, running the Microsoft Windows operating system.

workstation A computer designed for a single user that is more powerful than a personal computer. The term is relative, as today's personal computers are more capable than the workstations of a few years ago. Workstations are typically designed for a dedicated use, such as CAD or video special effects.

World Wide Web One of the **Internet services**, the Web has become the leading gateway to the Internet because of its support for multimedia and **hypertext**.

WYSIWIG What You See is What You Get, pronounced *wiss-ee-wig*. Refers to the ability of a computer system to display a document being edited more or less exactly the way it will appear in final form.

Bibliography

Abdel-Qader Al-Qawasmi, Jamal, Mark J. Clayton, Robert E. Johnson, and Yunsik Song. 1997. "Collaborative Facility Management Using Intranet Technology." CRS Center for Leadership and Management in the Design and Construction Industry, Texas A&M University, October 1997.

Allweyer, T. 1996. "Model Based Re-Engineering in the European Construction Industry." Unpublished paper. (Available at: http://delphi.kstr.lth.se/w78/)

Alshawi, M., & I. Faraj. 1995. "Integrating CAD and VR in Construction." Proceedings of the Information Technology Awareness Workshop, University of Salford, United Kingdom, January 1995.

Alshawi, Mustafa, and John Underwood. 1999. *The Application of Information Technology in the Management of Construction*. London: The Royal Institution of Chartered Surveyors.

American Institute of Architects. 1996. "Redefinition of the Profession: Report to the AIA Board of Directors." Washington, DC: The American Institute of Architects, September 1996.

Ames, A., et al. 1996. *The VRML Source Book*. New York: John Wiley and Sons.

Anon. 1995. "A Survey of Cities: Turn up the lights—The Dalton Story." *The Economist*, 29 July 1995.

Anton, Ted, and Rick McCourt, eds. 1995. "Email from Bill." In *The New Science Journalists*. New York: Ballantine.

Aouad G., M. Betts, P. Brandon, F. Brown, T. Child, G. Cooper, S. Ford, J. Kirkham, R. Oxman, M. Sarshar, and B. Young. 1994. "Integrated Databases for Design and Construction: Final Report." University of Salford, UK (internal report), July 1994.

Aouad, G., F. Marir, T. Child, P. Brandon, and A. Kawooya. 1997. "Construction Integrated Databases: Linking Design, Planning and Estimating, The OSCON Approach." Proceedings of the International Conference on the Rehabilitation and Development of Civil Engineering Infrastructures, American University of Beirut, June 1997.

Augenbroe, Godfried. 1998. "Executive White Paper Steering Committee on Building Product Information." Construction Research Center, College of Architecture, Georgia Institute of Technology, 16 July 1998.

Australian STEP Demonstration Project. 1995. Vol. 1.6–26. "Improving Efficiency in the Construction Sector."

Barlow, John Perry. "The Economy of Ideas." *Wired*, 3 February 1995. (Available at http://www.hotwired.com/wired/2.03/features/ economy. ideas.html.)

Barrie, D., and B. Paulson. 1992. *Professional Construction Management, Design-Construct and General Contracting.* 3rd ed. New York: McGraw-Hill.

Benedikt, Michael, ed. 1991. *Cyberspace: First Step.* Cambridge, MA: MIT Press.

Berners-Lee, Tim. 1989. "Information Management: A Proposal." Unpublished memo at CERN, March 1989. (Available at: http://www.w3.org/History/1989/proposal.html)

Black, Roger. 1997. *Web Sites That Work.* San Jose, CA: Adobe Press.

Bort, Julie, and Bradley Felix. 1997. *Building an Extranet: Connect Your Intranet with Vendors and Customers.* New York: John Wiley and Sons.

Bosak, Jon, and Tim Bray. 1999. "XML and the Second-Generation Web." *Scientific American,* May 1999.

Bourdakis, V. 1996. "From CAAD to VRML: London Case Study." Proceedings of the Third UK VRSIG Conference, De Montfort University.

———. N.d. "Virtual Reality: A Communication Tool for Urban Planning." Unpublished paper, Centre for Advanced Studies in Architecture, University of Bath, U.K.

Bourdakis, V., and A. Day. 1997. "The VRML Model of the City of Bath." Proceedings of the Sixth International European VRML Conference, Europia Productions.

Brand, Stewart. 1995. *How Buildings Learn: What Happens after They're Built.* New York: Penguin.

Broadbent, G. 1990. *Emerging Concepts in Urban Space Design.* New York: Van Nostrand Reinhold.

Brook, James, and Iain A. Boal, eds. 1995. *Resisting the Virtual Life: The Culture and Politics of Information.* San Francisco: City Lights Books.

Brooks, John. 1975. *Telephone: The First Hundred Years.* New York: Harper and Row.

Brown, Alex, Yacine Rezgui, Grahame Cooper, Jim Yip, and Peter Brandon. 1996. "Promoting Computer Integrated Construction through the Use of Distribution Technology." Unpublished paper, October 1996.

Brown, Judith, et al. 1995. *Visualization: Using Computer Graphics to Explore Data and Present Information.* New York: John Wiley and Sons.

Brown, Stuart F. 1997. "Building Business Buildings Better." *Fortune,* 8 September 1997.

Buchanan, Hugh, Paul Stevenson, David Fairbairn, David Parker, George Taylor, and Jason Wall. 1999. *Using Geogaphic Information Systems for Site Selection.* London: The Royal Institution of Chartered Surveyors.

Burdea, Grigore, and Philippe Coiffet. 1994. *Virtual Reality Technology.* New York: John Wiley and Sons.

Bush, Vannevar. 1945. "As We May Think." *The Atlantic Monthly,* July 1945.

Byrne, C. 1996. "Water on Tap: The Use of Virtual Reality as an Educational Tool." Unpublished doctoral dissertation. (Available at: http://www.hitl.washington.edu/publications/dissertations/Byrne)

Cairncross, Frances. 1997. *The Death of Distance: How the Communications Revolution Will Change Our Lives.* Cambridge, MA: Harvard Business School Press.

Campbell, Dave, and Maxwell Wells. 1994. "A Critique of Virtual Reality in the Architectural Design Process." Human Interface Technology Laboratory Technical Report R-94-3 Seattle: University of Washington. (Available at http://www.hitl.washington.edu/projects/architecture/R94-3.html)

Castells, Manuel. 1996. *The Rise of the Network Society*. Oxford: Blackwell Publishers.

Chalmers, Matthew, Kerry Rodden, and Dominique Brodbeck. n.d. "The Order of Things: Activity-Centred Information Access." Unpublished paper, Ubilab, UBS, Zürich, Switzerland.

Clark, David D. 1999. "High-Speed Data Races Home." *Scientific American*, October 1999.

Clayton, Mark J., Robert E. Johnson, and Yunsik Song. 1998. "A Study of Information Content of As-Built Drawings for USAA." CRS Center for Leadership and Management in the Design and Construction Industry, Texas A&M University, January 1998.

Cohen, Jonathan. 1998. "The Voice of the Village." *Urban Land*, November 1998.

Cooper, Alan. 1995. *About Face: The Essentials of Interface Design*. Foster City, CA: IDG Books.

Coopersmith, Jonathan. 1993. "Facsimile's False Starts." *IEEE Spectrum*, February 1993, pp. 46–49.

Crawford, Tad. 1995. "Clients vs. Creators." *Communication Arts*, September/October 1995.

Creighton, James L., and James W. R. Adams (contributor). 1997. *Cybermeeting: How to Link People and Technology in Your Organization*. New York: AMACOM.

Danahy, John W. 1990. "Irises in a Landscape: An Experiment in Dynamic Interaction and Teaching Design Studio." In *The Electronic Design Studio*. Cambridge, MA: MIT Press.

Davis, Stanley M., and Christopher Meyer. 1999. *Blur: The Speed of Change in the Connected Economy*. New York: Little Brown.

Day, A. 1994. "From Map to Model: the Development of an Urban Information System." *Design Studies* 15(3).

Day, A., V. Bourdakis, and J. Robson. 1996. "Living with a Virtual City." *Architectural Research Quarterly* 2: 84–91.

DeFillippi, Robert I., and Michael B. Arthur. 1998. "Paradox in Project-Based Enterprise: The Case of Film Making." *California Management Review* 40(2), Winter 1998: 125–39.

Deutsch, Claudia H. 1999. "Digital Polish for Factory Floors: Software Simulations Lead Manufacturers to Better Assembly Lines." *The New York Times*, 22 March 1999.

Dixon, Janice I. 1999. "On the Hook, in the Lead." *Design-Build Magazine*, February 1999.

Dodge M., S. Doyle, A. Smith, and S. Fleetwood. 1998. "Towards the Virtual City: VR and Internet GIS for Urban Planning." Proceedings of the Virtual Reality and Geographical Information Systems Workshop.

Doherty, Paul. 1996. *CyberPlaces*. Kingston, MA: RS Means.

Dyson, Esther. 1997. *Release 2.0 : A Design for Living in the Digital Age*. New York: Broadway Books.

Eastman, C., ed. December 1998. "OSCONCAD: A Model-Based CAD System Integrated with Computer Applications." *ITcon* 3. (Available at http://itcon.org/1998/3/)

Fallows, James. 1996. "Caught in the Web." *New York Review of Books*, 15 February 1996.

Friedlander, Mark C. 1997. "Design-Build: Legal Obstacles and Solutions." *Consulting-Specifying Engineer*, 1 April 1997.

Froese, Thomas. 1996. "STEP and the Building Construction Core Model: Computing in Civil Engineering." Proceedings of the Third Congress, American Society of Civil Engineers, Anaheim, June 1996.

Fruchter, Renate, Mark J. Clayton, Helmut Krawinkler, John Kunz, and Paul

Teicholz. n.d. "Interdisciplinary Communication Medium for Collaborative Conceptual Building Design." Department of Civil Engineering, Center for Integrated Facility Engineering, Stanford University, Stanford, CA. (Available at: ftp://cstanford.edu//pub/CDR/Publications/Reports/ICM.ps)

Ghosh, Shikhar. 1998. "Making business sense of the Internet." *Harvard Business Review*, March-April 1998.

Gibson, W. 1984. *Neuromancer*. London: Gollancz.

Gilboy, Colin. 1996. "Deliver Your Product Information Using the Internet." *CSI Specifier*, November 1996.

———. 1997. "Developing Your Construction Product Internet Web Site." *CSI Specifier*, February 1997.

Global Internet Project. 1996. The Emergence of a Networked World—Commerce, Society and the Future of the Internet. (Available at: http://www.gip.org)

Gralla, Preston. 1997. *How Intranets Work*. New York: Ziff-Davis.

Grant, Mike. 1993. "ISSUE: Interactive Software Systems for the Urban Environment." In *CAAD Futures 1993*. New York: North-Holland.

Graziani, Giovanni. 1998. "Globalization of Production in the Textile and Clothing Industries: The Case of Italian Foreign Direct Investment and Outward Processing in Eastern Europe." *Berkeley Roundtable on the International Economy Working Paper* 128, May 1998.

Grenier, Raymond, and George Metes. 1995. *Going Virtual: Moving Your Organization into the 21st Century*. New York: Prentice Hall Computer Books.

Griffin, M. 1995. "Applications of VR in Architecture and Design." Proceedings of the Information Technology Awareness Workshop, University of Salford, UK, January 1995.

Grossman, Wendy. 1997. *net.wars*. New York: NYU Press.

Gutman, Robert. 1988. *Architectural Practice: A Critical View*. Princeton: Princeton Architectural Press.

Hafner, Katie, and Matthew Lyon. 1996. *Where Wizards Stay Up Late*. New York: Simon and Schuster.

Han, Charles S., John Kunz, and H. Kincho. n.d. Law Performance-Based Automated Building Code Checking." CIFE Seed Research Proposal, Center for Integrated Facilities Engineering, Stanford University.

Hinks. J, G. Aouad, R. Cooper, D. Sheath, and S. Kagioglou. 1997. "IT and the Design and Construction Process: A Conceptual Model of Co-Maturation." *The International Journal of Construction IT*, July 1997.

Hoinkes, R., and R. Mitchell. 1994. "Playing with Time: Continuous Temporal Mapping Strategies for Interactive Environments." Proceedings of the 6th Canadian GIS Conference. Ottawa: Natural Resources Canada.

Hurlburt, A. 1977. *Layout: The Design of the Printed Page*. New York: Watson-Guptill.

Industry Canada. 1998a. *Sector Competitiveness Frameworks Series: Architecture*. 8 June 1998.

———. 1998b. *Sector Competitiveness Frameworks Series: Construction*. 22 June 1998.

Iovine, Julie V. 1999. "Architecture for a New Century: Fierce Poetry from Young Turks." *The New York Times*, 11 March 1999.

Jin, Yan, and Paul Teicholz. n.d. "VPMC Proposal: Virtual Project Management and Control." Research proposal, Center for Integrated Facilities Engineering, Stanford University, Stanford, CA.

Johnson, Robert E., and Mark J. Clayton. 1997a. " 'Best Practices' of Facility Management Organizations." CRS Center for Leadership and

Management in the Design and Construction Industry, Texas A&M University, October 1997.

———. 1997b. "The Impact of Information Technology on Facility Management Practice." CRS Center for Leadership and Management in the Design and Construction Industry, Texas A&M University, January 1997.

Johnson, Steven A. 1997. *Interface Culture: How New Technology Transforms the Way We Create and Communicate.* San Francisco: Harper San Francisco.

Kellner, Mark A. 1998. "Cities, Counties Turn to Online Systems to Serve Up Permits." *Government Computer News/State & Local*, October 1998.

Kellogg, Nelson R. 1997. "The Internet, Conversational Communities, and the Future of Planning." Unpublished Ph.D. dissertation.

Kiesler, Sara, ed. 1997. *Culture of the Internet.* Mahwah, NJ: Lawrence Erlbaum Associates.

Konchar, Mark. 1998. "Project Delivery Systems: What's the Difference?" *School Planning and Management*, July 1998.

Koskela, Lauri. 1992. "Application of the New Production Philosophy to Construction." Center for Integrated Facilities Engineering, Technical Report #72, Stanford University, Stanford, CA, August 1992.

Kostner, Jaclyn. 1996. *Virtual Leadership: Secrets from the Round Table for the Multi-Site Manager.* New York: Warner Books.

Kristof, Ray, and Amy Satran. 1995. *Interactivity by Design.* San Jose, CA: Adobe Press.

Kumar, Kuldeep, Han G. van Dissel, and Paola Bielli. 1998. "The merchant of Prado—revisited: toward a third rationality of information systems." *MIS Quarterly*, June 1998: 199(28).

Laiserin, Jerry. 1999a. "Computer Intranets Move Firms Closer to the Seemingly Elusive Goal of a Well-Connected practice." *Architectural Record*, March 1999.

———. 1999b. "Emerging Standards for Computer-aided Design Will Improve Communication within the Design Industry." *Architectural Record*, May 1999.

———. 1999c. "Firm Principals Should Consider the Many Ways That New Technologies Will Transform Their Staff Composition." *Architectural Record*, July 1999.

Larijani, L.C. 1994. *The Virtual Reality Primer.* New York: McGraw-Hill.

Latham. Michael. 1994. *Construction: The Team.* London: H.M.S.O.

Lauf, Stephen, Merlyna Lim, and Marcus Ormerod. 1999. "The Benefits of Virtual Place for Real World Design." In *Quondam: A Virtual Museum of Architecture.* (Available at: http://www.quondam.com).

Lawrence, Steve, and C. Lee Giles. 1999. "Accessibility of Information on the Web." *Nature* 400 (8 July 1999): 107.

———. 1998. "Searching the World Wide Web." *Science* 280 (3 April 1998). (Available at www.sciencemag.org)

Leiner, Barry M., Vinton G. Cerf, David D. Clark, Robert E. Kahn, Leonard Kleinrock, Daniel C. Lynch, Jon Postel, Larry G. Roberts, and Stephen Wolff. n.d. "A Brief History of the Internet, version 3.1." (Available at http://www.isoc.org/internet-history/brief.html)

Liggett, R., S. Friedman, and W. Jepson. 1995. "Interactive Design/Decision Making in a Virtual Urban World: Visual Simulation and GIS." Proceedings of the 15th Annual ESRI User Conference, Palm Springs, CA.

Line, Lars. 1997. "Virtual Engineering Teams: Strategy and Implementation." Program on Applied Coordination Technology, Norwegian University of Science and Technology, October 1997.

Lipman, A. D., A. D. Sugarman, and R. F. Cushman, eds. 1986. *Teleports and the Intelligent City*. Homewood, IL: Dow Jones-Irwin.

Lipnack, Jessica, and Jeffrey Stamps. 1977. *Virtual Teams: Reaching across Space, Time, and Organizations with Technology*. New York: John Wiley and Sons.

Lohr, Steve. 1999. "The Economy Transformed, Bit by Bit." *The New York Times*, 20 December 1999.

Lubar, Steven. 1993. *InfoCulture: The Smithsonian Book of Information Age Inventions*. Boston: Houghton Mifflin.

Lynch, Patrick J., and Sarah Horton. 1999. *Web Style Guide: Basic Design Principles for Creating Web Sites*. New Haven, CT, and London: Yale University Press.

Malone, Thomas W. and Robert J. Laubacher. 1998. "The Dawn of the E-lance Economy." *Harvard Business Review*, September-October 1998.

Malone, Thomas W., Robert J. Laubacher, and the MIT Scenario Working Group. 1997. "Two Scenarios for 21st Century Organizations: Shifting Networks of Small Firms or All-Encompassing 'Virtual Countries?'" MIT Initiative on Inventing the Organizations of the 21st Century Working Paper 21C WP 001, January 1997.

Malone, Thomas W. et al. 1999. "What do we really want? A manifesto for the organizations of the 21st Centry." MIT 21st Century Manifesto Working Group, MIT Initiative on Inventing the Organizations of the 21st Century Discussion Paper, November 1999.

Markoff, John. "An Internet Pioneer Ponders the Next Revolution." *The New York Times*, 20 December, 1999.

McDaniel, George, ed. 1994. *Dictionary of Computing*. 10th ed. New York: McGraw-Hill.

McDonald, Jared. 1994. "Biometric Authentication." Unpublished dissertation at the University of Otago, Dunedin, New Zealand, August 1994.

Meggs, P. B. 1989. *Type and Image: The Language of Graphic Design*. New York: Van Nostrand Reinhold.

Mitchell, William J. 1995. *City of Bits: Space, Place and the Infobahn*. Cambridge, MA: MIT Press.

Mitchell, William J., and Malcolm McCullough. 1995. *Digital Design Media*. 2d ed. New York: John Wiley and Sons.

Mitgang, Lee D. 1994. *Building Communities: A New Future for Architecture Education and Practice*. New York: Carnegie Foundation.

Mok, C. 1996. *Designing Business: Multiple Media, Multiple Disciplines*. San Jose, CA: Adobe Press.

Naisbitt, John. 1995. *Global Paradox*. New York: Avon Books.

Nasrallah, Walid, and Raymond Levitt. n.d. "Beyond CPM: Dependencies That Arise between Construction Activities." Research proposal, Center for Integrated Facilities Engineering, Stanford University.

National Institute of Building Sciences for the Construction and Building Subcommittee of the Technology Innovation Committee of the National Science and Technology Council. 1996. "Draft Report: Workshop on National Construction Goals as Related to the Commercial and Institutional Building Sector." Issued 18 September, 1996.

Negroponte, Nicholas. 1996. *Being Digital*. New York: Vintage Books.

Nelson, Charles. 1995. *TQM and ISO 9000 for Architects and Designers*. New York: McGraw-Hill.

Nelson, Theodor H. 1967. "Getting It Out of Our System." In *Critique of Information Retrieval*, edited by George Schechter. Washington DC: Thompson Books.

———. 1974. "No More Teachers' Dirty Looks." In *Electric Media*, by Les Brown and Elma Marks,. New York: Harcourt.

Nielsen, Jakob. n.d. "Report From a 1994 Web Usability Study." (Available at http://www.useit.com/papers/1994_web_usability_report.html)

Novak, Marcos. 1995. "Transmitting Architecture: The Transphysical City." In *Ctheory*, 29 November, 1995. (Available at http://www.ctheory.com/a34-transmitting_arch.html)

Novitski, B. J. 1998. "Changing the Face of Practice with Digital Technologies." *Architectural Record*, June 1998, pp. 72–77.

———. 1999. "Software Being Developed Now Will Completely Change the Architects' Design, and How They Charge for Their Work." *Architectural Record*, February 1999.

Oliver, S. 1994. "Identifying the Future of Information Technologies within the Changing Trends of the Architectural Profession." Unpublished paper, Department of Surveying, University of Salford, UK.

Ormerod, M. G., and G. Aouad. 1997. "The Need for Matching Visualisation Techniques to Client Understanding in the UK Construction Industry." Proceedings of Information Visualization, London, August 1997.

Orvis, William J. and Allan L. Van Lehn, "Data Security Vulnerabilities of Facsimile Machines and Digital Copiers," National Technical Information Service, U.S. Department of Commerce, Springfield, VA: January 1995.

Penn, A. et al. 1995. "Intelligent Architecture: Rapid Prototyping for Architecture and Planning." Proceedings of the Information Technology Awareness Workshop. University of Salford, UK, January 1995.

Pepper, Chris. 1999. "What's a Firewall, and Why Should You Care?" *TidBITS* 468, 22 February 1999.

Peppers, Don, and Martha Rogers. 1999. *The One to One Future: Building Relationships One Customer at a Time*. New York: Doubleday.

Peppers, Don, Martha Rogers, and Bob Dorf. 1999. *The One to One Fieldbook: The Complete Toolkit for Implementing a 1-to-1 Marketing Program*. New York: Bantam.

Perez-Gomez, Alberto, and Louise Pelletier. 1997. *Architectural Representation and the Perspectival Hinge*. Cambridge, MA: MIT Press.

Petrie, Charles, Sigrid Goldmann, and Andrea Raquet. n.d. "Agent-based Project Management." Unpublished paper, Center for Design Research, Stanford University.

Piore, Michael, and Charles Sabel. 1984. *The Second Industrial Divide: Possibilities for Prosperity*. New York: Basic.

Porter, Tom. 1997. *The Architect's Eye: Visualization and Depiction of Space in Architecture*. New York: Routledge.

Quinn, Barbara, Richard Allen, and Michael Sweeney. 1999. "Moving Maintenance into the Mainstream: The Cagis Integrated Gis and Permit Management System." City of Cincinnati, June 1999.

Raymond, Eric S. 1994. *The New Hacker's Dictionary*. Cambridge, MA: MIT Press.

Reeve, Alan, Rowena Rouse, Catherine Tranmer, and Bill Worthington. 1997. "Urban Design on the Internet: RUDI, A Case Study in Practice." *Online Planning*, August–September 1997.

Reina, Peter. 1999. "Old World Methods Fuel Renaissance." *Design-Build Magazine*, August 1999.

Rheingold, Howard. 1994. *The Virtual Community: Homesteading on the Electronic Frontier*. Reading, MA: Addison Wesley.

Richtel, Matt. 1999. "MCI Net Snag Could Drive Small Providers out of Business." *The New York Times*, 17 August 1999.

Rochlin, Gene I. 1997. *Trapped in the Net: The Unanticipated Consequences of Computerization*. Princeton, NJ: Princeton University Press.

Roszak, Theodore. 1994. *The Cult of Information: A Neo-Luddite Treatise on*

High Tech, Artificial Intelligence, and the True Art of Thinking. Berkeley and Los Angeles: University of California Press.

Salus, Peter H. 1994. *Casting the Net: From ARPANET to Internet and Beyond.* Reading, MA: Addison-Wesley.

Sanders, Ken. 1996. *The Digital Architect.* New York: John Wiley and Sons.

Schorr, Joseph. 1998. 'The Heartbreak of MIME Attachments." *Macworld*, June 1998.

Schrage, Michael. 1990. *Shared Minds: The New Technologies of Collaboration.* New York: Random House.

Seabrook, John. 1997. *Deeper: My Two-Year Odyssey in Cyberspace.* New York: Simon and Schuster.

Shapiro, Carl, and Hal R. Varian. 1999. *Information Rules: A Strategic Guide to the Network Economy.* Cambridge, MA: Harvard Business School Press.

Shiffer, Michael J. 1995. "Multimedia Representational Aids in Urban Planning Support Systems." In *Understanding Images: Finding Meaning in Digital Imagery*, F.T. Marchese (ed.). New York: Springer-Verlag.

———. 1996. "Computer-Aided Technologies and Tools Used in Transportation-Related Decision-Making and Presentation." Unpublished paper, Planning Support Systems Group, Department of Urban Studies and Planning, Massachusetts Institute of Technology.

———. 1995. "Interactive Multimedia Planning Support: Moving from Stand-Alone Systems to the World Wide Web." *Environment and Planning B: Planning and Design* 22.

———. 1992. "Towards a Collaborative Planning System." *Environment and Planning B: Planning and Design* 19.

———. n.d. "Interactive City Planning Using Multimedia Representation Aids." Unpublished paper, MIT Department of Urban Studies and Planning, Cambridge, MA.

Siegel, David. 1997. *Creating Killer Web Sites.* 2d ed. Indianapolis: Hayden Books.

Sinton, Peter. 1999. "Permits Online Save Time: New Programs Allow Building Owners and Contractors to File Paperwork Online." *San Francisco Chronicle*, 3 November 1999.

Slater, M., and S. Wilbur. 1995. "Through the Looking Glass World of Presence: A Framework for Immersive Virtual Environments." In *Framework for Immersive Virtual Environments*, FIVE'95 Esprit Working Group 9122. London: Queen Mary and Westfield College.

Smith, A., and M. Dodge. 1997. "A Guide to the Internet for the Planning Professional." *Planning*, 11 April 1997, pp. 16–17.

Spiegel, Stacey. 1995. "Crossings." In *Mythos Information: Welcome to the Wired World.* New York: Springer-Verlag.

Sproull, L. and S. Kiesler. 1991. *Connections: New Ways of Working in the Networked Organization.* Cambridge, MA: The MIT Press.

Srinivas, Hari. 1995. "Urban Planning and the Internet: An Exploration." Proceedings of the ISOCARP Conference, Sydney, Australia.

Standage, Tom. 1998. *The Victorian Internet: The Remarkable Story of the Telegraph and the Nineteenth Century's On-Line Pioneers.* New York: Walker Publishing.

Stella, Frank D. 1986. *Working Space.* Charles Eliot Norton Lectures 1983–84. Cambridge, MA: Harvard University Press.

Stille, Alexander. 1998. "Invisible Cities." *Lingua Franca*, July–August 1998.

Stoll, Clifford. 1996. *Silicon Snake Oil: Second Thoughts on the Information Highway.* New York: Anchor.

Sudweeks, Fay, Margaret McLaughlin, and Sheizaf Rafaeli, eds. 1998. Menlo Park, CA, and Cambridge, MA: AAAI Press and The MIT Press.

Swiss Federal Institute of Technology Zurich (ETH). "A Tool Set for the Virtual AEC Company." (Available at: http://caad.arch.ethz.ch/)

Tanner, Victoria L. 1999. "IRS Center Passes Audit." *Design-Build Magazine*, June 1999.

Tapscott, Don. 1997. *Growing Up Digital: The Rise of the Net Generation.* New York: McGraw-Hill.

———. 1992. *Paradigm Shift: The New Promise of Information Technology.* New York: McGraw-Hill.

Teicholz, Paul, and Martin Fischer. 1994. "Strategy for Computer Integrated Construction Technology." *Journal of Construction, Engineering and Management* 120 (1), March 1994.

Thibadeau, Robert, Jorge Balderas, and Andrew Snyder. 1999. "E-Commerce Catalog Construction: An Experiment with Programmable XML for Dynamic Documents." *D-Lib Magazine* 5 (2), February 1999. (Available at http://www.dlib.org/dlib/february99/thibadeau/02thibadeau.html)

Tombesi, Paolo. 1999. "The Carriage in the Needle: Building Design and Flexible Specialization Systems. *Journal of Architectural Education*, February 1999.

Tranmer, Catherine. 1997. "Review: Urban Design on the Internet." *Urban Design Quarterly* 64, October 1997.

Tucker, Hugh, and Betty Harvey. 1997 "SGML Documentation Objects within the STEP Environment." (Available at: http://www.eccnet.com/step)

Tufte, Edward R. 1997. *Visual Explanations: Images and Quantities, Evidence and Narrative.* Cheshire, CT: Graphics Press.

———. 1992. *The Visual Display of Quantitative Information.* Cheshire, CT: Graphics Press.

———. 1990. *Envisioning Information.* Cheshire, CT: Graphics Press.

Turk, Z., ed. 1998. "A Proposed Open Infrastructure for Construction Project Document Sharing." *ITcon* 3, December 1998.

Turkle, Sherry. 1997. *Life on the Screen: Identity in the Age of the Internet.* New York: Simon and Schuster.

"Using the Web to Speed Up Fast-Track Construction." *CleanRooms,* March 1998.

Varley, Pamela, and Edward Lascher. 1991a. "Blip on the Screen—or Wave of the Future? 'Electronic Democracy in Santa Monica." Kennedy School of Government Case Program, Harvard University.

———. 1991b. "Civic Vision: Participatory City Planning in Cleveland in the 1980s." Kennedy School of Government Case Program, Harvard University.

Waldrop, M. Mitchell. 1996. "The Trillion-Dollar Vision of Dee Hock." Fast Companyh 5:75, October 1996.

Wallis, Keith. 1999. "Asian Tigers Roar into Privatization Tactics." *Design-Build Magazine*, October 1999.

White, J. V. 1988. *Graphic Design for the Electronic Age.* New York: Watson-Guptil.

Whitten, Jeffrey L., and Lonnie D. Bentley. 1998. *Systems Analysis and Design Methods.* 4th ed. New York: McGraw Hill/ Irwin.

Whyte, Jennifer, and N. M. Bouchlaghem. n.d. "Evaluating New Housing: The Potential for Developers and Planners to Use Virtual Reality Techniques." Unpublished paper, Department of Civil and Building Engineering, Loughborough University, UK.

Wilson, A. 1974. *The Design of Books.* Salt Lake City: Peregrine Smith.

Wolfe, Andria K. 1998. *FMI's 1998 Construction Industry Training Survey.* Raleigh, NC: FMI Finan Publishing.

Wurman, Richard Saul. 1997. *Information Architects.* New York: Watson-Guptil.

Index

Page numbers in *italic* refer to illustrations.